NO TIDE~~~ ~~ ~~~~~

A HISTORY
OF THE
MANCHESTER PILOT SERVICE

BY

DEREK A CLULOW

The painting on the front cover, entitled
"PASSING WESTON POINT LOCKS OUTWARD BOUND"
was by the late Mr. W. (Bill) Yates, Pilot First Class, and
reproduced by kind permission of his wife Mrs. D. Yates.

First published 1995 by Countyvise Limited, 1 & 3 Grove Road, Rock Ferry, Birkenhead,
Wirral, Merseyside L42 3XS in conjunction with the author Derek A Clulow.

Copyright © 1995 Derek A Clulow.

ISBN 0 907768 72 5

Printed and bound by MFP Design & Print. *Tel:* 0161 864 4540

To

My very dear wife, "Tulip", who for 35 years has suffered silently the unsocial hours of my profession, listened patiently to my endless accident reports, mended willingly my broken body from football, helped unfailingly to "dry" me out from time to time and yet through all this, never stopped loving me.

The Author
Manchester Ship Canal Pilot Service
1954-1988

ACKNOWLEDGEMENTS

The longer the task of writing the history of the MANCHES-TER SHIP CANAL PILOT SERVICE has been put off, the greater the work of the historian, who will find records get destroyed, the older generation passes on, memories fade and facts blend into legends. In writing this history I found no exception to this rule.

First and foremost, in writing this acknowledgement I must express my deep sense of gratitude to Mrs Jean Capper whose unstinting offer to give up her much loved leisure time to transfer my - at times, illegible writings in longhand - words to paper by way of the typewriter. Without Jean's help and happy disposition through these long years - five in all - I could not have ever finished this history of the Pilot Service. With no less a sense of gratitude, I sincerely thank Adrian Wood, Graeham and Fran Hulbert for their invaluable contribution in editing and correcting the manuscripts a task of no mean feat, and gratefully appreciated. A special thank you to Mrs Yates for her patience and forbearance with me whilst lending me her late husband's (Mr W (Bill) Yates - Pilot First Class) voluminous photographic and work records he so painstakingly collected and kept for posterity, and for her kind permission for me to use the superb paintings by her late husband of scenes of the canal, especially the one that adorns the jacket of this book.

I shall always be grateful to Miss M Patch and her staff at the Greater Manchester County Council Records Office for their unfailing courtesy and assistance so readily given to me during my researching at that establishment. To Mr David Thornley ex. P.R.O. of the old Manchester Ship Canal Company, very many thanks for allowing me to browse through hundreds of photographs in the archives thus preserving an era that has gone for ever. To all the Pilot's widows who so kindly lent me their treasured photographs of their loved ones so that they may be ever remembered in the pages of this book, my thanks to you all.

Finally, if I have forgotten to acknowledge anyone from the list overleaf, please forgive me, there has been so many and some are bound to be overlooked.

Mr H G Pringle ⎫
Mr M E Warren ⎪
Mr J H Warren ⎬ Manchester Ship Canal Pilots
Mr A E Cooke ⎪
Mr P K Rali ⎭
Mr G Collins
Mr J Southwood   River Dee Pilot
Mr H Thelwell   Ex Pilots Clerk
Mr Gib. Jackson   Eng. Dept. Manchester Ship Canal
Mrs D Marten ⎫
Mrs Jan Lemon ⎬ Pilots National Pension Fund
Mrs Sweet ⎭
Mr C H Milsom   Editor "Sea Breezes"
Mr Alan Green   Liverpool Pilot
Mr Peter Lamey
Mr A Potts   Privy Council Office, Whitehall
Mr J Pepper   Dept. of Transport
Mr B K Phillips   Public Records Office, Richmond, Surrey
Mr J Allan   General Council of British Shipping
Mr S K Conacher   General Council of British Shipping
Mr P Dunbavand   Captain, M.S.C. Tug Service
Captain D W Jones   "Dalmor" Nefyn Gwynedd,
                        Inspector, Board Of Trade
Captain R Kilby-Lennon Ex-master "Hemsley I"
Captain G Cubbins   T & J Harrisons, Liverpool
F Armitt & Son   Shipping Agents
H.M. Tax Inspectors   Head Office, London
British Rail   National Railway Museum, York
Whitbreads Brewery
Maritime Museum   Albert Dock, Liverpool
Mr E Morrison   Ex-pilot Clerk
Arthur Guinness, Son & Co.
Mr R A Jamieson   Archives Assistant, British Waterways
Central Library   Manchester
Mrs J J Pierpoint
Mrs J Lang   Currie (Business Equipment Ltd.)
                        Birkenhead
Merseyside Transport Ltd.
Mrs G Cartwright
Mr C Parsons   World Ship Society
John Mills Photography Ltd., Liverpool
Mr John Young and Family

vi

CONTENTS

(No. in brackets refer to Chapter)

ALL THAT MANKIND HAS DONE, THOUGHT, GAINED OR BEEN: IT IS LYING AS IN MAGIC PRESERVATION IN THE PAGES OF BOOKS.

THOMAS CARLYLE.

THE BEGINNING IS THE MOST IMPORTANT PART OF THE WORK.

PLATO.

PROLOGUE

It is hard to trace the progress of Manchester, the manufacturing capital of Lancashire during the period 1600-1700, being overshadowed by the emerging greatness of Liverpool as a sea port.

Previous to the Great Civil War it had attained a position of wealth and influence, so much so that in 1638 Manchester contended with York for the honour of becoming the seat of a University on the model of Oxford and Cambridge for the instruction of youth of the northern Counties. Manchester was the centre of northern ports, a town of great antiquity, great fame and great ability - it was ideally situated for the provision of food, fuel and cotton goods.

The manufacturers of Manchester were highly praised for their spirit of enterprise in purchasing cotton wool from Cypres and Smyrna. "The town of Manchester in Lancashire", writes the historian Lewis Roberts, "must be herein remembered worthily and their encouragement commended".

Many towns in the north were urged to emulate Manchester and establish the manufacturing of cotton, thread and tape. Andrew Yarranton, another historian, wrote "The comfort of any place may be that if they once fit well in the manufacture of their goods, then they will deter all others setting up the same and so, consequently, at last be the great masters of it as Manchester is of all things it trades in".

This high reputation for skill and enterprise continued, so it was hardly surprising that in the year 1712 a number of Manchester gentlemen employed Mr Thomas Steers, the engineer of the first Liverpool Dock, to survey the rivers Irwell and Mersey, with a view of rendering them navigable from Manchester to Warrington. The engineer, Mr Thomas Steers, was able to put forth his plan with the following announcement :-

"The inlands ports of Lancashire and Yorkshire, being favoured with great variety of valuable manufacturers in woollen, linen,

1894

The steam Yacht "Norseman" leading a procession of boats opening the Manchester Ship Canal. Pilot Mr A Cartwright.

Courtesy M.S.C. Co.

M.S.C. "Gower" 1894 dressed overall for the opening of the canal. The "Gower" was one of the few wooden paddle tugs. Built in 1868 at Garston, Liverpool. Dimensions; L 120' B 20'6" GR.145 Tons. Captain in 1894 W. Banner.

Courtesy Capt. P. Dunbavand

cotton etc., and that in very great quantities, has made that neighbourhood as populous, if not more so (London and Middlesex excepted) as the same extent of any other port of Great Britain. The trades of these counties extend considerably through the whole island, as well as abroad, and the consumption of groceries, wool, dyeing stuff and other goods, consequently very great; but as yet not favoured with the convenience of water-carriage, though Providence, from the Port of Liverpool up to the most considerable inland town of trade in Lancashire, Manchester, has afforded the best not yet employed rivers of Mersey and Irwell for that purpose".

One of the major and very important factors for this survey, so long ago, was the manufacturer's concern that 75% of the cost of exporting their wares from Manchester to the outside world, was consumed in the rates charged to transport them from Manchester to Liverpool overland.

Such was the position of Manchester and the surrounding districts of Lancashire and even in those far distant years in the past, the pressing need for a canal or waterway was plain for all to see, a doorway from the very heart of the northern Counties for northern goods to everywhere in the then known world, at greatly reduced cost.

That it took 169 years for this seed of an idea to germinate eventually in the fertile brain of Mr Daniel Adamson is somewhat a mystery, but that I leave to other historians.

That a canal was started in 1887 and open to ocean going traffic in 1894 was an engineering miracle of its time never to be repeated, then or now, and I hope this prologue will answer the often posed question 'Why on earth build a port 40 miles inland?" Now you know.

I thought it would be extremely beneficial to the reader in forming a potted history of the Canal, so I am using an article taken from the Daily Express dated Monday, February 3rd 1936.

The Seven Wonders of the North - subject of a "Daily Express" competition - form the theme of reporter Mr McKenzie Porter's

1891
General view of Eastham Locks cleared for the admission of water
Courtesy Mrs W Yates Collection

1802
Barton Road swing bridge and aquaduct under construction
Courtesy Mrs W Yates Collection

series. In his first article he tells of the wonders of the Manchester Ship Canal under the heading Giant Port Forty Miles From The Sea.

Number Nine Dock is on the site of the old Manchester racecourse. No doubt other docks now float liners where once farmers grazed their herds or early Victorians built a primitive cotton mill. A port that is one of the largest in the United Kingdom yet is forty miles from the sea must possess a thousand such curious traits of character. The tramcar passenger who sees towering above him a ship's funnel blistered by the Suez sun, or looks down upon Lascars, Scandinavians, Greeks in streets housing Lancashire workers... and it is not uncommon in the approach to Manchester docks..... surely thirsts for knowledge of the great canal that made possible so fantastic a clash of sights.

It was to slake that thirst we came one chill day to a vast pool wherein lay under rain-sodden, drooping bunting the ships of all nations, the ships that keep in circulation the riches of the world.

Joseph Aldcroft, who signals locomotives over the main gates crossing, told us that three thousand carters, stevedores, ship-wrights, and "bosses" pass him every day on their way to work. He claims to know all their Christian names. And they call him "The little Jockey", a title he has held since he was the nippiest errand boy on the docks, forty years ago.

As Captain Howard, late of the Royal Navy, now Harbour Master, led us in search of a tug, we espied a small figure rowing down the avenues of steamers. It was "Dog Joe" (Joseph Schofield) who sails the docks to fish out dead dogs, sheep, cows, pigs and sometimes-dead men. He collects a daily average of seventy animal carcasses washed into the canal from "feed" rivers. His is the most odious yet one of the most important jobs, for the Ship Canal Company is scrupulous in avoiding pollution of these heavily trafficked waters which lack a cleansing tide.

We embarked in a tug and swished among the busy cranes flanking the huge store sheds, beneath the dizzy height of grain elevators, passed the fireboat Firefly, whose steam is never allowed to fall, and on to the first locks at Mode Wheel.

1890

Weston Point Dock Entrance

The earthwork dam on the left was to prevent the River Mersey Entering the newly dug ship canal. Note the number of sailing vessels in port.

Courtesy of Captain P. Dunbavand

6

It was from there we saw slicing the smoky wilderness ahead, the first "straight" of a thirty-five-and-a-half-mile waterway that was dug to give an inland city access to the sea and thereby to save it from industrial suffocation.

The first man to visualise a canal between Manchester and the Mersey at Liverpool was a crippled ledger clerk. People laughed, dubbed him Mad Ben Draycott. Satirical songs of his idea were sung in the theatres:-

> "Alas! too, for poor Liverpool
> She'd surely go to pot, sir.
> For want of trade her folks would starve,
> Her Custom House would rot, sir;
> They might come down to Manchester;
> We'd find them work to do, sir".

Sixty years later, in 1881, 19,000 houses were empty in Manchester. The city was strangled by high railway rates and heavy port dues at Liverpool. It costs more than 19s. to send a ton of goods from Manchester to Calcutta. Of this, 12s.6d. was charged before the goods left Liverpool.

Had Ben Draycott been so mad? Daniel Adamson an engineer born of humble Durham parents, thought not. He called a meeting at his home in the suburb of Didsbury. The canal was planned.

Parliament rejected the Bill twice. Vested interests rose in wrath. The fight for the licence lasted two and a half years. It cost £350,000. At one time expenses were five guineas a minute. But victory was Adamson's. The first sod was cut in 1887. Joyfully, trade guilds paraded the streets. Bakers carried a bust of Adamson moulded in bread. In 1894, Queen Victoria traversing the canal in her yacht Enchantress, performed the opening ceremony.

In the construction, 16,361 men and boys were employed. Churches were built especially for them.

They used 223 miles of temporary railways, 6,300 wagons, 100 steam excavators, 172 locomotives, 194 cranes, 59 pile drivers, 209 pumps, and 182 portable and other engines.

They used 19,000 tons of coal a month, and 8,000 tons of cement. They removed 51,000,000 cubic yards of earth weighing 776,000,000 tons. Over a fifth of the distance had to be blasted through sandstone rock. Manchester Corporation, holding a controlling interest in the shares today, invested £5,000.00.

Trade revived; industries sprang up along the canal. By 1911 more than 32,000 new houses were built. The rateable value of the area within a twenty-mile radius of Manchester had sprung from £2,200,000 to £7,100,000.

Trafford Park, an earl's estate, was blotted out. From the swan lakes and ornamental gardens rose one of the biggest industrial zones in the world. Within a mile of Manchester Town Hall there lay ships of 15,000 tons.

Daniel Adamson died before his work was completed.

The tug's engineer, Mr Wrench, came on the deck. "The construction? Aye those were the days, I worked on the construction. I remember" - pointing to a spot on the bank - " I remember ten men being killed just there. Two locomotives collided on the bank above and came toppling down on top of them".

We descended fifteen feet at Mode Wheel Locks. A coal wharf and a corn mill stood on our left, a tar works and a cemetery on our right. A diver broke surface. Probably he had been repairing the gates. Half a dozen divers are employed on the canal for purposes ranging from the raising of sunken barges to the recovery of cargoes accidentally slipped overboard. When a cashier dropped the wages in the water, Diver A J MacDonald made the quickest descent in his life. He thinks canal diving a "bobby's job" ... after the Navy ... taking bodies out of sunken

1891

Runcorn foreshore with pilings in place to build the Canal retaining wall. Part of retaining wall visible in the background under left railway arch.

(Courtesy of Captain P Dunbavand)

9

German submarines ... twenty-seven fathoms at Scapa Flow ... octopuses off Italy: "They scuttled away - frightened of me!". "Where you bound?" hailed the lock-keeper. "Ellesmere Port" replied Skipper Dugdale. The destination of every vessel passing through the locks, whether it be the Manchester Producer outward bound to Montreal, or just the Fanny Williams taking a sack of oil cake to the cattle wharf, is carefully noted. Skipper Dugdale told us he played golf. A seafaring man playing golf? "Never been to sea in my life - except as a passenger" he said. "I don't think any of the canal tug skippers have. Mostly we start as boys in the tugs and work our way up. This is a different technique from sea or river tugging. We play with inches and we have to pull the tugs up 'on their haunches' sometimes". Vessels under 2,000 tons travel under their own power.

Vessels of greater tonnage dare not attain sufficient speed to give steering way. Their wash would bring the banks down. Hence the tugs. Every craft however, carries a canal helmsman and pilot. When a destroyer flotilla came down a few years ago, commanders of the King's Navy stepped aside to let the Willie Tompkinsons of Runcorn take control. As bridges swung aside to let us through,cyclists, motorists and omnibus passengers stared down on us. Then the factories gave place to suburbs. Little boys cheered us on our way. The suburbs gave place to soft Cheshire countryside, but cows did not even look up when a bunch of Greeks in the stern of a passing Easterner shouted mirthfully at a swarm of rabbits. We wondered where was the German who had painted on a quay, in letters five feet high: "Herasus mit Ernst Thalmann!" - probably in the Indian Ocean, or perhaps the Gulf of Mexico.

Said the engineer, pointing to a stretch of parkland: "The lady who owned that place during the construction - she held out for months before she let us cut through. Oh, she was proper awkward". Compensation was paid those days in hundreds of thousands.

We passed under five mainline railway bridges, nine trunk-road bridges, the Barton aqueduct, which carried other boats high over our heads, and the Runcorn transporter bridge, bearing in its cradle omnibuses, bicycles, motor-cars and pedestrians bound for Widnes.

At Runcorn we hooted twice to attract the engineer's daughter. She came to the door of her father's quayside home and waved. The engineer waved back. "A grand lass!" he smiled.

We noticed the banks were being sealed with limestone. It has been found this enables helmsmen to see better at nights. All ships carry searchlights. Five hundred men are battling constantly with bank erosion. Six dredgers work twenty-four hours a day maintaining depth. The canal passes through fourteen municipal areas and pays rates to them all. Many ships carry detachable tops to their funnels and masts so there will be no danger of catching bridges. At the entrance to the canal lies a "cloakroom" where funnel tops are parked.

For twenty-one miles from the entrance at Eastham Locks to Latchford Locks, the canal is tidal. Over the great part of this distance, it runs alongside the Mersey and the two waterways are separated by a wall.

The value of the canal to the north can be gauged when it is realised that it carries ships into the very core of the most densely populated area in the world. Within a sixty-mile radius, London has 12.7 millions, Manchester 12.2 millions. But within an eight-mile radius London has only 14.36 millions against Manchester's 16.25 millions. The relative weights of industry in these two areas are incomparable.

An average of six million tons of goods a year are handled in the Port of Manchester. An average of three stowaways a week fall into the hands of the dock police.

Manchester, by bringing the sea to herself, gave Lancashire, West Yorkshire, Nottinghamshire, Leicestershire, the Black Country and the Potteries, a nearer port.

Many men died in the cause. To quote the tug's engineer: "It was like a slaughterhouse". But it was a great cause. Has it not provided material welfare for millions?

MANCHESTER SHIP CANAL

BETWEEN THE START OF CONSTRUCTION IN 1887 AND THE OPENING IN 1894 THESE WERE THE CAPITAL COSTS.

LAND	£1,274,991.	6s.	3d.	(32p)
CONSTRUCTION	£9,905,896.	19s.	5d.	(97p)
Engineering and Surveying	£ 145,864.	7s.	5d.	(37p)
INTEREST	£1,170,733.	13s.	4d.	(67p)
Parliamentary Expenses	£ 165,913.	7s.	6d.	(37p)
General Expenses	£ 384,836.	3s.	8d.	(15p)
TOTAL	£13,048,235.	17s.	7d.	(87p)

AT TODAYS VALUE THIS TOTAL WOULD BE
WELL IN EXCESS OF £600 MILLION

THE DEFINITION OF A PILOT.

FROM THE GREEK PEDOTES, STEERSMAN: THE FRENCH PEDON A RUDDER OR OAR: ONE LICENSED TO STEER VESSELS INTO OR OUT OF HARBOUR OR ALONG CERTAIN COASTS: A GUIDE: TO DIRECT THE COURSE OF, ESPECIALLY WHERE NAVIGATION IS DANGEROUS: TO GUIDE THROUGH DANGERS AND DIFFICULTIES.
OXFORD ENGLISH DICTIONARY.

1.

RAISON D'ETRE

The question is often raised "Why do competent masters of ships require a pilot?". To the uninitiated shore person with little or no understanding of the complexities of restricted water navigation and ship handling it must seem hard to understand.

Whilst a master is supremely competent and confident to sail his vessel in deep waters over vast oceans and seas in all weathers, it takes little imagination to understand why a master would anxiously seek and employ assistance from a person with local knowledge when entering a harbour with its restricted waterway, fluctuating depths, docks, locks and divers other problems that beset ships when entering or leaving a port, especially for the first time.

There has always been moves to grant pilotage certificates to masters and mates as early as the Merchant Shipping Act (Part V) 1854. Under this Act the master or mate of any ship was entitled to apply to the relative Pilotage Authority to be examined as to his ability to pilot the ship of which he was master or mate.

The prime movers of this Act were the ship-owners themselves who saw this as a way to cut the costs of running a ship, irrespective of the additional hazards and the strain placed on masters and mates, a system they perpetrate to this day. Most pilotage committees were against the granting of certificates to persons other than those who in accordance with their long-standing practices had qualified themselves in their various apprenticeship schemes and given a most severe and searching examination. The pilots were of the opinion that, with a few exceptions, masters and mates would not be competent to carry out such a service.

1891

Moore Lane Straight looking towards Runcorn. Wiggs Works on the right. Lining the banks to prevent subsidence, is a fine example of Fascine Work. This was the intertwining of willow brances and was carried out by Dutch engineers who were brought over especially for that purpose.

(Courtesy Captain P. Dunbavand)

Previous to 1812, ships causing damage were held responsible even though compulsorily in charge of a pilot. However, in that year exemption was granted, the owner or master being free from liability for damage caused by neglect of any pilot. This applied not only when the master was under compulsion to avail himself of the services of a pilot but also when a pilot was compelled to render his services on the demand of the master, although the master was under no obligation to employ a pilot.

During the passage of the Merchant Shipping Act of 1854, an interesting point arose regarding the granting of a pilot certificate.

When a claim had been made against a shipowner for damage by his vessel in charge of a pilot, he repudiated all liability by putting forward the 'compulsory pilotage' plea. The basis of this defence being that whenever a man was compelled by law to employ a particular individual in the performance of a given service, the law which imposes the obligation upon him must take away his responsibility for the acts of that individual whom he is compelled to employ and on this principle a shipowner was not responsible for any damage his vessel might do whilst under the charge of a compulsory pilot. The question which emerged was as to whether, when a vessel was being piloted by a certificated master or mate, or in the event of the services of a licensed pilot being required although a certificated officer was on board - there appeared to be nothing in the Act to prevent such a demand - the shipowner would be liable, should the vessel cause loss of life or damage to property.

However, this was resolved and the shipowner was relieved of liability for loss or damage occasioned by the fault or incapacity of a qualified pilot, but confined the immunity to the case where the employment by the master was compulsory.

The Pilotage Act of 1913 abolished this ruling, when it pointed out that immunity of a shipowner from liability inflicted hardship and injustice on innocent persons whose property had been damaged by a vessel in charge of a pilot.

Thus there was until 1913 a good reason for employing a pilot - from 1913 onwards ships became larger by way of tonnage, length, breadth and depth and the use of pilots became an increasing practice due to such factors as the insurance for loss or damage to a vessel not under a pilot in designated pilotage waters and the unreliability of the steam engines and steering mechanism in those days. Even in this high-tec modern age of the 90s mechanical and electrical failures of one sort or another, are frequently met when piloting a ship.

A master cannot always cope with such exigencies in restricted waters, whereas a pilot, having no doubt been in this position before, is able to bring his knowledge and expertise to bear to avoid damage.

When one thinks of the highly dangerous, inflammable and toxic cargoes that are transported in vast quantities in ships these days when a spillage through a collision between ships or a ship going aground could destroy all known life in the Irish Sea and possibly beyond, or an explosion could destroy half a town of considerable size, a pilot's worth is incalculable, for he is the first and last safeguard in preventing such a catastrophic happening.

It is no wonder pilots have become increasingly alarmed and concerned at the ostrich-like attitude and reasoning of the ship-owners in their continued persistence to enforce masters to proceed in pilotage waters without employing a pilot, purely and simply as a cost saving exercise without having due regard to the inherent danger to the environment or human life of an accident on board an unpiloted ship.

2.

THE FORMATION OF THE MANCHESTER SHIP CANAL PILOT SERVICE.

The Manchester Ship Canal in 1894 was the first new port to be built for over a century and therefore had no system of regularised pilotage. The very first pilotage acts were conducted by the barge masters and their towage tug-masters who worked for the now Castner Kellner Works (ICI) at Weston Point.   Their experience and expertise in navigating and towing in the many smaller inland canals throughout the North of England stood them in good stead on the larger waterway of the Manchester Ship Canal.

There were no fixed fees but the barge or tug master would normally negotiate a fee with the ship's master and/or the ship's charterer, the general rule being that half the fee was to be paid before sailing and the other half on completion of a satisfactory pilotage service.   These terms and negotiations usually took place in some tavern over a "pot of ale" often at great length and much dissension, until all interested parties came to an equitable decision.   One must agree that it was a far from satisfactory system for a pilot service.

For these reasons the Manchester Ship Canal Pilotage Committee was formed and their mandate was to consider and form a regularised pilotage system for the safe conducting of vessels in and out of the Canal.

The very first meeting of the Pilotage Committee was held at the offices of the Ship Canal Company, 41 Spring Gardens,

1896
Eastham Locks viewed from the River Mersey.
(Courtesy Mr G. Jackson)

1893
Admitting water into the Canal at Latchford Locks.

as to the formation of a Pilotage Committee. The report recommended a committee to be formed consisting of the Manager and Assistant Manager of the Ship Canal Company, five Ship Canal Superintendents and eight licensed Ship Canal Pilots. Four were to be nominated by the Mersey Licensed Pilots and four by the pilots not so licensed. This recommendation was unanimously adopted and the following members constituted the first Pilotage Committee :

Chairman: Mr Marshall Stevens - Manager of the Canal Company

Mr J C Wilson	:	Assistant Manager Canal Company
Captain Heasley	:	Canal Superintendent
Captain Dudley	:	"
Captain Waring	:	"
Captain Whitehouse	:	"
Captain Williams	:	"
Mr G H R Lewis	:	Mersey Sea Pilot
Mr N Colquitt	:	Mersey Sea Pilot
Mr C F Felton	:	"
Mr Adam Cartwright	:	Independent Pilot
Mr H Hill	:	"
Mr Peter Sinnot	:	"
Mr Joseph Stuart	:	"

The first eight pilots so elected to this Committee were appointed to remain in office only until the end of 1896. Thereafter the pilot members of the Committee would be appointed annually. The Pilotage Committee having been constitutionally formed, the following recommendations were placed before this august body :

1) The pilots forming the Ship Canal Pilotage Committee were to be granted the first licences.

1) The pilots forming the Ship Canal Pilotage Committee were to be granted the first licences.

2) The holding of a licence as a Mersey Pilot would be sufficient qualification for a Ship Canal Pilotage Licence, provided the pilot can show to the satisfaction of the Committee that he has made himself thoroughly acquainted with the canal and that he has navigated it on board of large vessels.

3) All applicants for a Ship Canal Licence must have obtained the recommendation of at least three members of the Pilotage Committee.

All these recommendations were unanimously approved.

Captain W H Dudley, Canal Superintendent; Mr W Backshouse, Mersey Sea Pilot and Mr P Sinnott, Independent Pilot, were appointed to form an examining sub-committee. The primary object of this sub-committee was to assure themselves that only competent candidates would be granted licences to act as pilots and to draft a code of questions for the examination of applicants for licences. It was agreed - because of the newness of the Canal - that when applicants are notified to attend the sub-committee for examination, they be furnished with the heads of the subjects upon which they were to be examined. As to the classes of Pilotage Licences, between December 1895 and January 1896, a series of proposals were placed before the Pilotage Committee :

1) That licensed pilots on the Canal be divided into two classes, viz: first and second. A second class pilot being restricted to the pilotage of vessels up to and including 600 tons net register; and that a second class pilot may at the expiration of twelve months, make an application to be examined for a first class licence.

2) That the licence or certificate granted to an appropriated pilot of the Liverpool Pilotage Service working exclusively for a particular line of steamers, be available only for the pilotage of vessels belonging to or chartered by the company by whom the appropriated pilots are employed.

3) That no licence be granted to any person unless he is prepared to devote the whole of his time to the work of Pilotage unless he

1892

Irlam Locks under construction. Note steam crane specially designed for the Ship Canal Co. by Stoddart and Pitt.

Courtesy of the M.S.C. Co.

be an appropriated pilot, or a master of officer of any vessel navigating the canal regularly.

4) That excepting under special circumstances no application for a Pilotage Licence be entertained from persons under 24 or over 50 years of age.

5) The licensing fee to be set at two guineas (£2.10p) for the first year with an annual charge of one guinea (£1.05p) for renewal of licence.

All these recommendations were accepted by the full Pilotage Committee.

It is not unreasonable to assume that the manner in which the examinations were to be conducted and the proposals the sub-committee put forward, were influenced by the Mersey Sea Pilots who played a very large part in forming the foundations of the first organised and regularised Manchester Pilot Service.

On Monday the 4th November 1895, the first applications for Pilotage Licences were submitted to the Pilotage Committee, all suitably recommended by three members of that Committee. They were ordered to be passed to the examining sub-committee and on November 11th and November 18th 1895 the following men were duly examined to become the first licensed pilots in the Manchester Ship Canal.

John Ellis of Runcorn aged 43   Granted First Class Licence
George Green of Rock Ferry aged 41   "
Hugh Jones of Liverpool aged 54   "
(Appropriated pilot for Clan Line)

William Onion of Ellesmere Port aged 33}Granted Second Class Licence

William Matthew of Bootle aged 55 Application Declined
George Foster of Ellesmere Port aged 42   "

The following to be recalled for further examination upon the Rise and Fall of the Tides in the approaches to the Canal entrance.

Harry B Jones of Litherland aged 38

Joseph Shaw of Runcorn aged 25

Henry Hill of Runcorn aged 33

Joseph Inglesfield of Runcorn aged 32

In the case of Mr George Green, he was only granted a first class licence if he was prepared to devote the whole of his time to Pilotage on the Canal otherwise a certificate would be granted if he continued his present command of the tug COMMODORE. Of the remaining four who were to be recalled, all were granted first class licences in January 1896, with the exception of Joseph Shaw who was granted a second class licence. At the same time, Mr William Onion appealed against being granted a second class licence and after due consideration was granted a first class licence.

In December of 1895, 38 applicants applied for licences of which 32 were passed to the examining committee with a special recommendation that in respect of the 11 applications received from the Mersey Sea Pilots, the examining committee satisfy themselves that the applicants had obtained sufficient practical knowledge of the navigation of the Canal. The other 6 applications were rejected.

In those embryonic days of the Manchester Pilot Service, many were called; few were chosen. Applications poured in from every walk of life. The examining sub-committee, no matter how overworked they became - in one particular month the committee met on 20 different occasions - they judged each case on the applicant's merits and at all times in the most scrupulous manner. They often examined a candidate twice or even three times, always abiding strictly to the mandate given to them by the full Pilotage Committee, until they were quite satisfied that the said applicant was a truly competent and qualified person to act as a pilot. There were divers reasons for not granting a licence, the most common being:

1) Not willing to devote the whole of his time to Pilotage.

2) Could not or would not supply proof of his age.

3) Their knowledge and experience of the Canal was found to be of such a limited character that they could not recommend them as fit and proper persons to hold a Pilotage Licence on the Canal.

4) The dubious state of an applicant's health left a lot to be desired.

Eventually the Pilotage Committee resolved that the limit to the number of first class General Licensed Pilots be 60.

On January 22nd 1896, the following notice was advertised under the director of the Chairman of the Pilotage Committee:

The following is a copy of those historic byelaws.

MANCHESTER SHIP CANAL.

PILOTAGE BY-LAWS.

Whereas the Manchester Ship Canal Company, being the pilotage authority for the Port of Manchester, having made certain by-laws for the regulation of pilots employed on the Ship Canal. and such by-laws having been submitted to and confirmed by the Queen's Most Excellent Majesty in Council, notice is hereby given, that the Pilotage By-laws of the Manchester Ship Canal Company will be put into operation on the 1st day of February, 1896.

Pilotage on the Ship Canal is not compulsory (excepting for certain passenger ships as provided for in section 604 of the Merchant Shipping Act, 1894), but no pilot except qualified and licensed in accordance with the said by-laws will be permitted to navigate, conduct, or move any vessel within the canal, docks, and basins of the Company.

Copies of the by-laws may be obtained on application at the offices of the Company, 41, Spring Gardens, Manchester.

By order.

January 22nd, 1896.   A. H. WHITWORTH, Secretary.

25

AT THE COURT AT WINDSOR

The 21st day of November, 1895.
PRESENT,

THE QUEEN'S MOST EXCELLENT MAJESTY IN COUNCIL.

WHEREAS by the 582nd and 683rd Sections of the Merchant Shipping Act, 1894, it is enacted that a Pilotage Authority may, by Byelaw made under Part X of that Act, do all or any of the things specified in the said Section; but that a Byelaw so made shall not take effect until it is submitted to Her Majesty in Council and confirmed by Order in Council:

And whereas the Manchester Ship Canal Company, being the Pilotage Authority for the Port of Manchester, have made and submitted for confirmation by Her Majesty certain Byelaws as set forth in the Schedule hereto annexed: And whereas it has been made to appear to Her Majesty that the proposed Byelaws are proper and reasonable: And whereas the provisions of Section one of the Rules Publication Act, 1893, have been complied with:

NOW, THEREFORE, Her Majesty, by virtue of The powers vested in Her by the Merchant Shipping Act, 1894, and by and with the advice of Her Privy Council, is pleased to approve of and confirm the said Byelaws as set forth in the Schedule hereto annexed.

C. L. PEEL

SCHEDULE
BYE-LAWS

1. The following Bye-laws shall commence and take effect on the 1st day of December 1895:

2. In the construction of these Bye-laws "The Company" shall mean the Manchester Ship Canal Company, the expression "the Directors" shall mean the Directors for the time being of the Manchester Ship Canal Company, and "the Canal" shall mean the Manchester Ship Canal.

3. Pilotage upon the Canal is not compulsory, but no Pilot, except qualified and licensed as hereinafter mentioned, shall be permitted to navigate, conduct, or move any vessel within the Canal, Docks, and Basins of the Company.

4. The Company may, if they deem it expedient so to do, examine any person (or persons) who shall be desirous to act as a Pilot, and every person who shall be approved of by the Company shall receive a licence in writing, signed by the Company's Secretary, stating that he is duly qualified to act as a Pilot on the Canal, and also setting forth the name, age, stature, complexion, and place of abode of the person so licensed.

5. Every licence granted by the Company shall expire on the first day of the month of September which shall first happen after the granting thereof, and for the licence which shall be granted to any person upon his first admission as a Pilot, there shall be paid to the Company the sum of £2 2s. (£2.10p) and for the second and every subsequent licence which shall be granted to such person the sum of £1 1s. (£1.05p)

6. Every licensed Pilot shall exhibit his licence to the Master of the vessel, and give his name and address and behave with strict sobriety and respect, and use his utmost care and diligence to conduct the vessel to her destination safely, and without damage to any vessel or other property; and he shall obey and execute all lawful orders given by the Company's Superintendents,

Dockmasters, and Officials relative to the locking, towing, transporting, or removing of any vessel under his charge, and he shall not. when the signal is against him, bring or attempt to bring any vessel into any lock, dock, or basin without an order in writing from an authorized Official of the Company.

7. Every Pilot to whom a licence has been granted shall provide himself with a flag of the usual dimensions and of two colours, the upper horizontal half red and the lower horizontal half white, and on taking charge as Pilot of any vessel, and so long as he remains in charge, he shall cause his flag to be hoisted on board such vessel where it may be most conspicuously seen, and shall keep this flag continually flying until he is discharged or relieved by another Pilot.

8. Every Pilot shall, when on duty, always have with him a good watch, a tide table, copy of the Company's bye-laws, his licence, and his flag.

9. Every licensed Pilot shall, before leaving any vessel piloted by him either inwards or outwards, obtain from the Officer in command of such vessel a certificate of his services, and shall, upon landing, report himself to the Company's Superintendent or Official in charge at such landing, and deliver up to such Superintendent or Official every such certificate and all moneys received by him.

10. No person to whom a pilotage licence shall be granted by the Company shall add to or in any way alter such licence or make or alter any endorsement thereon, nor shall at any time lend such licence.

11. A licensed Pilot shall not, without the Company's consent, demand or receive in respect of any services any payment either in excess of or less than the amount which he shall under any resolution or regulation of the Company for the time being in force be entitled to receive.

12. Whenever any licensed Pilot shall observe any alteration in any of the banks or the depth of water in the canal, or that any buoys, beacons, or lights have been driven away, broken down,

damaged, or are out of place, or any circumstances affecting the safety of the navigation of the Canal, he shall forthwith send correct written information thereof to the Manager of the Company.

13. Whenever any accident shall have happened to or been caused by any vessel while in charge of a licensed Pilot, such Pilot shall, immediately after leaving the vessel, report the facts of such accident, so far as he knows them, to the nearest Canal Superintendent.

14. Any licensed Pilot losing his licence shall forthwith give notice thereof to the Company's Secretary, stating the circumstances under which the licence was lost, and the Company'S Secretary shall, unless he shall be satisfied that the loss has been caused by the Pilot's misconduct, cause to be issued to such Pilot a duplicate licence in a form to be approved by the Company. For a duplicate licence a licensed Pilot shall pay to the Company such a sum, not exceeding £2 2s., (£2.10p) as the Company may direct in each case.

The Manchester Pilot Service had at last become of age. The full list was as follows :-

GENERAL LICENCE : FIRST CLASS

ADAM CARTWRIGHT	MARINE PARADE	SEACOMBE
JOSEPH STUART	28 BRADFORD TRRCE	SEACOMBE
HENRY HILL	SURREY STREET	RUNCORN
PETER SINNOTT	5 HENTHORNE ROAD	NEW FERRY
*W H COLOUITT	4 TEILO STREET	TOXTETH PK.
*G H R LEWIS	57 MADELINE STREET	TOXTETH PK.
*THOS K DIXON	127 SALISBURY ROAD	WAVERTREE
JOHN ELLIS	137 CHURCH STREET	RUNCORN
GEORGE GREEN	35 GROVE ROAD	ROCK FERRY
WM ONION	OXFORD TERRACE	ELLESMERE PT
HARRY BOXER JONES	12 SEAFIELD ROAD	NEW FERRY
HENRY HILL	5 YORK STREET	RUNCORN
JOSEPH INGLEFIELD	13 UNION STREET	
JNS WM EDWARDS	23 HAVERGALE STREET	RUNCORN
CHAS YOUNG	NEW FERRY LANE	NEW FERRY
*RICHARD IDDON	14 PHYTHIAN STREET	LIVERPOOL
JAS HILL	8 MANN ISLAND	LIVERPOOL
GEO CARTWRIGHT	8 MARINE PARADE	SEACOMBE
W J HUNTINGTON	14 BELLE VUE ROAD	SEACOMBE
*ELLIS TAYLOR	21 EDITH ROAD	SEACOMBE
*MORRIS WM ROBERTS	54 GROVE ROAD	ROCK FY.
NICHOLAS MORGAN	90 BUCHANAN ROAD	SEACOMBE
DAVID SORTON JONES	8 TAYLOR STREET	LIVERPOOL
*WM EDMONDS	THE KENNELS	AINTREE V.
*JAMES COUSINS	1 KNOWSLEY STREET	WALTON
*GEO H CLARK	19 SCMERVILLE ROAD	WATERLOO
THOS GRIFFITHS	25 RIDLEY STREET	BIRKENHEAD
JOHN IRLAM JONES	7 YORK VILLAS	EVERTON
*DAVID JONES	88 JUBILEE DRIVE	LIVERPOOL
*CHAS. E. WILCOX	HOME LEA	LISCARD
*THOS. DARCY	40 BEDFORD STREET	N. L'POOL
*THOS F BOYD	16 STANFIELD ROAD	LIVERPOOL
*JNS WM PASS	32 DYSON STREET	WALTON
*W A SMITH	89 BERKELEY STREET	LIVERPOOL
*ALBERT LEVER	3 WHITFIELD STREET	HR TRANMERE
WM HY JEVONS	8 PARK AVENUE	SEACOMBE
WM PEAOOCK	29 WATERLOO ROAD	RUNOORN
*EDWARD C HARRIS	23 CLARENCE ROAD	SEACOMBE
*F W T PENNEY	8 CEDAR STREET	BIRKENHEAD
*ROBERT ALLEN	18 HOLLAND STREET	LIVERPOOL

*ERNEST N MORRISON	61 TOLLEMACHE ST.	N.BRIGHTON
*GEO McALLISTER	11 TANCRED ROAD	ANFIELD
*THOS HY PATERSON	38 DOVEY STREET	LIVERPCOL
*ALEX DONALDSON	17 BELMONT ROAD	N. BRIGHTON
*JOHN W P DURRANT	12 COMELY BANK ROAD	EGREMONT
CHAS STRINGER	4 HUTCHINSON STREET	WIDNES
*THOS ED. PARRY	54 DUNLUCE STREET	WATERLOO
B WHITEHOUSE	27 MERSEY ROAD	ROCK FERRY
ROBT. HAIR	29 ARIEL STREET	WEASTE
JAMES BARNES	50 BROUGHAM STREET	TRANMERE
JOHN HYNES	18 EASTBOURNE STREET	LIVERPOOL
DANIEL O'KEEFE	23 LEIGH TERRACE	ANFIELD
JOHN THCMPSON	156 HULTON STREET	SALFORD
GEORGE BARTLEY	14 SEAFIELD ROAD	NEW FERRY
WILLIAM MARKER	105 STAMFORD STREET	O.TRAFFORD
THOMAS BROWN	43 YATES STREET	LIVERPOOL

* DENOTES LIVERPOOL RIVER MERSEY PILOT

GENERAL LICENCES : SECOND CLASS

JOS SAML PEGG	14 PHYTHIAN STREET	LIVERPOOL
T H L JONES-HACRY	THELWALL HALL	WARRINGTON
JAMES ABRAM	9 WATERLOO ROAD	RUNCORN

LIVERPOOL APPROPRIATED LICENCES : FIRST CLASS

WM BACKHOUSE	37 ARNOLD STREET	LIVERPOOL
HUGH JONES	29 ROCKFIELD ROAD	ANFIELD
	CLAN LINE.	
JNS RANDALL JONES	24 ELGIN DRIVE	LISCARD
R J PEDDER	66 MENZIES STREET	DINGLE
	LIVERPOOL CLAN LINE	
JNO B SUMNER	MAGAZINE PARK	LISCARD
H E WILLIAMS	3 LATHAM VIEW	EGREMONT
THOS LEWIS	6 BELGRAVE STREET	LISCARD
JAMES McLEAN	HOLLY BANK	LISCARD
JOHN HENDERSON	RIVERSLEA	LISCARD
WILLIAM CRANE	MAGAZINE LANE	LISCARD
H J MANCHESTER	79 TRAFALGAR ROAD	EGREMONT
	CLAN LINE	
CHAS F FELTON	21 PROSPECT VALE	FAIRFIELD
C H BERNARD	20 ALROY ROAD	ANFIELD
	ELLERMAN LINE	

JAMES ALLAN	5 WESLEY AVENUE	LISCARD
LAMPORT AND HOLT		
ROBERT PARRY	14 RICE HEY ROAD	EGREMONT
FRANK WILKINSON	RIVERSIDE	EGREMONT
		ANCHOR LINE.

PILOTAGE CERTIFICATES

THOS PAUL	9 VICTORIA ROAD	RUNCORN
ANDREW FRASER	410 ST VINCENT STREET	GLASGOW
ALEX BLAIR	30 JAMAICA STREET	GLASGOW
HY ROCKETT	44 BROOKLAND STREET	WEASTE
DUNCAN KERR	123 HOPE STREET	GLASGOW

SHIPS IN THE CANAL ON THE 13th. OCTOBER 1894.

POMONA DOCKS

"TAFFY"	FROM	PENMAENMAWR	STONE.
"HELVITA"	"	TREVOR	SETTS.
"FLAGSTAFF			
"MARY SUTHERLAND"	"	CONWAY	CLAY.

NO. 8 DOCK.

*RALLUS"	FROM	ROTTERDAM	GENERAL.
"CARADOC"	"	KOKTA	GENERAL.
"GRAMPUS"	"	GLASGOW	WOOD PULP.
"TWILIGHT"	"	STETTIN	WOOD PULP.
"OUSEL"	"	ROTTERDAM	GENERAL.

NO. 7 DOCK

"ANNA"	FROM	BAY VERT	DEALS.
"PRINCESS HELENA	"	GLASGOW	GENERAL.
"2ERWICK"	"	TREPORT	"
"TRIESTE"	"	STETTIN	"
"STORMARN"	"	HAMBURG	"

NO. 6 DOCK

"UNCLE NED"	FROM	LIVERPOOL	LOADING.
"MAURITIUS"	"	GLASGOW	GENERAL.
"MINSK"	"	COPENHAGEN	"
"BIELA"	"	BRASIL	"

The original Barton Aqueduct built by James Brindley in 1761 looking down stream.

(Courtesy Mrs. W. Yates Collection)

1892
The new Barton Aqueduct can be seen behind the road swing bridge, with the old archways built in 1761 still visible on the right.

(Courtesy Mrs W. Yates Collection)

PARTINGTON COALING BASIN

"STAGHOUND"	FROM BELFAST	COAL.
"BERYL"	" GREENOCK	COAL.

TRAFFORDWHARF

"PIONEER"	FROM LE HAVRE	FLOUR
"SAVINA"	" ROSARIO	WHEAT.

MOORE LANE

"MURIEL"	FROM ORMES HEAD LIMESTONE.

WARRINGTON

"GEORGE"	FROM LIVERPOOL	RESIN.

RUNCORN DOCKS

"BARSHAW"	FROM KILLYBEGS	CHINA CLAY.
"HARVEST QUEEN"	" PLYMOUTH	STONE.
"ZILLA"	" LLANDULLAS	LIMESTONE.
"QUELLE"	" PUGWASH	TIMBER.
"EDDA"	" NEW RICHMOND	DEALS.

ELLESMERE PORT

"ELEANOR"	FROM PLYMOUTH	CHINA CLAY.
"MOSS ROSE"	" FOWEY	"

VESSELS IN TRANSIT.

OUTWARD BOUND.	INWARD BOUND.
"SEAL" TO GLASGOW	"SUNFLOWER" FROM LIVERPOOL
"MARGARET" LIVERPOOL	"KATIE CLEUDD" PARR
"DHOON GLEN" SLIGO	"TELEGRAPHIC" LONDON
'EASTHAM" LONDON	"JUNO" BORDEAUX
"ARCHITECTI" LIVERPOOL	"AVALON" VALENCIA
"ROYAL PRINCE" TUNIS	"CASTOR" PATRAS
"MARTIN" ROTTERDAM	

In addition to these movements transits were made by 12 Tugs, 5 Hoppers, 62 Cargo Barges and three passenger steamers.

34

1890
The Magazine
This was a purpose built store for all the explosives to be used
when blasting through rock during the digging of the Ship Canal
between Eastham and Latchford Locks. It is still standing today
in1993

(Courtesy of Mrs J. J. Pierpoint)

3.

THE PILOTAGE WORKING SYSTEM
1894-1896

With the establishment of an organised Ship Canal Pilot Service in 1896 , which had been greeted with great acclaim by all participating parties, the problems that were to assail this fledgeling service so soon after its formation could hardly have been envisaged let alone imagined by the Pilotage Committee. Little could they have realised what bitter seeds of discord had been sown and what a chequered and stormy future lay ahead.

The Ship Canal pilot service was divided into two very distinctive and separate bodies, viz: 'the haves' and 'the have nots'. The Liverpool Pilots (Appropriated Pilots) represented 'the haves' and the Ship Canal Pilots (Independent or Free Pilots), 'the have nots'.

Even before the formal setting up of the Ship Canal pilot service, the major bone of contention and frustration among the non-appropriated pilots had always been the large discrepancies in the earnings of individual pilots, due to the unequal and iniquitous pilotage working system. The question uppermost in the minds of all the Ship Canal pilots was, "When will an equitable and fair working system be introduced to alleviate the present pernicious system of earnings?".

The pilotage system that prevailed in 1896, from the time the very first services were rendered on the Ship Canal in 1894, was the time honoured custom whereby the fees from each vessel piloted were directly paid to that pilot who provided such a service. On paper this appeared fair and equitable but in actual practice this was not so and left a lot to be desired in the equal sharing of work and consequently earnings.

In 1896, forty-three Liverpool Pilots were licensed to perform pilotage duties on the Manchester Ship Canal. One fourth of the pilotage earned by these pilots for their services on the canal went into their own accounts and the balance to a common fund for the benefit of the whole Liverpool Pilot Service. The Liverpool Pilot Service had a pooling system of earnings as early as 1773 and again in 1798. A new pooling system came into operation in 1896.

These pilots were already very well established and known by Ship Owners, Ship Brokers (Agents), Freight Clerks, etc. Liverpool's first authorised pilot service commenced in 1776, and they looked upon the Manchester Ship Canal as a natural appendage to their pilotage district, especially the appropriated pilots. The original appropriated pilots were described as "Attached" or "Steam" pilots. This took its rise from the time when sailing vessels far outnumbered steamers, in 1824. Then masters of coasting steam vessels, trading between certain ports, were permitted to retain their outward pilot on board during the whole of the voyage so that he would be available to pilot the vessel into Liverpool when she returned; in other words he was "attached" to the "steam" vessel for the duration of the voyage and an appropriate fee was paid into the general pilot fund.

When this practice ceased certain Liverpool Pilots were selected to pilot vessels of particular companies, the first of these being appointed in 1860 to the Montreal Steam Ship Company. They were officially designated Appropriated or Choice pilots and have remained so unto this day.

Each of these appropriated pilots earned more pilotage fees than the Ship Canal pilots, the type of ship they handled being more remunerative, being in the main larger and more frequent in entering and leaving port. They jealously guarded this privi-

Mr Marshall Stevens. Born in Plymouth in 1852 First Chairman M.S.C. Pilotage Committee 1895-1897
Courtesy of the M.S.C.Co.

Mr Ernest Latimer. Born Drocheda 1869. Chairman of Pilotage Committee 1900-1928.
Courtesy the M.S.C. Co.

leged position and any attempt to break down or infiltrate this influential and affluent cadre was quickly repelled. These pilots had another great advantage over the Ship Canal Pilots, they being Liverpool Pilots had regular employment and their earnings were equally divided according to their rating but were allowed to compete with the Ship Canal pilots on equal terms.

The crumbs that were left from the rich man's table that is to say, those vessels requiring a pilot service that did not come under the auspices of the Liverpool Appropriated Pilots, were "appropriated" in yet another manner.

The invidious situation that prevailed here was that the remaining pilotage services were monopolised and under the control of four senior Ship Canal Pilots, Adam Cartwright (Licence No.1), John Stuart (Licence No.2), Peter Sinnot (Licence No.4) and George Green (Licence No.9). They had an advantage over the other Ship Canal Pilots by having a seat on the Pilotage Committee and therefore had the confidence and respect of all the powers that be, Ship owners, Agents, Brokers and the Ship Canal Authority. From this privileged position they had managed to convince the Pilotage Committee that they could and would organise an efficient system of Pilotage to ensure all vessels requiring pilots would be manned.

The four "Master Pilots" as they were known, were unable to perform all the pilotage themselves and allocated a portion of their work to other pilots (usually favourites). These pilots so employed had to sign an agreement to assist or work under one of the Master Pilots and on completion of a pilot service, sign the pilotage bill stating that the fee earned was to be paid into the private account of the Master Pilot who employed him.

The Master Pilot then paid the said pilot such a sum he thought fit and proper which at times was as little as 10% of the authorised pilotage fee but never on any occasion in excess of 50%. This arrangement became known as the "Contract" or "Farming Out" system.

Standing W. Peacock
Seated L-R J. Inglesfield, G. Green(?), P. Sinnot, J. Hill

1900
Mr C. Stringer of Widnes

1899
Mr J. W. Edwards of Runcorn

40

It only remains to account for the third class of pilots who were neither Liverpool Pilots nor "Contract" pilots. They objected on moral and professional grounds to the "Contract" or "Farming Out" system and refused to condone and co-operate with the Master Pilots. These pilots could be truly called the "Free" or "Independent" Ship Canal Pilots. They pursued their search for piloting work by personally calling on the Freight Clerks in the Shipping Brokers (Agents) offices that proliferated along the Dock Roads and in the cities of Liverpool and Manchester in those days.

It was a precarious and often unrewarding way of attaining a living from piloting, most of the pilotage work in the Ship Canal having already been "appropriated" in one way or another. The most saddening aspect of this situation was, that the very system of "commission" they so totally abhorred forced them to pursue their vocation in this manner, and they discovered to their undoubted dismay, it was rife in the Shipping Brokers (Agents) offices by way of the Freight Clerks who were accustomed to charge a "commission" for all piloting work they delegated to individual pilots.

If a pilot refused to pay this "commission" he very quickly discovered that the offer of piloting work from the Freight Clerks was drastically reduced, almost to become non-existent and a more receptive pilot was offered the work. It was the classic "Catch 22" situation of yesteryear.

The final calamity that could befall a "Free" pilot would be at the time he applied to be re-examined for the renewal of his Ship Canal Licence on September 1 of each year. Under an Article in the Canal Pilotage Bye-Laws it states "a pilot must have completed at least three full length passages between Manchester and Eastham or vice-versa in the capacity as a pilot, during the pilotage year, August 31st to September 1st the following year, to qualify for re-examination for the renewal of his licence.

The Master Pilots were not slow in realising how effective this Bye-Law could work for them in conjunction with their control of pilotage on the Ship Canal. From this position of power during the pilotage year, they could and did prevent any "Free" (non-co-operative) pilots from completing the requisite three full length pilot services. This successfully and permanently removed any disturbing factions to their affluent way of life.

The infamous "Richard Edwards Affair" which is given a full and frank coverage later in this book, is a perfect testimony that this odious practice was carried on by the Master Pilots. This was the chaotic and troublesome state that existed as the working system of the Ship Canal Pilotage Service in 1896.

EVENTS ON THE MANCHESTER SHIP CANAL

The first sod was cut at Eastham on the 11th November, 1887.

Thurs, 19th June, 1891. Ellesemere Port to Eastham section completed.

2nd July, 1891. Water admitted in Eastham Locks.

16th July, 1891 Traffic to Ellesmere Port Via Ship Canal commenced.

28th September, 1891, canal open to Weston Marsh lock.

22nd July, 1892, Saltport established.

9th June, 1893, water admitted to the Runcorn section.

8th July, 1893, water admitted to canal from Runcorn docks to Old Quay.

18th October, 1893, the official opening of Ellesemere Port pontoon dry dock.

17th November, 1893, water admitted between Runcorn and Latchford.

25th November, 1893, Canal filled from end to end at 10.30pm.

7th December, 1893, first journey of directors by water over the whole length of the canal.

1st January, 1894, canal opened for traffic to Manchester when 71 vessels opened the docks, leading the procession from Latchford was the steam yacht "Norseman" with the canal directors on board, next was the "Snowdrop" with members of the city corporation, the "Brackley" and "Dagmar" carried ship canal officals.

21st May, 1894, official opening by Queen Victoria on admiralty yacht "Enchantress".

The first cotton ship at Manchester was the "Finsbury" of London on 17th January, 1894, unloading 4,170 bales.

18th January, 1894, first steamer from New Orleans, "Glenisle", unloaded 4,390 bales for 21 cotton spinners.

January, 1894, "Venango", first heavy cargo, 21'-3" with 4,000 bales of cotton and 2,222 tons of corn and general cargo.

25th September, 1894, first telephone installed at Runcorn.

4.

THE FIRST ATTEMPTS TO FORM
A ROTARY SYSTEM

March 9th 1896 was to become an historic day in the annals of the Ship Canal Pilot Service. At the regular meeting of the Pilotage Committee held at Spring Gardens, Manchester, presided over by Mr Marshall Stevens, Mr Norman Colquitt, representing the Liverpool Pilots who held a Ship Canal licence and therefore an elected member of that said committee, placed the following proposition before that august body:

"That the Ship Canal Pilots be divided into two bodies to be called "Appropriated" and "Term" pilots; the term pilots to attend at times and places to be hereafter agreed so that pilots may always be available at these places for Shipmasters requiring their services.

Pilots to be given the choice of whether they will be "Appropriated" or "Term" pilots, but if they prefer to be appropriated pilots that they be limited to the pilotage of vessels of one firm only". It is not hard to perceive the great influence of the Liverpool Pilot Service in this proposal.   One of the greatest tributes that can be paid to the Liverpool Pilot Service is that other pilot systems in the UK and indeed all over the world, have been modelled on their service.

This was the first contentious attempt to achieve some semblance of uniformity and to lay the foundation for a regular, properly organised rotary system of pilotage in the Ship Canal. For some pilots the thought of such a revolutionary change from

1900
The docks at Ellesmere Port

1904
The docks at Runcorn. The bowler hatted pilot is Mr John Ellis of Runcorn.

unbridled freedom to some form of rigid discipline with all its connotations, must have come as quite a shock.

After hearing the views of some of the members of the Committee, the chairman suggested that before the Committee made any recommendation, the matter should be thoroughly considered by the whole of the pilots. To enable this to be done, he suggested that a short statement should be proposed by Mr Colquitt giving his views and that this should be distributed amongst the Ship Canal Pilots and if necessary, a general meeting should be held to discuss the matter.

It was resolved that the Chairman with Messrs. Colquitt and Cartwright should form a sub-Committee to draft a short statement on Rotary Pilotage. This was embodied in the form of the following letter and forwarded to each of the pilots licensed upon the Ship Canal in April 1896:

"It has been proposed that with the exception of Pilots specially appropriated to particular firms the Manchester Pilot Service shall be worked upon what is known as the "Turn or Rotary System". The proposal to work this system of Pilotage is as follows: "That pilot stations should be established at Dukes Dock Liverpool, Eastham, Runcorn, Partington and Manchester. That pilots shall be placed on the list and attend at one of the stations as arranged and that they take turns with each other, each pilot taking that vessel which comes in his turn."

The proposal was fair minded and impartial but it proved to be an almost insurmountable hurdle, so much so that it continued to be contested for the next two decades and caused a great deal of animosity between the two piloting factions of that time, the Liverpool Pilots holding a Canal Licence and the Ship Canal Pilots,the legacy of which lasted well into the 1960's.

For the next twelve months no progress was made in implementing the major points in the proposal that was embodied in the letter sent to all pilots. One can only assume that the majority of the pilots were unwilling to adopt themselves to a new working system with such rigid discipline. Unfortunately, there are no records of the pilots' replies to that particular proposal.

However, the disenchantment with the present system of pilotage did not abate and on May 6th 1897, Mr Benjamin Whitehouse, a Ship Canal Pilot elected by the Ship Canal Pilots to represent them wrote the following letter to the Pilotage Committee:

"Sir

Manchester Ship Canal Bye-Laws

The Pilotage on the Manchester Ship Canal is carried on in a very unsatisfactory manner which causes great dissatisfaction amongst a great number of the licensed pilots - Article 15 in the Canal Pilotage Bye-Laws reads as follows:

" All Pilotage rates shall be collected by the Company and paid to the pilots who earn the same, less a reasonable deduction for the cost of collection. Such pilotage rates shall be as follows..."

Our complaint is that the Pilotage is in the hands of two or three pilots who are on the Pilotage Committee. These pilots cannot do all the work themselves so let other pilots (favourites) do a portion of the work for them.

These men have to sign the pilot cards that the money is to be paid into the private account of the pilot who employed them and not into the man's account who earned it. They then pay the man any sum they may think proper. In fact, nearly the whole pilotage is farmed and monopolised. We are very much dissatisfied with this system and consider it unfair and we respectfully ask you to assist us and insist that the Bye-Laws be carried out as they stand; and that the pilotage money should be paid by the Canal Company only to the man who does the work and earns it.

Trusting you will be able to help us
(signed) B Whitehouse
For the pilots. "

At the same time a copy of a letter addressed to "The Rt. Hon. The Duke of Devonshire K.G., Lord President of the Privy Council in London sent by Mr B Whitehouse on behalf of the Ship Canal Pilots was read to the Pilotage Committee:

"Sir

River Mersey Pilots re Manchester Canal Pilots

There are upwards of 30 River Mersey Pilots holding Licenses for pilotingon the Manchester Canal. The pilotage on the River Mersey is compulsory.These pilots have an unfair advantage over us Canal Pilots. They being Liverpool Pilots have regular employment and their earnings are equally divided according to their rating and they are allowed to compete with us on equal terms. We do not consider this just as the competition is not equal: We, the Canal Pilots (by one of the Minutes passed by the Canal Pilotage Committee), have to devote the whole of our time to piloting on the Canal.

Will you be good enough to take this matter up and kindly cause me to be informed whether the Liverpool Pilots have a legal right to work in other pilotage waters than their own, and if not, what steps should be taken to put a stop to it.

Trusting you will be able to help us in this matter,

(signed)   B Whitehouse

For the pilots. "

These two letters and all their implications were discussed at great length by the Pilotage Committee without coming to any conclusive recommendations. Eventually it was agreed that the Committee needed more time to consider the subject matter of the two letters and it was proposed that this matter be placed on the Agenda for the June Pilotage Committee meeting.

The June Pilotage Committee meeting once again offered much discussion, after which it was proposed by Mr N Colquitt (Liverpool Pilot), and seconded by Mr Dixon (Liverpool Pilot):

"That the present system of working the Manchester Ship Canal Pilotage service is unsatisfactory and ought to be amended."

Upon a show of hands there appeared:

For the motion - 4   Against   - 6.

The Chairman declared the motion to be lost. Once again the barrier to a fair and equitable rotary working system proved impenetrable and the "Gang of Four" still sat snugly behind their defences.

But the pilots were now determined not to be denied their right to a fair working system and on August 31st 1897 a deputation from the pilots holding licences on the Ship Canal met with the Chairman of the Pilotage Committee. They complained bitterly that under the present system of pilotage on the canal, a portion of the pilots were unable to earn a living and that other aspects of the Pilotage service left a lot to be desired and required changing.

A nine point Charter was placed before the Chairman and read as follows:

1. Contracts: To cancel the contract business as carried on by Messrs. Cartwright, Stuart, Sinnot and Green and to allow no pilot to contract for more work than he can personally attend to and then only with one firm.

2. Employment of Pilots: No pilot shall employ any other pilot to assist him in completing his contracts, but any work he cannot personally attend to shall be given to the first Canal Pilot offering his services, either in the river or at Eastham Locks; any infringement on this rule should incur a severe penalty.

3. Article 15: Earnings: Article 15 should be carried out in its entirety, i.e. the pilot earning the money should have it collected in his own name, paid into his own number and receive the money himself. On no account shall he be allowed to sign his card over to another man's number.

4. Signing Agreements: No pilot be allowed to sign an Agreement to assist or work under any other pilot on the Canal without the authority of the Pilotage Board and then only under exceptional circumstances.

5. Committee Men: The Canal Pilots should be allowed to choose their own representatives on the Pilotage Board with power to supersede them and to elect others in their place from time to time. At present we know nothing of the proceedings of those of the Committee who pretend to represent us. We think the Pilotage Committee should be reconstructed at once as it is not representative.

6. Liverpool Pilots Licences: Some of our members think the Liverpool Pilots should not be allowed to take up their Canal Licensces after the expiration of their present Licences in September, the reason for this is that they have a good living already which is protected by law. We thus have to compete with them at a disadvantage; we respectfully ask you not to grant any more Licences to the Liverpool Pilots as we consider there are too many on the Canal already.

7. Liverpool Pilots: Any Liverpool Pilot who may be broke or suspended from the Liverpool Pilot Service for drunkenness, insubordination, incompetency or any other cause should also be broke or suspended from the Manchester Ship Canal Pilotage Service as if he is not fit to pilot on the Mersey he is not fit to pilot on the Canal.

8. Agreements: No Liverpool Pilot should be allowed to make an agreement with the Captain of a ship for his Canal Pilotage until he has first completed his River Mersey Pilotage at Eastham under a severe penalty.

9. Boat at the Manchester Docks: We do not consider it right that Pilot Sinnott should be allowed to have a boat working in the Manchester Docks. We are not allowed to do anything but pilot but he is allowed to do both boating and piloting - through this he gets a lot of cheap information which is a disadvantage to us generally - we should like this to be stopped or we allowed the same privilege.

1895

WHEN A SAILING SHIP CAME TO MANCHESTER
"TIMARU" GAT: 1363. l.239' B.36'

In the early days of the Manchester Ship Canal three and four masted sailing ships came to the Pomoma Docks to discharge, One such ship was a refrigerator ship the "TIMARU." pictured above passing through the Barton Aqueduct channel outward bound. The vessel had loaded the first full cargo of frozen mutton from Melbourne, Australia, It was a long voyage, a memorandum dated October 11th 1895 stated:- The latest news of the "TIMARU" is that she left Melbourne on June 3rd. She was reported spoke on July 11th in 56 S 74 W off Cape Horn, but this is not to be relied upon she may arrive any day. This memo is still preserved by the Manchester Ship Canal Company.

(Courtesy of the M. S. C. Co.)

The Chairman accepted the document of recommendations from the pilots but refrained from commenting on their contents and intimated he would place their recommendations before the full Pilotage Committee meeting on September 27th. This was duly done and after considerable discussion and after hearing the views of some of the members of the Committee (who I wonder?), the following replies were minuted:

Nos: 1, 2, 4 & 8: The views of the pilots holding General Licences should be obtained as to whether the present system of pilotage should continue or whether they would prefer the "turn system"; and the Secretary was instructed to issue a circular accordingly.

No: 3 Earnings: The Chairman stated that from the 1st October the Company could not recognise any pilot for receiving the earnings of any group of pilots and that they would only pay the pilotage fees collected by them to the individual pilot earning the same and the Secretary was so instructed to inform the pilots.

No:5 Composition of Committee: This question would be dealt with at the end of each year of office, the representatives on the Committee being re-elected annually as provided for in the Minutes of the Committee dated October 21st 1895.

Nos: 6 & 7: Liverpool Mersey Pilots: No action was deemed necessary with regard to these but the Chairman stated it was not likely that any more Licences would be granted to pilots holding River Mersey Licensces.

No:9 Boat at the Manchester Docks: As the boat referred to does not belong to Pilot Sinnott, no action was considered necessary.

In accordance with the September minutes on October 14th 1897 a circular was sent to all pilots holding a General Licence on the Ship Canal. - The Liverpool Pilots holding a Canal Licence were excluded by the Secretary of the Pilotage Committee which read as follows:

"Sir

As it is represented to the Pilotage Committee that the present system of working the pilotage on the Canal does not give satisfaction to the whole of the pilots, the Committee are prepared to consider whether a rotary or turn system might be adopted, but before doing so are desirous of having the views thereon of the whole of the Pilots holding General Licences on the Canal and for this purpose I enclose a card which I shall be glad if you will fill up and sign and return it to me at your early convenience.

The rotary or turn system would be worked somewhat on the lines of stations being established at Dukes Dock, Liverpool, Eastham, Manchester and elsewhere as may be found desirable to which a certain number of pilots would be attached, each pilot taking his turn of piloting such vessels as may require the services of a pilot."

The wording was almost identical to the original document sent to all pilots eighteen months earlier in April 1896.

At the Pilotage Committee meeting of January 1898, the Secretary made the following statement:

"In reply to my circular sent to all pilots holding a General Licence on the Ship Canal, I have received the returned voting postcards as follows:

In favour of present system - 20.

In favour of Rotary system - 17.

Total Pilots eligible to vote: 44

The Pilotage Committee proposed and passed that in view of these returns it was not considered necessary to alter the present system of working.

How the Pilotage Committee could ignore that nearly 50% of the Ship Canal pilots were totally against the present working system and wanted a radical change, I cannot, for the life of me, understand.

It seems totally inconceivable that yet another attempt to end the blatant monopoly of pilotage and establish a fair system of working could, again, be thwarted. One can only assume that a considerable amount of lobbying must have gone on between October and January. What the Liverpool Pilot Service thought of the Ship Canal Pilots Service is not recorded; maybe it was unprintable.

COLLISION & DAMAGE.

19/1/1893	BORING BARGE "HESKETH" IN EASTHAM CHANNEL,SUNK BY A TONETE CHARGE EXPLODING UNDER THE BARGE,MANY TOOLS LOST,NO ONE HURT.
10/2/1893	TOWNSON,A DREDGER HAND,SUSTAINED BROKEN ARM,RECEIVED £8-2-6 COMPENSATION ON 15/3/1893.
5/9/1893	COAL BARGE "EVA" SUNK AT WESTON MARSH LOCK,CARGO OF 41 TONS.
2/12/1893	BARGE "ALICE" SUNK BY SALT UNION STEAMER "LORD DELAMERE" BLOCKING THE WEAVER CANAL,CLEARED 4/12/1893.
2/2/1894	A COAL BARGE SUNK AT WESTON WALL,BARGEMEN RECOVERING COAL AT 2/- PER TON.
31/7/1894	"ACCUMULATOR" CAUGHT A WIRE IN PROPELLER WHEN RUNNING "BARRY'S" PORT HEAD MOORING.
10/5/1894	ROYAL YACHT "ENCHANTRESS" WITH GUNBOATS "SPEEDY" & "SEAGULL" WENT UP THE CANAL,"ENCHANTRESS" COLLIDED WITH THE PONTOON AT ELLESMERE PORT.RETURNED OUTWARD BOUND ON THE 22/5/1894.
10/8/1894	A NARROWLY ESCAPED ACCIDENT ON BORING BARGE,THE ANCHORAGE OF TONETE IGNITED WHILE BEING CUT.

MAY DAY/95	COAL BARGE "MAYFLOWER" SUNK AT NO MANS LAND,24 TONS OF COAL.
17/11/1894	S/S"ELSE" ASHORE AT WIGG'S,BROKEN STERN POST. 4/4/1895 .
4/4/1895	DREDGER "MANCHESTER" BROKE TWO BLADES OFF STARBOARD PROPELLER, FOULED THE BANK.
10/4/1895	S/S"HAROLD" RAN THROUGH 65 FT GATES AT LATCHFORD,SMASHING THE INTERMEDIATE GATES,DEBRIS REMOVED BY "GORGON". FIRST INCIDENT OF LOCK GATES BEING RAMMED.
24/4/1895	STEEL BARGE "No 15"SUNK AT WESTON POINT.NO DETAILS
26/6/1895	STEEL BARGE "No 10"SUNK IN THE WEAVER CANAL.
27/6/1895	STEEL BARGE "No 8' CAPSIZED AT WESTON POINT.
22/7/1895	LAUNCH "JENNY" SUNK AT HER MOORINGS AT RUNCORN BRIDGE.
12/8/1895	SYNDICATE STEAMER SUNK IN THE ENTRANCE TO OLD QUAY LOCK.
20/9/1895	A VERY HIGH TIDE LIFTED THE PONTOON "GORGON" & BREAKING HER ADRIFT AT OLD QUAY,SHE DRIFTED UP RIVER GROUNDED ON SAND BANK OPPOSITE MR LITTLER'S WORKSHOP,TOWED OFF AT NOON.
22/9/1895	AN OLD DRILLING BARGE AT ELLESMERE PORT ADRIFT IN THE CANAL, FLOATED UPSTREAM TO INCE FERRY,TOWED TO OLD QUAY BY "MINNIE".
8/10/1895	BARQUE "CHRYSOLIS" AGROUND AT SHROPSHIRE UNION ENTRANCE.
5/10/1895	"GWENNIE" TOWING "GORGON",ROPE FOULED PROPELLER.
16/10/1895	TUG "YORK" BROKE PROPELLER IN THE MIDDLE OF CANAL AT FRODSHAM.
13/1/1896	"BETA" PICKED UP "BOLLIN'S"SIDE CHAIN WITH PORT PROPELLER.
14/2/1896	S/S"ASTONHILL",OUTWARD,DRAFT24'GROUNDED AT SECTION 72, REFLOATED ON TIDE.
25/2/1896	TUG "REGULATOR" AGROUND IN THE RIVER WEAVER.

1897

Tug M.S.C. "Charles Galloway" towing two sailing ships past Weston Point Docks. The pilot would have been on the forward sailing ship.

1897

A loaded steamer outward bound passing through Runcorn railway bridge, Tug M.S.C. "Teaser" aft. Note the amount of fenders over the side of the vessel.

(Both photographs Courtesy of Captain P. Dunbavand.)

56

MORE COLLISIONS & DAMAGE.

26/1/1893	BRUNNER MOND FLAT "PARAGON" IN COLLISION WITH THE HOPPER "JUMBO" AT DUTTON LOCK.
29/5/1893	STEEL BARGE "No 2"IN TOW OF THE HOPPER "WHALE", COLLIDED WITH "MANX FAIRY" WHILE PROCEEDING DOWN THE CANAL,DAMAGE SLIGHT.MASTER OF THE "WHALE" & 2 BARGE-MEN WERE DISCHARGED FOR NEGLIGENCE.
17/6/1893	S/S"JASON" COLLIDED WITH DREDGER "BARRY" AT ELLESMERE PORT. "DROMEDARY" COLLIDED WITH "CULZEAN CASTLE" AT WESTON MARSH LOCK.
20/7/1893	SCHOONER "MERIDIAN" COLLIDED WITH "BUF-FALO" AT WESTON MARSH LOCK,SCHOONER'S FIGURE HEAD DAMAGED.
26/10/1893	"MANX FAIRY" COLLIDED WITH TUG "PIONEER" AT FRODSHAM.
9/11/1893	TWO NARROW BOATS,"JOHN"&"JAMES" COL-LIDED WITH "ACCUMULATOR".
22/11/1893	A COAL STEAMER WITH A PONTOON.
6/12/1893	A STEEL BARGE COLLIDED WITH No 62 SWINGBRIDGE ABUTMENT.
11/12/1893	STEEL BARGE "No 1"CAPSIZED,TOWING LOADED FROM THE DREDGER "BARRY" AT OLD QUAY BRIDGE.SKIPS ALL IN CANAL BOTTOM.
15/1/1894	BARGE "TAPP" IN TOW OF TUG "ACCUMULATOR" DAMAGED PICKERINGS BRIDGE IN THE WEAVER CANAL.
2/2/1894	S/S "OPAL" OF HULL COLLIDED WITH STEEL BARGE "No 5".
6/6/1894	TUG "ROSE" & FLATS IN TOW COLLIDED WITH S/S"TELEGRAPH" NEAR RUNCORN BRIDGE.
2/7/1894	DREDGER "BARRY" COLLIDED WITH BARGE "NO 5" AT WESTON POINT.
30/7/1894	TUG "ACCUMULATOR" WITH BARGE "No 5", OUT-WARD BOUND. "No 5" COLLIDED WITH BRIDGEWATER FLAT"CAMBRIDGE". ENGINEER OF THE TUG WAS NOT STANDING BY HIS ENGINE.

1903
The Manchester Navigation Committee on board the
"Charles Galloway"
Back Row left to right: R. Fairclough, J. Pritchard, W. Collier,
T. Hales, W. Thorne, H. Boddington, E. Inman, W. Hunter,
J. Meadowcroft.
Seated left to right: J. K. Bythell, Sir David Gamble,
G. Jebb (Chairman), Sir Joseph Verdin, F. Hawkins.
(Courtesy of M. S. C. Co.)

1892
Dutch "Fascine" workers.
(Courtesy of M. S. C. Co.)

29/9/1894	TUG "GLADIATOR" COLLIDED WITH BARGE "No2".(FOG).
14/12/1894	BARGE "No 24" COLLIDED WITH R.EVAN'S FLATS.
11/4/1895	"CLAN MONROE" FOULED "BOLLIN",INWARD BOUND.
23/5/1895	S/S"VELISHELI" COLLIDED WITH HOPPER "BETA" & THE DREDGER "BOLLIN".(FOG).
21/6/1895	BARGE "No 5" COLLIDED WITH SS "STANLEYFORCE" AT SALTPORT. BARGE DAMAGED.
5/7/1895	HOPPER "BETA" COLLIDED WITH S/S "STANLEY FORCE" IN EASTHAM CHANNEL AT 12-20 AM."STANLEY FORCE" SUNK,SEVEN HANDS SAVED BY "BETA".FIVE HANDS MISSING.(SEE 9/8/1895).
6/7/1895	S/S"MAURITIUS" COLLIDED WITH A COAL FLOAT AT NO MANS LAND, FLOAT RENDERED USELESS.
9/7/1895	TUG "GLADIATOR" COLLIDED WITH WESTON POINT WALL,SHIFTING THE BOILER 1 INCH.

1897
Barton Lock. The Private Tug "Agnes Seed" leased to the M. S.
C. Co., towing two sailing ships outward bound from Manchester.
The Pilot would have been on the leading sailing vessel no doubt
claiming Double Pilotage.

(Courtesy Captain P. Dunbavand)

5.

CANAL PILOTAGE TARIFF : 1895 - 1915

With the formation of a Pilotage Committee and the consolidation of a Canal Pilot Service in 1895, it naturally followed that a properly regulated and legal Canal Pilotage Tariff for every class of vessel should be implemented. The laws of the land decreed the Canal Company were responsible for the code of Canal Pilotage Bye-Laws along with the authority to grant licences to suitable men. These responsibilities were confirmed by Her Majesty's Privy Council on 21 November 1895 and incorporated the right for the Canal Company to set a suitable Pilotage Tariff.

The first schedule of pilotage tariffs was as follows :-

1. All pilotage rates shall be collected by the Company and paid to the pilots who earn the same, less a reasonable deduction for the cost of collection. Such pilotage rates shall be as follows :-

An initial fee shall be paid for each vessel when requiring pilotage service entering or leaving the Canal, according to the net registered tonnage.

	£ s d	
300 Tons and under	0. 10. 0.	(50p)
600 Tons and under	1. 0. 0.	(£1.00)
1,200 Tons and under	1. 10. 0.	(£1.50)
All over 1,200 Tons	2. 0. .0.	(£2.00)

and in addition thereto a sum at the rate of 1s.0d.(5p) per mile or portion of a mile for the distance navigated. Vessels in ballast shall pay the full initial fee, but only half of the mileage rate.

2. When pilotage service is rendered to a vessel in the Canal, but when not entering or leaving the Canal, one half the above-named initial fee is to be charged, in addition to the mileage rate of 1s. (5p) per mile.

3. In any case any licensed pilot shall refuse to pilot any inward or outward bound vessel upon the request of the Master thereof, or in case it shall be proved to the satisfaction of the Company's Directors that any Pilot shall in any manner have failed in or neglected his duty as a Pilot, or in any manner acted contrary to any of these Bye-Laws, or if any Pilot shall refuse to obey any summons of the Company's Directors to appear before them, or to obey any order of the Directors, the Company may recall the licence granted to such Pilot and declare the same to be void, or may suspend the same for such time as they shall think proper.

4. Every person offending against or contravening any of the preceding Byelaws shall, for every such offence, forfeit and pay a sum not exceeding five pounds.

5. If any person other than the Master or Mate shall pilot any vessel into, or out of, or along the Canal, Docks or Basins of the Company, without having been first duly licensed by the Company to act as a Pilot or after the expiration of his licence and before the same shall have been renewed, he shall for every such offence be liable to a penalty not exceeding twenty pounds.

It is interesting to record that in 1895 the Income Tax was 8d.(4p) in the pound for incomes over £150 per year. Twenty Pilots exceeded that figure.

At the Pilotage Committee held on 2 December 1895, a discussion took place as to the collection of Pilotage Fees. After the system adopted by the Mersey Docks and Harbour Board for the collection of the fees for the Mersey Pilots had been fully explained, it was proposed by Mr Colquitt (Liverpool Pilot) and seconded by Mr Hill (Canal Pilot):

1. "That the Canal collect the Pilotage fees to be charged by the Ship Canal Pilots through the National Provincial Bank, along

with their own charges against the ship piloted - the Company charging a commission of 5% for such collection.

2. That each pilot send in to the Company an account of the amount due to him for pilotage service, either fortnightly, monthly or quarterly, as he may elect to be paid.

3. That a Sub-Committee be formed to consider and formulate a certificate for giving particulars of the services rendered by a Pilot which is to be signed by the Captain of the vessel piloted and then handed by the pilot to the Company's Superintendent or Official on landing, to be forwarded to the Dock Office.

All these points were unanimously approved.

On March 21 1896, a memorandum was sent to the Heads of Department at the Dock Office which stated "It will be observed from the Bye-laws that the Canal Company have to collect the pilotage charges from the Shipowner or Agent and pay the amount to the pilot earning the same, less a commission for collecting the charge. The modus operandi is that for each vessel piloted, the pilot shall obtain the signature of the Captain of the vessel upon a printed card provided by the Pilotage Committee for that purpose; upon which is shown the amount due for the service and any other information. The Pilot to countersign the card and afterwards send it at once to the Dock Office wheie an account for the pilotage is to be promptly sent to the Shipowner or Agent and immediate payment required.

This will be done by the Tolls department and before preparing the account, it will be the duty of the Clerk to check the debit entered on the Pilot's card and should the amount shown for pilotage differ from the scale of charges set forth in the Bye-Laws, the amount must be amended to the correct amount. A typical example of the procedure is detailed below :

Pilotage of s.s."WELLRAVEN" - 499 Tons

A letter was received by the Company's Tolls Department from Messrs George Simpson & Co., the Agent of the above steamer, complaining that Pilot Mr Hare who had piloted the

1904

The first Crane Berth - known as "Sheer-Legs" - used for removing top of funnels and non-telescopic masts on vessels proceeding beyond Runcorn Docks.

1984

New Crane Berth. Now mainly used for removing Radar Masts. "City Line" funnel on quay.

(Courtesy Mr G. Gibson)

vessel from Manchester to Acton Grange on 10 December 1898 and from Acton Grange to Eastham on the 11 December, had made a charge of £3.15. 0. (£3.75) instead of £3.5.0. (£3.25) for his services.

After due consideration, the Committee instructed the secretary to inform the Tolls Department that the amount to which the Pilot was entitled in accordance with the Company's Pilotage Bye-laws was £3.5.0. (£3.25) made up as follows :-

	£ s d	
Manchester to Acton Grange (Vessel not entering or leaving Canal - Half initial fee)	0.10.0.	(50p)
Mileage Manchester to Acton Grange ls (5p) per mile	0.18.0.	(90p)
Acton Grange to Eastham (Full initial fee)	1. 0. 0.	(£1)
" " " Mileage	0.17.0.	(85p)
	3. 5. 0.	(£3.25)

Such mistakes were not uncommon in the early years of implementing the new Tariff.

On the other hand there were some Pilots who still thought the Rules and Regulations made by the Pilotage Committee regarding the collection of all pilotage dues did not apply to them. It was reported that on the 5th June 1897 the S.S. "CORSAIR" was piloted from Eastham to Weston Point the pilotage charge amounting to £1.1s.0d. (£1.05p) but on application being made by the Company for payment the owners stated the pilotage had already been paid to another Pilot who they had engaged to Pilot the vessel and declined to pay a second time.. It transpired this Pilot usually does any pilotage for them in the Canal. He had charged the inward pilotage at a "rate per foot" instead of the mileage rate in accordance with the Byelaws, such payment was sufficient to cover the pilotage both inward and outward, and that the owners had frequently paid such pilotage fees to him direct.

The Pilot admitted he had received the pilotage fees because it had been offered to him without his asking for it, but had not received any other fees direct from that Company. Investigations proved that the British and General Express Company had paid the Pilot direct for the pilotage of the "CORSAIR" on a number of occasions and for which he had not accounted to the Company. It was also revealed he had over-charged them in four cases of such pilotage to the amount of £3.4s.0d. (£3.20p). The Pilot did refund this amount when questioned by the shipping company stating that these pilotages did not concern the Ship Canal Company at all. He also returned the amount for the pilotage fee £1.1s 0d(£1.05p) collected by him and expressed his sorrow at having violated the Pilotage Byelaws, which he stated should not occur again.

The Pilotage Committee was not impressed with his contriteness nor were the two Pilots' representatives (Messrs. Colquitt and Sinnot) who moved :-

"That a second class licence is issued to the Pilot in place of his first class licence and that the renewal of his first class licence not to be considered before the issue of new licences in August 1898."

The resolution was unanimously adopted.

It was proposed that for the present the earnings shall be paid to the pilots monthly. Not all the pilots were pleased or in agreement with this proposal, nor the restraints placed on them regarding the collecting of pilotage fees after the free-for-all method they had used for a few years. On 18 May 1896, a short but pointed statement was made at the Pilotage Committee that it had been brought to their notice that some pilots collected their own fees without advising the Canal Company in the usual way. The Pilotage Committee resolved that a return be kept at Eastham for one month from all pilots taking vessels up and down the Canal, so that it may be checked with the cards sent in to the Dock Office by the pilots.

It must be appreciated that in collating the first ever schedule of Canal Pilotage tariffs, it would be unavoidable and inevitable that certain omissions would occur. One such omission immediately noticed by the Canal Pilots' representatives was a charge for a vessel being detained on passage which necessitated that vessel to moor alongside a berth. At the Pilotage Meeting of 18 May 1896, it was proposed by Mr Colquitt (Liverpool Pilot) and seconded by Mr Stuart (Canal Pilot) "that in the case of a passage up or down the Canal being broken for the convenience of a vessel, this Pilotage Committee think the pilot should charge the sum of ten shillings (50p) in addition to the standing Tariff". After some discussion it was agreed that a Sub-Committee should be formed to consider the question of charges made by pilots for extra services. On 10 August 1896, a letter containing the following recommendations from that Sub-Committee was put before the Pilotage Committee :

1) "That with regard to any pilotage rendered to vessels in the River Mersey outside the Canal, the account for such services should be rendered by the pilot direct to the owners or Agents and not through the Canal Company, such pilotage not being within the Canal Company's jurisdiction.

2) That when for the purpose of bunkering or otherwise for the convenience of the owners, a vessel on her passage up or down the Canal, calls at Partington, Acton Grange, Runcorn or other place of call and proceeds on her journey within two hours, a charge of five shillings (25p) be made for berthing; but when detained for a longer period but not exceeding six hours a charge of ten shillings (50p) be made for berthing and detention, provided that the charge of ten shillings (50p) does not exceed one half of the initial fees set out in the Company's Bye-laws."

Both these recommendations were accepted and passed by the Pilotage Committee and added to the Schedule of Pilotage Tariffs. But on 30 January 1901, this agreement was rescinded and the following amendment substituted in place of same, viz:

"That when for the convenience of owners a vessel on her passage up or down the Canal calls at Partington or other place for bunkering or any other purpose and proceeds on her journey within two hours, thereafter a charge shall be made by the Pilot of 5/- (25p) for berthing, but when detained for a day or part of a day in excess of two hours a charge of 10/- (50p) per day or part thereof be made for berthing and detention provided that such charge of 10/- (50p) per day does not as a total charge exceed one half of the initial fees set out in No.16 of the Company's Pilotage Bye-laws. If a vessel is detained beyond 24 hours at any one point of call, she shall be treated as moving from point to point in the Canal."

The Secretary was instructed to forward a notification of the amended agreement to all Pilots immediately. On 7 March 1901 a letter addressed to the Pilotage Committee from the Secretary of the Pilotage Association read as follows :-

"Gentlemen,

At a meeting of the above society held at Liverpool on the 4th instant it was resolved that a letter be written to your Committee asking for your reconsideration of the Pilotage Charges for detention at Partington and other places. The pilots consider that the time is far too long (24 hours for 10/- (50p) and think that the charge say for 2 hours of 5/-(25p) and for a longer period up to 12 hours,10/-(50p) and if detained beyond that time to be treated as moving from point to point. I am also requested to state that the Pilots consider that Oil Tank Ships navigating the Canal outward bound loaded with water ought to be treated as loaded ships with Oil inward bound as to the Pilotage Charges.

Hoping this will receive your favourable consideration."

A discussion took place on the reading of the letter and the Secretary of the Pilotage Committee was instructed to inform the Pilots' Association that the question of payments to pilots for detention had been very fully and carefully considered by the Committee before coming to the decision at the last meeting and that they saw no reason to alter that decision now. With regard to the piloting of Oil Tank Steamers outward bound in the Canal when in Water Ballast, the Committee had, again, after careful consideration, decided that the charge for such vessels remain the same as for vessels in ballast.

There ensued a period of relative calmness on the subject of Pilotage Tariff until 29 February 1904, when the Chairman of the Pilotage Committee submitted and read the following letter from Pilot G Green respecting the present rates of Pilotage chargeable on the Canal:

"Dear Sir

I wish to bring before your notice the question of the Canal Pilotage Tariff. I think the time has now arrived when the initial fee for large ships (such as are being navigated on the Canal at present) should be increased, because it seems to me there is no comparison in that I piloted the S.S."HOLNIS" from Eastham to Manchester on Friday last, she being a vessel of 609 tons, her initial fee is £1.10/-, the mileage added to that makes her pilotage £3.5.0. (f3.25); on Saturday I also piloted the s.s. "SPONDILUS" of which you know she being a vessel of 4,700 tons and her initial fee is £2.0.0. and the mileage added to that to Eccles makes the pilotage £3.13.0. so that you see, sir; the difference in the tonnage is 4,100 tons and the difference in the pilotage fee is 8/-(40p) and no doubt you will see there is no comparison whatever.

There is not much inducement for a pilot to cater for large ships for the extra anxiety and responsibility which is attached to navigating the Canal. If I may be allowed to make a suggestion, I think that the initial fee for vessels over 2,000 tons should be not less than £3.0.0.

Hoping that my letter will receive your due consideration,

I remain

Your obedient servant,

(s'd) G Green."

The Chairman explained to the Committee that they were aware the fees charged for pilotage service on the Canal had originally been fixed with the consent of the Ship Canal Directors and were governed by the Pilotage Bye-laws which had been sanctioned by Her Majesty's Privy Council and, therefore, before any alteration could be made the question would require to be further considered by the Canal Directors. He further stated that Mr Latimer would bring the matter before the Chairman of the Ship Canal Directors and report to a future meeting of this Committee.

Before a report could be presented to a future Pilotage Committee meeting the following communication, date 13 May 1904, was submitted and read to the June Pilotage Committee :-

"Dear Sir

We the undersigned Ship Canal Pilots beg to bring before your notice the question of the present tariff. As the size of the Steamers now navigating the Canal has so increased, we think the tariff should also be increased - that is to say, that the initial fee for Steamers from 2,000 tons - 3,000 tons should be not less than £3.0.0. and from 3,000 tons - 4,000 tons, £3.10.0. (£3.50).

You are no doubt aware of the extra anxiety and responsibility attached to the navigation of vessels of this class and in many cases (particularly in winter), it means two days work" (Vessels only navigated during the hours of daylight in those days due to the pilots' lack of experience in night navigation and to lack of lighted channel markings). "We should also like to call your attention to the Oil Tankers that are berthed at Barton and Eccles oil berths. These vessels have to be brought from those berths into the docks, a distance of three miles, to be swung around before proceeding down the Canal.

This also means the added responsibility of taking these tankers twice through Mode Wheel Locks. The extra money allowed for this work is 3s.0d. (15p) from Barton Oil Berth and 2s.0d(10p) from Eccles to be added to the tariff charge, which we think is grossly insufficient for the amount of work done.

The Ellesmere Port Pontoon Dry Dock built in 1893.
(Courtesy Captain P. Dunbavand)

Hoping that these matters will receive your due consideration, we remain, Your obedient servants." - there was appended to this letter seventeen signatures of senior Canal Pilots.

The Chairman reminded the Committee that this question had been raised in a letter from Pilot Geo. Green, one of the signatories of this letter, and had been submitted to the Pilotage Committee on 29 February when it was referred to the Chairman to bring this matter before the Ship Canal Directors. The present communication was ordered to be passed on to Mr Latimer for his information when taking up the matter with the Canal Company Directors and to report back at a future meeting.

The Ship Canal authority have always been masters of procrastination whenever dealing with all matters appertaining to Pilotage, most especially Pilotage Tariff and this early example was no exception. Whilst it must be appreciated that in the very competitive world of shipping then and now, ever more so then, when Manchester was a new port, costs had to be kept at a minimum to attract tonnage to the port and pilots fees were no exception. On the other hand, if the Harbour Authority could delay an increase in Pilotage Tariff long enough, and there were many devious ways of doing so, any financial benefits would be lost by the time the increase was implemented by the natural rising living costs.

This system provoked a great deal of resentment over the ages amongst all pilots but fortunately a new system was introduced in the 1970s whereby from the day a percentage increase was placed before the Pilotage Committee until the day a successful agreement had been implemented, a percentage surcharge was made on the Tariff to cover for any lost revenue during the negotiations. This new system considerably hastened all future negotiations on Pilotage Tariff, but sad to relate it had taken nearly 90 years to reach that position. On 3rd October 1904 the Chairman of the Pilotage Committee informed the meeting that after careful consideration of the requests for a review of the pilotage tariff, the Canal Company Directors could find no real justification to alter any of the pilotage tariff and unanimously rejected both appeals. This matter was now closed.

Closely following the total rejection for an increase in the Pilotage Tariff, during the next months an attempt was made to reduce the earnings of Pilots on certain vessels. The question was raised by Messrs. George Simpson and Co.; Shipping Agents/ Brokers, that vessels coming to Manchester with part cargoes for other ports and leaving the Ship Canal without having taken on board any additional cargo while in the Ship Canal, should be treated for the purpose of Pilot charges as vessels outward bound in ballast i.e. half the mileage rate. The unanimous view of the Pilots was that as the cargo carried by such vessels paid freight to the Shipowners, the Pilots should not be asked to treat them as vessels in ballast. The Pilotage Committee said that they regretted the views expressed by the Pilots in this matter as the Canal Company was anxious to encourage vessels to the Ship Canal which were only able to procure part cargoes for ports. The Canal Company levied no tolls on the cargo brought into and taken out of the Ship Canal for other ports. By offering some inducement to such vessels to use the Ship Canal the Company was also providing more work for the Pilots. Under these circumstances they regretted the Pilots did not voluntarily agree to assist the Canal Company in their efforts.

This wheedling attempt to sway the Pilots to agree to their request was unanimously rejected by the Pilots. This reaction was hardly surprising, the Pilotages' Committee plea coming but one short month after the Pilots' request for an alteration in their tariff had been rejected so adamantly by them. The matter was not brought before the Pilotage Committee again. The next decade saw no alteration in the Pilots' tariff, the only change of note came in December 1914 when the Chairman (Mr. Browning) of the Pilotage Committee reported that a letter had been received from the Pilots' Association requesting that the Company should deduct 2½% from the monthly earnings of the twenty-three pilots who had signed below to go towards the National Relief Fund. The Chairman said that he would make the deductions requested and forward the amount to the National Relief Fund.

Adam Cartwright No.1 Pilot Manchester Ship Canal
1895-1905
(Courtesy Mrs G. Cartwright)

6.

THE PIONEER PILOTING FAMILY
1894-1976

This accolade goes undisputedly to the Cartwright family, who were one of the most respected families ever to grace the Manchester Pilot Service. The Cartwrights came from a family of Liverpool Pilots and it was this qualification that enabled Mr. Adam Cartwright to become the holder of the first First Class Licence in the Manchester Pilot Service at the age of 45 years. His knowledge of the administration and working system of the Liverpool Pilot Service was of invaluable assistance to him when he and three other Pilots - Messrs. Hill, Sinnot, and Jos. Stuart - were instrumental in forming the Ship Canal Pilot Service in 1894. That he did not achieve the high ideals and working conditions he strove so hard to introduce, was entirely due to the lack of integrity and propriety of many Ship Canal Pilots of that time.

On January 1st 1894 the Manchester Ship Canal was opened over its full length. To lead the procession from its starting point at Latchford Locks to the Manchester Docks, was the steam yacht "NORSEMAN" with all the Canal Directors and friends aboard. Mr. Adam Cartwright was appointed to Pilot the "NORSEMAN" on this epoch-making voyage. In May of the same year, Queen Victoria, on board her steam yacht the "EN-CHANTRESS", performed the official opening ceremony and again Mr. Adam Cartwright was appointed to act as Pilot on Her Majesty's yacht for this historic and auspicious occasion. Afterwards he was personally introduced to and congratulated by

Queen Victoria for his piloting ability in navigating her vessel safely through the new waterway.

Mr. Adam Cartwright died suddenly on January 1st. 1902 aged 53 years. His only son George had commenced his sea going career as a Liverpool and Garston Pilot and in January 1896 he had passed the examination for a First Class Ship Canal Licence at the age of 25 years. George Cartwright became associated with many historical events during his 39 years service as a Pilot on the Canal. Mr. Cartwright was the first Canal Pilot to be officially employed by a shipping company - Manchester Liners - the harbinger of the Choice/Appropriated Pilot system. His most notable feat was undoubtedly the piloting of the largest vessel ever to attempt a full transit of the Ship Canal, the famous S.S. "MANCHESTER CITY", in January 1899. A full account of that epic voyage is documented later in this book. At the time, it was thought impossible to take a vessel of such length and breadth up the Ship Canal to Manchester, there being too many acute bends to negotiate.

When Mr. Cartwright announced his intention of attempting this feat he was ridiculed none more so than from his own Ship Canal Pilots, no doubt jealous that they had not been given the opportunity. The popular saying at the time being that a vessel would "need hinges" to get round the bends in the Ship Canal. The fact that he accomplished the feat and at the same time proving his detractors irrefutably wrong, when still in his first years as a First Class Pilot and at the age of only 27 years, rapidly established his reputation and ability as a Ship Canal Pilot. As time went on he became more and more respected by all with whom he came into contact . He became so renown for his piloting expertise that any Master who knew he was bound for the Manchester Ship Canal would from any distance write and secure the services of Mr. George Cartwright. A copy of just such a letter is reproduced in this Chapter. Towards the end of his piloting career he did not enjoy good health and in 1935 at the age of 63 years he was forced to retire through failing health. He died in May 1942 aged 71 years. Such Manchester Pilots were

Mr George Cartwright 1896-1935

1920
*Mr T. N. Gorst 1911-1924.
On the right of the picture is Mr J.
Baxter, another pilot on the left.*

(Courtesy of Mr T. Cartwright-Gorst)

*Mr George Cartwright Jnr. 1933-
1976*

Photographs
courtesy of Mrs G. Cartwright

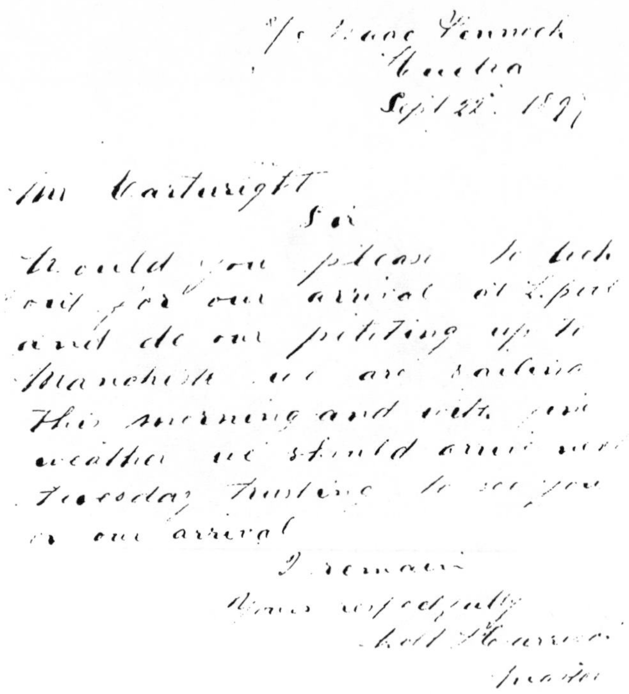

1897

THE FIRST FORM OF CHOICE/APPROPRIATION PILOTAGE

S.S. ISAAC PENNOCK
HUELVA
SEPT. 22nd. 1897

Dear Mr. Cartwright

SIR,

Would you please to look out for our arrival at Liverpool and do our piloting up to Manchester. We are sailing this morning and with fine weather we should arrive next Tuesday, trusting to see you on our arrival.

I remain

Yours respectfully

Walt Harrison

Master

1899

S. S. "Manchester City" Length 461', Breadth 52'. Gross Tonnage: 8,600.

The first large vessel to transit the full length of the Manchester Ship Canal. January 15th 1899. Pilot Mr G. Cartwright. Helmsman Mr John Kaye. Tugs. "Andrew Seed" and "Merry Andrew"

(Courtesy of Manchester Liners LTD.)

the Cartwrights the likes of which we will never see or produce again.

Mr. George Cartwright had a family of ten children, nine daughters - three daughters died in infancy between 1897 and 1901- and one son, the youngest of the family, who was named after his father George. He was the last of the pioneering family of the Cartwrights to hold a Ship Canal Licence. He commenced his sea career as an apprentice deck officer in 1927 with Manchester Liners and joined the helmsmans service in 1933 eventually obtaining his Second Class licence in 1946 and two years later passed the examination for a First Class Licence. In June 1957 he was appointed Choice Pilot for the Furness Withy Company. He did not inherit the flamboyant approach to piloting of his illustrious predecessors in the family, times had changed and all the "Firsts" in piloting in the Ship Canal had been accomplished.

Nevertheless he was no less respected than his grandfather and father for his quiet demeanour and no nonsense attitude he approached his piloting duties. If ever a Ship Canal Pilots sobriquet of "GEORGE THE GENTLE" it would indeed have been Mr. George Cartwright Jr. He retired at the age of 65 years and died in 1980.

There was a further connection, through marriage with the Cartwright family and the Pilot Service. The eldest daughter of Mr. Cartwright senior married Mr. Thomas Naylor Gorst. Mr. Gorst joined the helmsmans service in 1911 and passed his examination for a Second Class Licence in 1918. Unfortunately before he obtained his First Class Licence he died in June 1924 at the age of 33 years the youngest Pilot to die in service in the history of the Manchester Pilot Service. His widow was the first to receive a gratuitous payment of any kind from the Pilot Service. The sum was £50. Mr. Gorst had one son - Mr. T. Cartwright Gorst - who went to sea from his mother's influence - in 1938 with the United Molasses Company (Athel Line) with the sole intention of eventually becoming a Ship Canal Pilot. By the time the war had ended he had obtained a Masters Certificate and he remained at sea with the Athel Line for the next 40 years. He is still alive and well to-day at the age of 69 years.

7.

PILOTING THE FIRST
LARGE VESSEL TO MANCHESTER
SUNDAY: JANUARY 15th 1899

Of the many ships that passed the Liverpool Landing Stage on that Saturday afternoon there was one whose passage excited an extraordinary interest. She had been reported from Kinsale on Friday afternoon and from Holyhead and Point Lynas on Saturday morning; she entered the river soon after 1600 hrs and as she threaded her way up to an anchorage in the Sloyne, no-one acquainted with shipping could doubt either her identity or her destination. Obviously she was bound up the canal,for her four telescoped masts and telescoped funnel gave her that appearance of squatness which has become the peculiar advertisement of Manchester all over the seven seas; but she was distinguished by her great size from all other ships that have used the Canal and although she had never before been seen on the Mersey, she was recognised at once as the famous "Manchester City".

Famous already in several ports and for several reasons. Famous at Middlesbrough as the largest ship ever built on the Tees; famous on the Tyne and on the coasts of Wick and Cromartyshire as the steamer that broke her quadrant during a gale in the Pentland Firth and made her way back zig-zag fashion into the North Sea without the help of a rudder, only to lose her anchors and be driven ashore in the Firth of Cromarty; famous at St. Johns in New Brunswick as the greatest ship that was ever seen there; famous in Liverpool as a ship built to do that which had often been declared by Liverpool shipowners to be impossible for any vessel of her size; and famous in Manchester as the first ship built for the Manchester Liners Limited - the first great steamship company identified with the port and the biggest steamer by a thousand tons or more that ever attempted to navigate the Manchester Ship Canal.

There were many shakings of heads, not only in Liverpool - Manchester's greatest rival - over the audacity of the attempt. It is a curious fact, not wholly inexplicable perhaps, that nearly every captain who takes or has taken a ship to Manchester believes his own ship, be it only a coasting steamer of three or four hundred tons register, to be "quite big enough for the canal". He knows the difficulties and anxieties that have beset him during long vigils upon his own bridge and he desires none greater, whether for himself or his worst enemy. But the pilots not wedded to a particular ship and almost welcoming fresh taxes on their skill as a means of increasing their reputation and the profits of their calling, take a bolder view; and Mr George Cartwright (aged 27), who has earned the credit of piloting the "MANCHESTER CITY" up the canal betrayed not the least distrust of its capacity.

The Liverpool river-pilot, on the other hand, who had brought her into the river did not approve of large steamers. There were more than two, hundred licensed river pilots attached to the port of Liverpool - they share the work, pool their earnings and draw an equal dividend. Formerly there were more pilots but the number had to be reduced; now would-be pilots must serve an apprenticeship until a vacancy occurs - perhaps for eight or nine years. It was true that the tonnage of shipping entering the Mersey had greatly increased but the pilots' profession was being spoiled by the "Whales". When asked his opinion of the "MANCHESTER CITY", he said :- "Fine steamer, no doubt about it, but we call them pilots' robbers . Now this vessel" he enlarged" has in her the cargo of three decent size ships, each of those three ships would take a pilot and have a draught of perhaps nineteen feet. This vessel's draught is about twenty-four and a half feet". The pilot's face was sad looking, for a pilot's fees are assessed according to the vessels tonnage and draught.

The owners of the "MANCHESTER CITY" hoped that this momentous experiment would be conducted with a modicum of privacy. The night fell dark but clear and when the tide began to ebb an hour after midnight, the anchor was weighed and the vessel steered towards Eastham Locks under the expert guidance of Mr George Cartwright, the Liverpool River Pilot had disembarked in the Sloyne as was the practice in those days. The channel to Eastham is winding and on Saturday night it was dotted with the red, green and white lights of shipping. But the "MANCHESTER CITY", despite her great proportions, steered (as one enthusiastic admirer remarked) "just like a yacht" and was guided surely through them all. As the vessel approached the locks, an incident occurred to remind one and all that a liner - not a mere ocean tramp of no pedigree - was docking.

From the deck there rose up a fountain of fire which leapt into the dark air, first a green ball then another green ball, then a third and finally a red ball. A minute or two later a similar firework was let off on the Lock-pier. They were the house-signals of the Manchester Liners to be used at sea when the ships pass in the night and speak to one another in passing. The "MANCHES-TER CITY" had presented herself at the gate of the port that was to be her home and had been bidden to enter.

Eastham Lock is nearly 25ft wider than the ship and she went in easily and quietly. Mr Cartwright who controlled her was perched high up on the flying bridge whistling tunelessly through his teeth, interrupted now and then by a word to the steersman or an engine order rung down to the engine-room. Then she was moored in the lock to wait for daybreak and the commencement of another famous chapter in her career.

The day dawned, grey overcast and bitterly cold. An easterly wind blew unchecked over the river and at 0800 hrs, preparations for the voyage up the Canal to Manchester began. The tug "Merry Andrew" with her twin funnels and paddles, was in her accustomed place, made fast astern under the command of Capt.

Sam Edwards and the tug "Agnes Seed", a single screw steam tug capable of 8 knots, commanded by Capt T A Seed was made fast forward. One long blast of the "MANCHESTER CITY" whistle was the signal to the tug- boats that all was ready to proceed on this epic voyage, the engine-room telegraph rang out orders to go ahead and this momentous voyage began at 0815 hrs. The keen, cool young pilot (Mr G Cartwright) high up on the open bridge was supreme; the fortunes of the Canal, in some sense at least and the safety of a ship and cargo worth nearly a hundred thousand pounds (about ten million pounds at today's prices) lay in his hands.

For the first half-mile or so the idle spectators of this experiment betrayed a little anxiety but those who were doing the work betrayed none at all.   At the first bend a mishap seemed imminent. The helm was ordered "hard-a-starboard", the Canal helmsman Mr John Kaye, spun the wheel obediently round but some mysterious derangement of the steering gear reversed the design. The vessel's head continued to swing to port from her mid-channel course and the telegraph was put over to "full speed astern".   The engine-room was not caught napping and the danger of colliding with the Canal bank was instantly averted. A few minutes sufficient to restore the steering gear to a sense of its first duty and the tug-boats in the meantime had manfully kept their mistress from erring; the way was never off her. After this little scare, everything went reasonably perfectly.

The "MANCHESTER CITY" really did steer "like a yacht", she never again "took a sheer" - a vice common to most large ships in narrow waters and comparable with the shying of a nervous horse.   She got through the most awkward places and round the sharpest corners, including Runcorn Bend - the bogey of Liverpool Shipowners - without touching anything or having to send mooring ropes ashore to warp her round.   She passed several steamers moored in the Canal, a large Spanish vessel called the "NOVIEMBRE" at Old Quay Lock amongst them. The locks gave not the least trouble and the success of this great experiment was unqualified.   She arrived in Irlam Locks at 1800

1899

M. S. C. "Agnes Seed" Head Tug on that epic voyage to Manchester. A single screw steam Tug built in Plymouth in 1892 for Captain T. A. Seed of Birkenhead and chartered to the M. S. C. in 1893. Dimensions L. 86', B. 17', G. R. T. 93, B. H. P. 60. In February 1932 her boiler exploded and she was broken up at Tranmere.

M. S. C. "Merry Andrew" stern Tug to the "Manchester City" in 1899. Only twin funnelled steam Tug ever on the Canal. Could only use both paddles in the same direction having a lockable rudder at each end.

Dimensions L.140', B. 21', G. R. T. 222. B. H. P. 80

Photo's courtesy of Captain P. Dunbavand

hrs - ten long weary hours after leaving Eastham and although she might safely have made her way up to the Manchester cattle lairages in the dark, it was decided to give the pilot, helmsman and deck officers and engineers a well-earned night's rest.

Such a feat described above is, of course, not accomplished for the first time without a great deal of human strain on all the ship's personnel. Down four long flights of iron ladders, far below the level of the water, stood the chief and one of his staff. One had stood by the reversing gear and the other by a wheel that regulates the speed. Beside them was a telegraph recording a bewildering and rapid succession of orders from the bridge, each order prefaced by a warning note on the bell and repeated back before execution. They had stood there for ten hours. The Chief Engineer mopped his brow with a lump of cotton waste, smiled sardonically and said "So this is the Manchester Ship Canal is it? I want no more of it".

The pilot and helmsman looked as if they had not been in bed for a week after they had moved safely into Irlam Locks, for their eyes were bleary with exhaustion, whilst Captain Forrest on the bridge, responsible for the ship's safety, all the time, was drawn and haggard with fatigue. Hence it is that the Ship Canal is not much loved by ships' personnel.

The following morning (Monday) she resumed her voyage at daybreak and arrived at her discharge berth to land her livestock at 0930 hrs, thirteen and a quarter hours steaming time from leaving Eastham and passing through four Locks without so much as scratching the paint.

The voyage of the "MANCHESTER CITY" proved that the Canal could be navigated safely by cargo steamers of the largest modern class. She herself is 461 feet long overall and 52 feet beam with a deadweigh capacity of 8,600 tons. Her cargo consisted of 450 head of cattle, 150 sheep, two horses and 7,300 tons of general cargo, part of which was refrigerated.

Her arrival was of great significance for the port of Manchester on 16 January 1899.

8.

THE COST OF LIVING 1901

In the year of 1901, the average earnings for a first class and second class pilot was £112 and £59 respectively, but it must be fair to say while their earnings appeared low, in 1901 only 400,000 persons in the United Kingdom declared earnings of £400 or more for Income Tax purposes and less than one million people earned £160 or more - this being the level for liability for Income Tax. There were six pilots who were in the latter bracket and were taxed at 1/2d (6p) in the pound.

To make the comparison with other trades and professions, a fully qualified Fitter or Turner was earning £88 per year for a 54hr week, skilled Labourers £104 per year for a 54hr week. On the land, a top agricultural worker was paid £76 per year for unlimited hours, although he did have certain concessions such as low rent and reduced food prices.

On the high seas, a Master of a vessel of 6,000 tons gross, would have earned £198 per year, whilst a Chief Officer would be earning £114 per year; an Able Seaman first-class earnings stood at £42 per year.

It is interesting to note, outside of pilot earnings, wages increased by 11% between 1895 - 1900 and from 1900 - 1910, the real wages of workers declined by 13%, but the wholesale and retail prices rose by 13.4%. The value of the purchasing power of the sovereign declined by 2/6d. (12½p) during that same period.

In the 1900's, very few canal pilots, if any, owned their own houses, preferring to rent them for various reasons. They would have been able to rent a modest three-bedroom house within easy reach of their pilot boarding points for 1/11d.(9p) a week.   The cost of running the home would have been per week : Gas for cooking @ 2/1d(14p) to 6/-d(30p) per cubic foot; electricity for light was charged between 2d(1p) and 6d(2½p) per unit and to keep the home warm coal was priced between 1/-d(5p) and 1/6d(7½p) a hundred weight. An average total of cost of 10/-(50p) per week.

Food was easily the biggest outlay and in May 1901 the following list of victuals for one month and their cost, was considered necessary for a family consisting of two adults and two children under 16, to maintain a healthy life :-

		s. d.
FLOUR	1 stone (141bs)	1. 5. (7p)
LARD	11b	0. 6. (2½p)
BUTTER	2½1b	2. 11. (14½p)
MILK	3½ gals	1. 1½ (6p)
EGGS	17	1. 0. (5p)
CHEESE	11b	0. 9. (3½p)
TEA	½1b	1. 0. (5p)
SUGAR	41b	0. 3. (1½p)
JAM	21b	0. 9. (3½p)
CONDENSED MILK	1 tin	1. 5½ (7½p)
COCOA	¼1b	0. 6. (2½p)
POTATOES	1 stone	0. 8. (3p)
OATMEAL	31b	0. 7½ (3½p)
C/FWD	12.	0.1½
RICE	12oz	0.2 (1p)
BEEFSTEAK	21b	2. 0. (10p)
BEEF	4½1b	3. 4½ (17p)
MUTTON	½1b	0. 4. (1½p)
BACON	½1b	0. 3½ (1½p)
FISH	21b	1. 1. (6p)
APPLES	31b	1. 6. (7½p)
ORANGES	6	0. 6. (2½p)

ONIONS	6	0. 6.	(2½p)
VEGETABLES	various	2. 3.	(11½p)
SOAP	llb	0. 2½	(1p)
TOBACCO	4oz	1. 0.	(5p)

TOTAL :   £1 .5. 4. (£1.32)

A loaf of bread cost 2½d(1p) but most homes baked their own and the cost of a pint of beer, 2d(1p) or the cheaper beer called "Dinner Ale", was 1½d(½p) a pint, a glass of spirits was 3d (1½p).

Clothing for the family was relatively cheap - a pilot's need for a year was as follows :-

s. d.

2 PR BOOTS			
(SUMMER/WINTER)	@ 5/-d (25p)each		
	(Repairs:4/-(20p)	14. 0.	(70p)
4 PR SOCKS	@ 6d. (2½p) each	2. 0.	(10p)
2 COATS			
(SUMMER/WINTER)	@ 3/9d(19p)each	7. 6.	(37½p)
WAISTCOAT		1. 6.	(7½p)
2 TROUSERS			
(SUMMER/WINTER)	@ 3/-d(15p)each	6. 0.	(30p)
2 SHIRTS	@ 2/-d (10p) each	4. 0.	(20p)
HAT AND SCARF		1. 0.	(5p)
TIE		0. 6.	(2½p)

TOTAL: £1. 16. 6. (£1.79½)

His wife would be expected to spend on herself for one year the following :-

		£ s d
2 PAIR OF SHOES	@ 2/lld (15p) each (Repairs 2/-d(l0p))	7. 10. (30p)
2 DRESSES (SUMMER/WINTER)	@ 5/- each	10. 0. (50p)
2 APRONS	@ 6d. each	1. 0. (5p)
2 SKIRTS (SUMMER/WINTER)	@ 3/6d each	7. 0. (35p)
2 PAIR STOCKINGS	@ 6d each	1. 1. (5½p)
UNDERCLOTHING (Two of each article)		5. 10. (29p)
2 PAIR STAYS	@2/lld each	5. 10. (29p)
1 HAT		1. 0. (5p)
1 JACKET		1. 6. (7½p)
1 SHAWL		1. 0. (5p)
TOTAL :		2. 2. 1. (2.09½)

The cost of clothing children was hard to identify, but on average for 1901, £3.0.0d. would be a reasonably accurate figure; for two children, the youngest child mainly wearing second hand clothes.

Therefore, the total cost for a Canal Pilot to house, feed and cloth himself and family for one month in 1901 would have been £3.0.0d., with an average wage for a first-class pilot of £9.4.0d. per month; and a second-class wage of £5.0.0d. per month, bearing in mind some first-class pilots were earning £15.0.0d. per month due to the working system already described.

The majority of the Canal Pilots' wives had to be excellent house-keepers for there was little room for squandering money. They also had to be exceptionally innovative when it came to culinary adroitness. I am sure it was during these years many of our traditional north country dishes were concocted out of the fertile minds of the wives of that period in English History, in what must have been a never-ending battle to make ends meet.

TRAGEDIES, DROWNINGS ETC.

1/8/1894   Dead body raised by the dredger "Barry" at Runcorn laybye believed to be the engineer of S.S. "Albertain".

2/8/1894   A flatman was drowned outside Weston Mersey Lock last night, body recovered this morning.

13/8/1894   A man found drowned off the "Elk" at Weston Wall.

30/12/1894.   John Woodhouse, master of "Barry" missing since late last night grave fears are entertained that he has fallen in to either the Weston or Ship Canal

8/4/1895.   Marsh, drowned off a dolphin at Eastham, brought to Runcorn by the tug "Virginia".

27/12/1895.   Harry Smitham, master of the tug "Wigan" was carried over-board and drowned at 5.20pm, the tug had been in collision with the tug "Florida" and Brunnermond's steamer "Cambria". At the inquest on 30/12/95 a verdict of accidental death through error of judgement. Later a collection for his widow was made, raising £9-2-10.

28/7/1902.   Waspey, watchman at Weston Point. His body was found by a barge.

9/8/1902.   Fireman of "Minnie" drowned at Old Quay.

4/11/1904.   A man fell off transporter bridge construction and killed.

12/5/1911.   Awoman's headless body found in Weston Mersey Lock.

6/10/1911.   At 5.00pm, Friday, the body of H. Congreve, M.S.C. Chief Engineer, was found in the ship canal under Latchford cantilever bridge.

20/5/1911.   Motor launch "Una", used for sounding, was sunk by the s.s. "Caledonia" near E4 buoy, 2 drowned.

22/5/1911.	"Una" lifted by "Beta", brought into the canal, dead body of Price the engineer on board.
10/2/1903.	Stanlow Jack (Hughes) was drowned at the Gowy outfall, he was duck shooting and had a heart attack and was engulfed by the tide. "Eva" conveyed the coffin to Ince from Stanlow 13/2/1903.
24/8/1914.	Bridgewater tug "Walton" collided with S.S. "Yorkshire" at the Mersey weir. The tug sank, the engineer and lad were drowned. The master was thrown clear and escaped. The tug was salvaged by pontoon sheerlegs.
20/6/1918.	Aeroplanes collided at Hooton, both airmen killed. This was witnessed by Lomas, cashier on cash boat.
21/4/1920.	A woman's headless body was found in the pontoon recess at Ellesmere Port, later the head was found at Frodsham pumps.
28/2/1925.	A human foot was found in a shoe in a barge from Mersey weir.
28/1/1928.	A man jumped off Runcorn Railway Bridge into canal, suicide.
22/2/1928.	A man jumped off Runcorn Railway Bridge onto the canal wall
12/2/1928.	W. H. Musker, first master of dredger "Gowy" died at home (Partington) on Sunday.

9.

THE STRUGGLE CONTINUES 1900-1911

In October 1900 a letter was submitted and read to the Pilotage Committee in which it stated that a number of Canal pilots had formed an Association with the object of assisting in the defence and maintenance of an equitable and just system of pilotage on the Canal. It would also adopt rules and regulations for their benefit and guidance. They respectfully requested that the Pilotage Committee would give assistance in their endeavour to break up the unjust system of pilot "Farming out" or "Contracting out" at present practised on the Canal by four Ship Canal Pilots who they named viz: Mr A Cartwright, Mr P Sinnot, Mr J Stuart and Mr G Green.

Mr Latimer, the Chairman, said that although the Committee had some time ago adopted the plan of paying to each pilot the money earned by him, there might be some matters with regard to the existing system of pilotage on the Canal, which it would be well to enquire into and he proposed that this matter be left to the Deputy Chairman and himself to investigate.   They were both duly authorised to take this matter in hand.

Mr W Onion, Secretary of the newly formed Pilots Association, wrote on December 17th 1900, to the Pilotage Committee detailing their proposed system of working the pilotage on the Canal.   The Pilotage Committee considered that the information given therein on the proposed new scheme was insufficient for them to deal with the matter and it was left for their further attention at a later date.

A new year dawned, undoubtedly with great hopes of change for on January 30th 1901, Mr Latimer reported that he had interviewed all the pilots against whom he understood charges had been made of "Farming out" pilotage work on the Canal and receiving a percentage of the tariff for doing so; viz Messrs. Cartwright, Stuart, Sinnot and Green.   He had informed the pilots concerned of the charges made against them and stated that if there had been any such actions on their part it was totally wrong and contrary to Canal Pilotage Bye-laws and must at once be discontinued.

The Chairman warned them that if in the future any case was brought before the Pilotage Committee, that a pilot had demanded or received any monies for transferring work to another pilot, then such pilot's licence to pilot on the Canal would certainly be suspended or withdrawn altogether.

Then came the amazing statement and admission from the Master Pilots that when they had transferred work to other pilots they had made a practice of charging from ten to twenty-five per cent on the earnings of such pilotage.   The figure was nearer to fifty percent of the pilotage fee.   The Master Pilots had judiciously decided to err on the lower scale for obvious reasons. The excuse they gave for justifying such a charge was the "very great expense in looking after the vessels on their arrival in the river, attending on the owners, providing boats for boarding the vessels and other incidental expenses of telegrams, etc., in order to avoid any delay in getting steamers up to Manchester".

The enormity of the admissions made by the Master Pilots, one would have thought, could hardly have been ignored by the Pilotage Committee, considering that for nearly three years they had steadfastly denied to the Pilotage Committee, all charges brought against them that such a system had ever existed. The Master Pilots' rather weak excuses for charging a percentage of the pilotage fee, especially concerning the boating in the river, held no credence with the Pilotage Committee.   They had already been informed twelve months previously that Canal Pilots who boarded vessels in the river, inward bound, did so for their own convenience and never charged a fee for this service. There was another more sinister reason for boarding in the river besides avoiding delay to vessels, which will be revealed in a later chapter. Here was a clear case for the Pilotage Committee to act under the powers granted to them by the Canal Pilotage Bye-Laws of 1896, to either suspend or withdraw the Master Pilots' Licences.

The Master Pilots were no fools and they had not made their admissions lightly nor without having given it a great deal of thought and possibly judicious lobbying prior to this meeting. They knew only too well the consequences of being found to have received or asked for monies from "Farming out" pilotage work, therefore they planned their strategy to perfection.

Firstly, the Chairman reported the Master Pilots had stated that after hearing the Chairman's views and remarks of the matter to hand, they all agreed with him that the system of levying such charges which had been made was most definitely wrong and after expressing great regret, each one assured the Chairman that for the future they would not charge anything more than the actual cost of telegraphing to the Pilot whom they wished to do the work.

The Chairman also reported (this was the second master-stroke) that he had received from Mr P Sinnot, one of the Ship Canal Pilots representatives on the Pilotage Committee, the following report of a meeting of Canal Pilots held at Seacombe on the 21 January:

TO THE MANCHESTER SHIP CANAL PILOTAGE COMMITTEE

Gentlemen,

At the meeting of the FREE PILOTS SOCIETY (this Society was set up in direct confrontation to the Canal Pilots' Association) at Seacombe on January 21st, it was proposed by Mr Campbell and seconded by Mr Hill Junr and carried unanimously that the Rotary System be not enforced.

It was further proposed by Mr Stuart and seconded by Mr ACartwright, the two senior Master Pilots, that for the future there will be no percentage charged for any pilotage done on the Canal, only expenses incurred, and this proposal was also carried unanimously.

We, the undersigned Pilots on the Ship Canal agree to the above proposals and we have voluntarily signed our names to work on the above conditions. (This was another revelation - for the first time ever the names of those pilots who condoned the "Farming out" or "Contracting out" system practised by the Master Pilots, were disclosed) :

Adam Cartwright	James Abram
Jas. Stuart	Ashton Waterworth
Peter Sinnot	Geo. Batty
George Green	A. E. Postlethwaite
John W. Pass	W. M. Marker
M. Campbell	H. Boxer Jones
George Cartwright	W. J. Huntington
John Edwards	John Hynes
Henry Hill Snr.	F. Smith
John Ellis	Dan O'Keefe
Joe Inglesfield	H. Hill Jnr.

The Chairman stated that as it would be seen from the above statement, the most pressing complaint of the Pilots Association, viz the question of farming the pilotage on the Canal with its percentage payments and which appeared to be the centre from which all their grievances arose, had been satisfactorily dealt with in the interests of all pilots holding a Canal Licence. The Chairman went on to say that he did not think it was necessary at the present to take any further action towards the letter of December 17th 1900, received from Mr W Onion, Secretary of the Pilots Association regarding the forming of a rotary system. These statements were unanimously approved by all the Committee. Had not the Master Pilots planned it well?

The members of the Pilotage Committee were undoubtedly gentlemen of commerce as well as being gentlemen in society and must have assumed they were negotiating with the Master Pilots on the basis that they were gentlemen also. They accepted without hesitation the Master Pilots' regrets for their past conduct and that they were truly chastened, also the Master Pilots' assurances that they would never ever again ask for or receive monies for pilotage work they farmed out.

How these members of the Pilotage Committee, men of good standing in the community, could have been so gullible in accepting these assurances is beyond the author's comprehension.

Here was a cast-iron case, based on the most damaging self admissions, to once and for all, put an end to the pernicious working system that existed. That the Pilotage Committee did not pursue this case to its logical conclusion, nor did they even admonish or censure the Master Pilots for their conduct, remains a mystery to the author.

Without question, a major disadvantage to the advancement of a rotary system, was the lack of a representative on the Pilotage Committee of the Canal Pilots who were desirous of such a system. At that moment of time, there were 44 Licensed Canal Pilots of which 22 were in favour of a rotary system and 22 were against. They had no one to make their views heard or to press the pro's and con's in debate at Committee level. This was a serious mistake on their behalf and eventually proved to be their undoing. There are questions that have always remained unanswered:

1) Why did the Pilotage Committee agree with the so-called Free Pilots who did not want a Rotary System?

2) Why did the Pilotage Committee favour the iniquitous system they knew existed?

3) Why did the Pilotage Committee dismiss the Pilots' Association's representations for a Rotary System so offhandedly?

1899
Constructing No.9 Dock
(Courtesy of M.S.C. Co.)

1905
Blasting the last of the retaining wall of No. 9 Dock.
(Courtesy of M. S. C. Co.)

4) Why did the Pilotage Committee continue to support and agree with the Master Pilots, even after they had admitted to a serious charge of breaking a most stringent Pilotage Bye-Law?

5) Why did the Pilotage Committee not pursue the blatant contravention of that Bye-Law or even censure the Master Pilots?

Because the passage of time has erased all the prominent personnel of that said Pilotage Committee, we will never be able to find the answers to all those questions and many others; suffice it is to say that one must draw one's own individual conclusions.

No doubt weary and sadly disillusioned by the continual setbacks to establish a rotary system, especially the latest rebuttal, this was the last serious attempt to change the working system, for twelve years. The Canal Pilots frustrated in the extreme, turned inwardly on themselves and the working system became a free-for-all system one with no holds barred in the manner they obtained pilotage work. They did this to the detriment of the other Canal Pilots, friend and foe, and became colloquially known as the "Catch-as-Catch-Can" system. This system was to hold sway for over a decade.

So bitter were the feelings that this system engendered between the Canal pilots, causing so much heartache, that its legacy lasted for another incredible 60 years.

An incident occurred in March 1903 which caused a certain amount of displeasure and dismay amongst the Pilots. A complaint was received at Pilotage Committee regarding the practice of Pilots leaving a vessel before the completion of pilotage. The Chairman (Mr. Latimer) stated:-

"That it was of frequent occurrence for Pilots in charge of vessels navigating the Canal and which were moored temporarily for the night, to leave the vessel and go to their homes joining the vessels again in the morning and that it was considered very undesirable that vessels should be left in such a manner seeing that it might be necessary for them to move during the night and they would be unable to do so if the Pilot was not on board"

During the discussion which followed it was mentioned that on some of the vessels there was no sleeping accommodation for Pilots and that in such cases where a vessel tied up at say Latchford, Runcorn or any other place where accommodation could be obtained near at hand the Pilots did not think they ought to remain on board. The Chairman however stated that the complaint more particularly referred to Pilots leaving their vessels in order to return home for sleeping whether the vessels had accommodation or not. It was ultimately resolved that the secretary of Pilotage Committee be instructed to issue the following letter to all Pilots:-

"I am instructed to draw your attention to the practice of leaving a vessel whilst temporarily moored before completion of pilotage. In future wherever possible the Pilot must remain with the vessel from the commencement of the journey to its completion and that should it be necessary to moor at any point on the journey for the night the Pilot should not leave the vessel unless there is no sleeping accommodation on board and in such cases only where accommodation can be obtained in the neighbourhood of the place where the vessel is moored. "

The letter had the desired effect and the Pilots who dearly coveted their own bed at night were forced to stay aboard some of the most inhospitable ships imaginable. Often the settee in an unheated chartroom or wheelhouse was the place for a night's rest. A stiff backed cane chair tilted into a corner of the ship's galley was warmer, but no less comfortable, even if the Pilot found that the ship's galley was left unlocked at night.

The practice has been perpetuated until this day although conditions on ships regarding accommodation for Pilots have improved immensely since 1945.

In October 1911 a more important issue came to the surface when it was discovered that there had not been a serving Pilot on the Sub-Committee for examining applicants for a Pilots Licence or Certificate since August 1907. Accordingly a letter from Mr. Hindle (Pilot's representative) was submitted to the Pilotage Committee in November:-

"I am instructed by the Pilots to write and ask if you would make arrangements for one of our representatives to sit on all examining committees for either Pilotage Licence or Certificate. This has always been a practice but of late years our representatives appear to have been left out. "

The Chairman read the resolution on this matter dated 27th. August 1907 which stated:-

That the four Canal Superintendents of this committee be appointed a sub-committee to examine all applicants for Pilotage Licences and report the result of such licence examinations. Three members to form a quorum and for each attendance a fee of 5s.0d. (25p) and travelling expenses to be paid."

The Chairman then asked Mr. Hindle if he had anything to say in support of his letter. Mr. Hindle replied that all he could say was that this Examining sub-committee was the only one in the United Kingdom on which the Pilots were not represented. At Liverpool there were two Pilots on the examining sub-committee. He did not wish to make any reflection on the present members of the sub-committee as he was convinced that all the examinations were conducted with perfect fairness, but it was the wish of the Pilots Association that it should be brought in line with other Pilotage Districts.

The Chairman then made a most amazing statement when he pointed out that the circumstances in Manchester differed from other ports, as the Canal was an inland waterway with certain fixed physical conditions which were better known to the Canal Superintendents than to any other persons even the Pilots themselves. How the Chairman arrived at such an outlandish conclusion remains a mystery even unto this day. He went on to say that at other ports where the navigation was more open the position was different and the Pilots were very properly represented on the examining sub committee. He did not regard the reason advanced for the proposed change as a very substantial one and asked if any other grounds could be put forward. Mr. Hindle replied he was not aware of any. It was also pointed out to Mr. Hindle that if the Pilots were represented on the sub-committee it would have to be either one or two of the sitting or substitute representatives and such Pilots would thus be kept from their work more than at present. The Pilots were not on a pooling system in 1911.

There seemed to be a great reluctance on behalf of the Pilotage Committee to allow a serving Pilot to once again sit on the examining sub-committee. The Chairman's (Mr. Browning) statement that the Canal was "better known to the four Canal Superintendents than to any other persons, even the Pilots themselves" was a most derogatory and inflammatory remark to make even in those early days and must have incensed all Pilots. At the December Pilotage Committee Mr. Hindle reported that after having spoken to the Association on this matter once again the opinion had been expressed that as existing Pilots had to meet newly appointed Pilots day after day on the Canal it would inspire confidence if one of their number was put on the examining sub-committee . That was all there was new to say on the matter. It would merely revert to the condition of things which existed on the Canal from 1894 to 1907, the alteration being made in 1907 because the Pilots' representatives did not attend..

The Chairman pointed out that a full list of Pilots was published in the monthly Sailing List and there was a list posted up in the Dock Masters Office together with the names of the vessels for which there were appropriated Pilots. Thus a Pilot need never be in ignorance of the names of other Pilots nor of the vessels they were in charge of. Mr. Hindle replied that the list in the Dock Masters Office was at the wrong end of the Canal and suggested one should be posted in the Lockmasters Office at Eastham and another at the Eastham Pilot station. These lists should contain not only the names of the Pilots but also of Masters and Mates holding certificates and the vessels they were authorised to Pilot. The Chairman promised that this would be done. It appears the Pilotage Committee would do anything to placate the Pilots other than reinstate them on the examining sub-

1950

M. S. C. "Old Trafford" leaving Runcorn under tow for the last time
(Courtesy of Captain P. Dunbavand)

"Old Trafford". A steel steam paddle tug built by Jos. T. Eltringham at Stone Quay, South Shields, in 1907, registered at Manchester no. 5/1907. Off:No:124285. 100'-0" x 20'-2" x 9'-9". (O.A. 106'6" x 36'-9"). 155-61 Gross. 1-64 Reg. 66 N. H. P. 400 I. H. P. 11 Knots.
New boilers fitted in 1933.

Sold to the Ridley Steam Tug Co. of Newcastle on the 29th September, 1950. Left Old Quay in October and sailed south about to that port where she was re-named "Reliant", registration transferred to Newcastle. Sold again in 1956 to the Seaham Docks & Harbour Co.

Now in the Greenwich National Maritime Museum.

committee. During the discussion the Canal Superintendents expressed an opinion that there was a reflection cast on the manner in which the present examining sub-committee did its work, but both Mr. Hindle and Mr. Postlethwaite assured the Committee that nothing of the kind was intended.

After many more Pilotage Committee Meetings a very reluctant examining sub-committee appointed a Pilots' representative to sit on that committee. It was August 1914 and a Pilots' representative has remained on that sub-committee ever since.

"I have never heard one argument in point that the respectability of pilots will be destroyed. It is not my wish to cast reflections on any body of men , but as to the respectability of the business of a pilot, it never was respectable, it will never be respectable and he who looks forward to the respectability of his son, will never place him in a position to be a pilot. "

MR. FAWDINGHAM THEAKSTONE
LIVERPOOL MERCHANT ON PILOTAGE COMMITTEE 1826.

10.

PILOT -v- PILOT

From the very beginnings of the Manchester Pilot Service, it was a constant battle to obtain work, it naturally followed there would always be a certain amount of friction, disagreement and confrontation between pilots. The Pilotage Committee had the unenviable task of being judge, jury and peacemaker in all manner of pilotage disputes; at times, demanding the wisdom of King Solomon and the patience of Job. To their undying credit they acquitted themselves with commendable acumen.

Individual pilots became most devious and unscrupulous and diverse methods were used to obtain pilotage work. The lengths to which some pilots would go to obtain work knew no bounds. The paying of gratuities to the Captain of a ship to obtain the pilotage was particularly unpalatable, so much so that on the 26 August 1904, the following letter from the Secretary of the Pilots' Association was submitted and read at the Pilotage Committee :

Dear Sir

At a meeting of this Association on the 22nd instant, I was instructed by the members present to ask you to be good enough to make the following "bye-law" and to have it printed on all the Pilotage Cards that have to be signed by shipmasters, i.e.

"Gratuities are not allowed to be given or received. Any infringement of this Bye-Law will subject the pilot to instant dismissal".

At present, we are aware that gratuities are given both to Captain's clerks and others and also that pilots pay other pilots to secure employment which we consider is detrimental and a disgrace to the service and ought to be dealt with severely.

1905
No.9 Dock Completed

(Courtesy of M.S.C. Co.)

MANCHESTER SHIP CANAL
Opening of New Dock (Nº 9)
By Their Majesties

KING EDWARD VII
AND QUEEN ALEXANDRA

THURSDAY JULY 13TH 1905.

ADMIT ONE PERSON.

To
Transit Shed

No. 2

Ground Floor.

Entrance to Docks
by
Aubrey Street only

(See Plan on Back.)

1910

*Elders and Fyffes "Chirrapo", GAT. 4041, L. 374', B. 48', bound
from Modewheel, with a full cargo of bananas.*

(Courtesy Mrs W. Yates Collection)

1900

*Anglo-American "Tonawanda", GAT.3416, L.330', B.43'. Note the
position of the Pilot Flag below the Ensign aft. Stern tug "Merry
Andrew".*

(Courtesy Mrs W. Yates Collection)

It is a frequent occurrence on a ship's arrival at Eastham and before the pilots' cards are delivered up to the pilot, for the captain to demand a gratuity and inform you that his last pilot paid it and if you don't pay it you will not pilot his ship up or down the canal again. We think when you are making new pilots this matter should be brought forceable before them and that they should undertake an obligation not to commit these abuses. In fact, all pilots holding Canal Pilot Licences should be obliged to take the same obligation.

If you decide in favour of the above Bye Law, you would oblige us very much by notifying the same to each pilot separately.

We are, Sir, your obedient Servants

The M.S.Canal Pilots Assoc.

B Whitehouse, Secretary protem.

After some consideration of the same, it was :-

Moved by : Captain Williams

Seconded by : Captain Waring and Resolved:

that the following notification be printed on the pilotage cards issued to pilots which have to be signed by shipmasters in connection with pilotage services performed on the Ship Canal and the Secretary was instructed to so advise Pilot Whitehouse:

"Gratuities must not be given or received as this would be an infringement of the Company's Pilotage Byelaw No. 11 and render the pilot liable to a heavy penalty."

Although every pilot received a copy of this resolution, it did not deter in any way the continuation of this practice; the hardest part was proving any allegations. A typical complaint was heard by the Pilotage Committee in November 1904 when two pilots were summoned to appear before them. The Chairman stated that a pilot, the holder of a first-class Licence, had complained to Mr Latimer that he had piloted the s.s."UDSIRE" up the canal on her voyage here on the 3 September last and also had received instructions from the ship's agents in Manchester to attend and pilot her on her outward journey that voyage and also when she again came to the canal on the 22 October. (This substantiates the method of obtaining pilotage mentioned in an earlier Chapter). He found on the ship's arrival at Eastham on her second voyage that the captain had written to another pilot to attend and pilot the vessel on that occasion, which circumstance gave the pilot the impression that the change of pilotage had been brought about owing to the other pilot having given a gratuity to the Captain of the "UDSIRE" and although he had no actual proof that this has been done, the reason for his thinking so was that when he was obtaining the signature of the captain to the card for the inward pilotage on 3 September, the latter had asked him for a gratuity out of the pilotage fee but which he declined to give him. The pilot also complained that he had lost two days and had incurred 12/6d. (62p) in attending at Eastham waiting the ship's arrival which he contended might have been saved if the other pilot had advised him that he had received the instructions to attend the vessel on arrival.

It appeared that on the "UDSIRE"'s outward voyage on the 7 September, the inward pilot being engaged with the S.S.JUNO, gave the pilotage of the S.S.UDSIRE to the other (farming out) pilot and he imagined the subsequent engagement of this pilot by the captain to pilot his vessel upon her next voyage inwards, was the result of the pilot having given a gratuity to the captain out of his fee for piloting her outwards on her previous voyage. Mr Latimer had written to the pilot in question to see what reason he could give for the change of pilots. The following letter denying the accusation had been received :-

Dear Sir

I beg to report that at the request of a pilot, I piloted the (7 Sept) S.S. UDSIRE down the Canal and on arrival at Eastham Locks, the captain told me that if ever he came to the canal again he would give me the pilotage of his ship. I asked him why he wished to change his pilot and he answered me as follows. "I prefer you to the other as I consider you have handled the ship more to my satisfaction than he did". On Thursday 20th Oct,

I received a letter from captain of UDSIRE (copy enclosed) asking me to meet him at Eastham which I did.

I have no knowledge only what you tell me about what the captain said to the other pilot in reference to a gratuity, but in my own case I can most solemnly assure you, Sir, and am prepared if necessary, to swear oath that the captain of the UDSIRE has never either directly or indirectly spoken about a gratuity, neither have I at any time offered or given a present, gratuity or any money to the captain of the UDSIRE; and if the other pilot is a gentleman, which I very much doubt, he will apologise to me for making such a false accusation. Before leaving Eastham Locks last voyage, I asked the captain of UDSIRE if he was aware that his agent in Manchester had sent the other pilot to his ship. His answer to me was that he was master of his own ship and he wanted no advice from agents or brokers about pilots.

Yours respectfully

(signed) H B Jones.

Mr Latimer considered the question of giving gratuities by pilots thus raised, to be of such great importance. Both pilots were called into the room and during a long investigation, one pilot was severely cross-examined, during which he strenuously denied that he had been asked by the captain of the UDSIRE for a gratuity or that he had given him one and expressed himself as surprised at being asked by the captain to pilot the vessel on her subsequent voyage inward, as he had given him no encouragement to refuse the other pilot. While the Committee felt they could not do otherwise than accept the pilot's statement on the subject of the gratuity, they thought he was deserving of censure for not advising the other pilot under all the circumstances that he had received the captain's instructions to pilot the vessel on her next voyage and so at least have saved that pilot's time and expense and the Chairman conveyed to the pilot the Committee's opinion on that point. The case was considered closed.

It appears that the actions of some pilots were determined by the circumstances that prevailed and not by principles, the more inconvenience a pilot could cause another, the greater the satisfaction they derived from it.

The S. S. ROLAND arrived at Eastham Locks inward bound for Ellesmere Port during the level of the p.m. tide. The steamer as is usual would have been brought up on the west side of the lock for the river pilot to land and the canal pilot to go on board, but the vessel landed on the east side of the lock. Immediately the ROLAND was brought up in the lock, a pilot who was on the east side went on board and offered his services as pilot, and the captain engaged him.

A pilot had been instructed by the agents of the ROLAND to attend the ship and that he was on the west side of the lock at Eastham, but that owing to the steamer bringing up on the east side of the lock, he was unable to board her before the other pilot got on board. However, he crossed the lock in his small boat and went on board the ROLAND and handed the captain his letter from the agents. The captain then told the first pilot that the second pilot was his pilot.

The first pilot was well aware that a pilot had been ordered to attend and was awaiting the vessel's arrival on Eastham Lock, but being the opportunist he was, he took full advantage of the vessel docking on the east side where he was stationed. His only mistake was not realising the other pilot, ordered by the Ship's Agents, had access to a small boat and was able to cross the lock while the river and the canal were level. Had his pilot been unable to do so he would have had the pilotage of that vessel taken right from under his nose. Some pilots in those days could have taught Dick Turpin a lesson or two.

The antagonism between pilots engendered by the method some pilots used to obtain work from one another, was often transferred to actually piloting a vessel. This abrasive pilotage attitude became a constant source of complaint to the Pilotage Committee. In an incident when damage was sustained whilst two vessels were passing each other in the canal, the Pilotage

Committee felt if ordinary care and consideration had been exercised by one of the pilots, no damage would have been incurred. The Chairman addressed one of the pilots, saying 'he understood there was a feeling amongst pilots generally, that when he was piloting vessels on the canal he had no consideration for anyone he might meet underway, neither for other pilots ships or his own'.

The pilot defended himself pompously, by saying he thought the feeling of the pilots regarding the manner of his piloting was the outcome of his refusing to become a member of the Pilots Association and he certainly thought there was no ground for complaint against him. The pilots statement was totally refuted by the Pilotage Committee. The Chairman's final remarks summarised the incident perfectly by saying, he hoped that not just the two pilots before him, but all pilots would work together in future and any private feelings or friction there was between them would be put on one side, not only for their own sake but for the sake of the Manchester Pilot Service as a whole.

This appeal from the Chairman of the Pilotage Committee did not appear to have the desired effect upon the pilots in question. The following month the self same pilots were again summoned by the Pilotage Committee to answer a complaint of aggressive and inconsiderate piloting. After a long and searching enquiry, it resulted in one of the pilots being warned that if a similar complaint was brought before the Committee again and it was proved, the Committee would take a very serious notice of the matter. This second incident prompted the Chairman of the Pilotage Committee to once again make a genuine, heartfelt plea to the pilots regarding their personal feelings towards other pilots.

The Chairman - almost in despair I would think - stated he thought it was a very serious matter that two senior pilots on the canal should be so opposed to each other. Indeed, it was a matter of great regret to find that such feelings existed between pilots and he considered they should all try to establish a better understanding between themselves. If they would only endeavour to carry this out, it would, he felt sure, make for a more efficient and compatible pilot service. He did not think they could do anything more in the case before them except to say that he sincerely hoped that no pilot would have to appear before the Committee in any similar case in future.

No such similar case was ever recorded again.

Arising above all this acrimony between the pilots, there were pilots of stricter morality who had a sense of propriety and a dedication to see justice fair play and a properly organised pilot service established on the Manchester Ship Canal. Not for them the catch-as-catch-can or 'farming-out' systems; not for them the gratuitous payments. What they wanted was a pilot service of which they could be justifiably proud.

They worked long, hard, voluntary hours in an attempt to achieve their aims and ideals. The Manchester Pilot Service should have been eternally grateful for these unselfish men, but unfortunately in this imperfect world we live in, they were not always appreciated or understood.

Certain Pilots did not confine their "Dirty Tricks " department exclusively to their fellow Pilots. One of the most despicable pilotage practices ever used on the Ship Canal was the refusal of a Pilot to allow another vessel that they were delaying - usually through their own inept piloting- to overtake them. I cannot think of a better example or illustrate more clearly the enmity created by this selfish practice than the complaint from Captain Brennel, Master of the S.S. "VANELLUS".

" I regret to inform you that since my company ceased to regularly employ Canal Pilots, some Pilots have wantonly and maliciously laid themselves out to retard the passages of the steamers on the Ship Canal. With great respect permit me to state I am perfectly aware of the serious charges I am making and I also beg you to distinctly understand I am prepared to fight these creatures to a finish. Their conduct to us, unoffending Ship Masters,Company servants, who are obliged to obey,or resign their commands is beneath contempt. I will quote just two cases to prove my charge.

1st. Case July 10th. 1926:-

I left No. 6 Dock bound for Antwerp cast off my tug boat (MERCIA) and ordered her to proceed to the small lock at Modewheel to be lowered down in the short end and await my vessel below. Two large vessels were ahead of me, a Clan Boat and an American vessel the "CONEHATTA". There was also a very large vessel, a Federal Liner waiting to leave No. 9 Dock. I passed the Clan Boat underway in the swinging basin with the permission of her Pilot and I entered the small lock just as they closed the top gates of the big lock behind the "CONEHATTA". We were lowered down at the same time. I asked the Pilot of the "CONEHATTA" to allow me to proceed first, stating I will take the small lock at Barton again and you will not see me again. His reply is unprintable and not worthy of a person holding such a position as a Pilot.

He left the big lock exactly 3½ minutes before I steamed out of the small lock. I again took the small lock at Barton and again this Pilot would not let me pass after another plea for him to let me go ahead,to which I received a similar answer in the same tone as the former. He was that anxious to gratify spite that his intelligence was not acute enough to grasp the fact that he was also holding up his colleagues on the Clan Boat and the Federal Liner, because I decided to take the big locks at Irlam and Latchford, there was no object in taking a risk with nothing to gain by entering the small lock whose dimensions - you hardly need reminding of - are 350 feet by 45 feet, and my vessel is 290 feet between the perpendiculars and has a beam of 42 feet,

Author: What the Master of the "VANELLUS" possibly did not appreciate was that the Pilot of the "CONEHATTA" could not have cared less about the delay or inconvenience he was causing his 'Colleagues' astern of him. No doubt it was giving him great delight:

2nd. Case September 14th. 1926:-

My vessel was in Eastham Locks when I was ordered by a lock

official to proceed ahead. I accordingly blew prolonged blast on the vessels whistle as per bye-law,to indicate to all vessels I was under-way. I rang half speed ahead and again blew a prolonged blast on the vessel's whistle. I observed, at that time, a large vessel commencing to leave from the East Dolphins, she did not sound her whistle that she too was proceeding up the Ship Canal and it was not full daylight. On my enquiries later I learned that the boatmen in attendance to the vessel had informed the Pilot "there is a Cork Boat leaving the lock" to which the Piot replied "I want to get ahead of that 'expletive'. I only prevented a collision with this vessel by going full astern on my engines. I presume that when the lock staff instruct a vessel to go ahead I am justified in proceeding without any interference from other vessels.

Owing to the paltry cussedness of this Pilot I did not reach Manchester Docks until 1915hrs some twelve hours later when I could have arrived at noon easily. We lost half a days work and we still had to proceed to Liverpool, discharge, load,and sail for Antwerp on Saturday the 18th. inst,or lose a week. I make no complaint against such Pilots as Mr. Cartwright, Mr. Postlethwaite, or Pilots of their type,from such I have always received kindness and courtesy. In conclusion permit me to state that I have piloted my own vessels on the Ship Canal for 24 years. I have never had a collision or a serious accident during that time."

An explanation or justification for this kind of conduct does not readily or easily come to mind. The author has experienced being a recipient of this behaviour from Pilots on many occasions. Pilots would go to such an extent to prevent a vessel overtaking them - especially at locks - to make unnecessary engine movements knowing full well this would cause a strong flow of water across the entrance of the small lock, thus causing the vessels entering that lock to get ahead of him, to sheer either to port or starboard and damage the lock or vessel or both. The Author has been exactly in such an incident when damage occurred.

This practice continued to exist throughout the entire history of the Manchester Pilot Service. It was the greatest single cause of ill will within the service and was extensively carried out,especially between the feuding families. The greatest exponents of this practice were undoubtedly the appropriated Pilots for the Shell Oil Tankers.

The lack of compassion and comradeship in the Pilot Service and the absolute example of Pilot v Pilot cannot be better illustrated than in an incident that occurred in March 1941. The German "Blitz" on Merseyside was at its most ferocious height and the home of Mr. N. Colvin (Pilot Second Class) was completely destroyed by enemy action. His family suffered injury, occasioning him to be absent from duty for six days and to seek fresh accommodation for himself and his family. The Pilots Association proposed a resolution that :-

Any Pilot compelled through enemy action to seek fesh accommodation for himself and family and being absent from duty for this purpose shall be granted leave of absence for a period of not more than seven days on a two-thirds share of earnings.

In all other professions - Liverpool Pilots included - full pay was granted during leave of absence as the direct result of the loss of your residence through enemy action. Nevertheless, this proposal had to be submitted to the twelve Pilots who were not members of the Association and from their replies it transpired that those Pilots were far from unanimous to this proposal. It was therefore agreed that no payment should be allowed to Pilots absent owing to enemy action,but if a Pilot found it necessary to be absent for this reason, no permission was required and he should ,if at all possible, communicate the fact he would be absent to the Pilot Clerk.

It must be pointed out that Mr. Colvin was one of the younger Pilots - 38 years old - and in terms of holding a Pilot Licence he had only been granted a temporary second class licence late in 1940. These two factors did not endear him to the twelve senior Pilots who were not members of the Association and some of the senior Pilots who were members. A modicum of sympathy prevailed when at the Pilotage Committee in August 1941 C.F. Young (Pilot) re-submitted the original resolution and the Pilotage Committee unanimously agreed that such a provision should be made after hearing that 21 Pilots had signed the resolution. There is no record of this resolution being made retrospective.

The antagonism between Pilots was not solely restricted to Piloting it was often motivated by greed. In 1901 a typical case came before the Pilotage Committee. The concession for the boating and mooring services had been granted to Mr. Cave (Second Class Pilot) by the Pilotage Committee and had become a very lucrative business. Covetous eyes looked longingly at this service and one Pilot, who had a strong desire to share in this money making venture, wrote to the Pilotage Committee criticising the lack of an efficient and regular boating service at Eastham, when more than one vessel required the services of a boat and had quoted examples of the lack of this service.

It was pointed out to the Committee that Mr. Cave only attended to the boating when he had no piloting duties to perform and therefore enjoys the monoply in its widest sense. It was further explained the boating work comes only fitfully, at times not enough work for one man but at other times there is more than he can manage. Arguing on these lines it was resolved that a second Pilot be allowed to use a boat in the Eastham Basin or on the other hand the concession granted to Mr. Cave be cancelled to save any further friction between these two Pilots which had become extremely noticeable. The boating and mooring concession was granted to the second Pilot. It is told that the relationship between these two Pilots deteriorated even further and the incidents that occurred between them during their attempts to procure work from one another in Eastham Basin had to be seen to be believed. This antagonism was carried on in their piloting work to such an extent that Mr. Cave was forced to relinquish his Pilots Licence through the actions of the Pilot who had invaded his private boating and mooring service.

There is a happy sequel to this story, Mr. Cave's ·Eastham Boating Service became a very remunerative business and served

1912

Coasting Vessel approaching Barton Road Swing Bridge. The gas lamp in foreground was the only navigation light between Barton Locks and Modewheel Locks, a distance of 4 miles.

(Courtesy of M. S. C. Co.)

him well for the rest of his life. The second Pilot relinquished his boating concession some 12 months after he had applied for it . He had not, after all, been able to secure enough boating work to make it worth continuing with.

An application in February 1906 was submitted from a second class pilot asking permission to suspend his licence for six months to enable him to instruct someone to take over the work of rigging certain ships at the docks on behalf of the wife of his late uncle, who had died rather suddenly leaving his business with no one to look after it and his wife not very well off.He intended to instruct a brother of the widow so that he could manage the business for her and which he would be fully capable of doing if he could be in regular attendance to instruct him for six months. The Pilotage Committee agreed that the Pilot be given temporary leave of six months.

The Pilot duly returned to work on September 1st but at the Pilotage Committee in September the Chairman said it had come to his notice that this committee had been grossly misled in granting the request of a Pilot to cease piloting for six months in order to instruct a relative in the work of shiprigging at the Docks, as he had been told that the shiprigging work had been carried out by the Pilot for his own benefit. The Pilot had obtained permission of the Committee to cease piloting for a specific object and had not carried out that object. He considered this a breach of faith with the committee and an abuse of the Pilot Service and notice should be taken of the matter.

The Pilot was seen by the Chairman of the Pilotage Committee at the Dock Office and after spending some considerable time with the matter he had to report that he had been unable to obtain any satisfactory explanation from the Pilot, although the Pilot admitted that his statements made in his letters to the committee requesting the six months leave of absence were not true. The pilot was brought before the Pilotage Committee in January 1907 and asked for an explanation on this matter. He stated that the widow's younger brother had declined to undertake the work and he had ultimately arranged for someone else to carry on the work and this he was now doing on his own account. The Pilot further stated that he had paid the widow during his six months period about £10 and that it was not true for the widow to say that he had only given her £2.

The Pilotage Committee decided that his conduct in this matter had been very unsatisfactory all through and he should be severely reprimanded. The Chairman warned the Pilot that should he ever have to ask for permission for any favours from this Committee again the statements repecting same should be correct ones and that if he at any future time was brought before the Committee on any pilotage matters and be found to be making misleading statements he would have his licence taken away. He should be thoroughly ashamed of himself in the manner in which he abused the Pilot service.

11.

THE CATCH-AS-CATCH-CAN-SYSTEM

In the early undisciplined days of the Manchester Ship Canal Pilot Service there were many unsavoury aspects of individual pilots obtaining work on vessels to the detriment of other pilots, none more so than the infamous practice of "Farming out" and the "Catch-as-Catch-can" system. When the attempt to form a Rotary System collapsed in 1902 the latter system became the most prevalent amongst the embittered Pilots. Some Pilots had access to tug boats or small "sculling" boats to enable them to board a vessel in the river, either off Dukes Dock, Liverpool, or in the Sloyne an anchorage for vessels at the entrance of the Eastham Channel, although one Canal Pilot was known to have boarded a vessel, bound for Eastham, off the Rock Lighthouse, New Brighton, in a small "sculling" boat.

The Catch-as-Catch-can system was based on the principle of the first Pilot to board the vessel received the pilotage in the Canal, irrespective of whether a Pilot had already been ordered by the Ships Agent/Broker and was awaiting the vessels arrival at Eastham Locks to present his own credentials. Obviously the Pilots without river craft were at a distinctive disadvantage having always to wait the inward bound vessel at Eastham Locks. There was another great advantage to piloting a vessel inward bound. It was the practice of some Pilots, to offer their services to the Master of the vessel for his outward passage in the Canal and this was often accepted.

Without doubt the classic case of the "Catch-as-Catch-Can" system, illustrating not only the inherent dangers of this system to life and limb but the tremendous tenacity of the Pilots in those days to obtain work. Such was the pilotage of the S.S.

"ARENDAL" on September 3rd 1909 At the September Pilotage Committee Meeting the Chairman submitted and read the following letter complaining of the action of a Pilot in obtaining the pilotage of the S.S. "ARENDAL".

Dear Sir,

I was appointed by Messrs. R.F. Sanderson and Co. Agents for the steamer "ARENDAL", to attend to her piloting and given a letter of introduction to the Captain. I attended at Eastham Locks for 3 tides, on the third tide after the vessel was due she came into Eastham and on boarding her my services were refused as the Captain had accepted the services of Mr. H.B. Jones who had got on board in the river and persuaded the Captain (who was an entire stranger to the port) to accept him, explaining that if he did not do so he would probably have difficulty in obtaining a Canal Pilot at Eastham.

On my pointing out to Mr. Jones the injustice of his action he told me he applied to the Captain for the work and the Captain could suit himself who he took and that neither I, Mr. E. Bowen (Manchester Steamship Owners Representative) or the Canal Co. could alter it and that I could do as I liked about it. If Mr. Jones' assertion is correct many of the Ship Canal Pilots are working under a false impression as they believe the method adopted to get work is disreputable and countenanced by the Canal Co. When the boat in which Mr. Jones and his two assistants were going alongside the "ARENDAL" she capsized and all three were thrown into the fast flowing river but Mr. Jones managed to get on board the "ARENDAL" while his son and another 2nd Class Pilot were rescued by the steam flat "HAROLD" and brought up to Eastham Locks.

I am reporting this clear case to you for the purpose of ascertaining for the benefit of such of the Canal Pilots who have no boat, whether the river method of obtaining work is the correct one. If it is fair competition, then I presume all Canal Pilots can do likewise when other Pilots who are appointed for the work by the Ships Agents are in attendance. As the

"ARENDAL" is still berthed in Manchester the enclosed facts can be verified by the Captain.

Yours respectfully

A.E.Postlethwaite.

After reading the letter the Chairman asked Mr. Jones if he had anything to say in connection with the complaint levelled at him. Mr. Jones admitted that he boarded in the river but the statements in other respects were not correct and could only be described as a tissue of falsehoods Mr. Jones stated that Captain Peterson of the S.S."VESTFOS" gave him a note for the Captain of the "ARENDAL" recommending him as a Pilot for the Canal. He presented this letter on boarding the "ARENDAL" in the river and the Captain at once engaged him to pilot the steamer in the Ship Canal. Mr. Jones denied he informed the Captain he would have difficulty in obtaining a Pilot at Eastham Lock. He also denied having mentioned Mr. Bowen's name or made the statements mentioned by Mr. Postlethwaite, viz. "that neither he (Postlethwaite), Mr. Bowen, or the Canal Co. could alter it. He said the Captain of the "ARENDAL" would confirm what he had said if he was seen by any of the Canal Co. Officials.

In answer to an enquiry from the Chairman of the Pilotage Committee as to whether he was aware before he went to intercept the "ARENDAL" in the river that Mr. Postlethwaite had been engaged to pilot the vessel in the Canal, Mr. Jones replied that he had not been so informed by anyone, although knowing that Mr. Postlethwaite did all Messrs. Sanderson's pilotage in the Canal and thought it possible that he might be ordered for the vessel. Mr. Jones considered that he had the perfect right notwithstanding that to obtain the pilotage if he could do so. (The Catch-as-Catch-Can system in all its glory. Authors note.) He further stated that if he had been informed that a Pilot was at Eastham Locks waiting for the steamer he would not have given up his endeavour to obtain the pilotage of the "ARENDAL" (Here the tenacity shows through. Author).

Mr. Jones also stated that Mr. Postlethwaite had previously obtained the pilotage of vessels he had been regularly piloting on the Canal and he did not think he had done anything unfair in obtaining the pilotage of the "ARENDAL" (Tit-for-Tat Piloting. Author). It was decided that Captain Williams (Canal Superintendent) should interview the Master of the "ARENDAL" as to the circumstances under which he engaged Mr. Jones and his refusal to accept Mr. Postlethwaite. Captain Williams was to report his findings at the next Pilotage Committee meeting.

Captain Williams duly interviewed the Master of the Norwegian steamer "ARENDAL". At the October Pilotage Committee Meeting he reported he had explained to the Master the purpose of his visit immediately he boarded the vessel in the Dock. To the questions put to the Master, he answered them in a straightforward manner. The Master stated that on his arrival in the River Mersey Mr. Jones boarded his vessel and reported himself as a Ship Canal Pilot and to questions put by the Master, Mr. Jones had replied " Yes, I do hold a Ship Canal Licence", which satisfied the Master who then said "That is good you may pilot my vessel in the Canal. Mr. Latimer (Chairman) pointed out to the Pilots, who had accused each other of having obtained pilotage work which they considered belonged to themselves, that whilst no doubt each thought he had a grievance against each other it was necessary both in the interests of the pilots generally and also of the Ship Canal Co. that they and the other Canal Pilots should work amicably one with the other and he suggested that they Messrs. Jones and Postlethwaite should meet and discuss and get rid of any grievance which they considered at present existed between them and work together in a friendly spirit in the future. If they were unable to do so then they should each put their grievances in writing when he would go into the question more fully with them, but he hoped this would not be necessary. The matter was to be considered at an end unless he heard further from either one or both Pilots.

The two Pilots in question were not to be appeased so easily and showed just how this Catch-as-Catch-Can system could engender so much bitterness between Pilots. At the November

1915
"War Sepoy", GRT.5557, L.400', B.52'. A converted cargo vessel
into an oil tanker.

(Courtesy Mrs W. Yates Collection)

1910
"Manchester Spinner", GRT.4227, L.360', B.48'. Torpedoed south
of Malta January 22 1918. The last Manchester Liner to be lost in the
1914-1918 War.

(Courtesy Mrs W. Yates)

Pilotage Committee Meeting the Chairman stated that contrary to expectations Messrs. Jones and Postlthwaite had not met for a friendly discussion to clear up their differences as had been suggested and he now submitted and read the following letters which had been received from both Pilots.

Dear Sir,

I am sending you the original order which I received for the first ship of the Foss Company which came into the Canal. After these ships were sold to the Thor Thorensen Co. they also sent me orders for the pilotage of their ships in the Canal. I am enclosing two letters from the Captain of the "ULEFOS", requesting me to attend his vessel on arrival in the canal which I always did, until Mr. Postlethwaite by some unmanly way took the work from me. I may also add, Sir, that on your advice I spoke with Mr. Postlethwaite and asked him to have a friendly discussion about this matter, but he absolutely refused to have any conversation with me and left me most abruptly.

Your obedient servant
H.B.JONES.

Mr. Postlethwaite's letter read as follows.

Dear Sir,

With reference to your request that Mr. Jones and I have a conversation with a view to coming to an amicable agreement, I refused his offer to converse on the matter simply because I cannot place any faith in what he says. I have been bluffed before by him. I have given a truthful answer to the charge he made against me of stealing three of the Thorensen Line steamers from him. I am informed by the Agents - Sandersons - that Mr. Jones letter of authority to pilot steamers of the Thorensen Line had been cancelled and the Masters of the three ships in question, who sent for me and offered me the pilotage, say they have no knowledge of the existence of this letter and they take any Pilot they choose.

I have never at any time acted in an ungentlemanly or unfair way to obtain work. Mr. Jones has answered my just complaint against him with falsehoods, which can be easily disproved by interviewing the Agents or any of the Masters. I have nothing further to say, I am just endeavouring to get fair play.

Captain Williams then submitted a report of a meeting held between himself, the Secretary of the Committee (Mr. J. Richardson) Mr. Postlethwaite and Captain Elger of the S.S."ULEFOS". Captain Williams stated he at once informed Captain Elger of the nature of their interview and asked him if he was willing to say under what conditions the pilotage of his steamer in the Canal had been transferred from Mr. Jones to Mr. Postlethwaite. Captain Elger agreed to do so. Captain Williams then stated he informed the Master that Mr. Jones had produced letters which he had received from him (Captain Elger) and also from the owners, requesting Mr. Jones to pilot his steamer in the Canal. Captain Elger had replied that some time ago he did engage Mr. Jones to pilot his steamer in the Canal, but although he regularly advised Mr. Jones when he expected to arrive at Eastham Locks, Mr. Jones with one or two exceptions, never personally attended to pilot the steamer but sent someone to act for him (Unsolicited proof the FARMING OUT" system of pilotage did exist.) and as he was never sure that Mr. Jones would be in attendance on his arrival he considered he might as well take the first Pilot that offered his services on his arrival at Eastham or in the river as to go to the trouble of writing to a Pilot to attend his vessel who instead of doing so sent someone else to do the piloting and he therefore, decided to give the piloting of his steamer to Mr. Postlethwaite with whom he was perfectly satisfied.

Captain Elger went on to say that the Captain of the "SKOTFOS" gave the pilotage of that steamer to Mr. Postlethwaite in consequence of that steamer meeting with an accident when piloted by Mr. Jones and the Captain of the "GRANFOS" also gave the pilotage of that steamer to Mr. Postlethwaite on his (Captain Elger) recommendation. He further stated that his firm do not interfere with the pilotage arrangements of their steamers but leave this entirely with the Captains and each Captain was at liberty to take any Pilot he chose. He had informed Mr. Jones of this when he presented a letter supposed to be from the owners . Captain Elger finally stated that no undue influence had been brought to bear on him or any other Captains in the company as to their employing Canal Pilots. He had simply engaged Mr. Postlethwaite because Mr. Jones did not personally attend to the pilotage of his steamer.

After hearing this report from Captain Williams the Chairman said it clearly showed that Mr. Jones was under some misapprehension in stating that Mr. Postlethwaite had in an unfair way taken the pilotage of these steamers. Due to Mr. Jones absence further consideration of the matter would have to be postponed until the next Pilotage Committee Meeting in order that Mr. Jones could read all the relevant information. Mr. Hindle (Pilots' representative) said that Mr Jones was very upset at having lost these three vessels after having piloted them for so long (ten years) and he had no doubt felt that something had been said to his disadvantage to bring this about. Mr. Latimer reiterated that whatever the opinion Mr. Jones held as to the reason of his losing the pilotage of the steamers it was quite evident from Captain Elgers statement that Mr. Postlethwaite was not to blame in this matter. The meeting was closed.

At the Pilotage Committee Meeting held on January 3rd 1910 the Chairman (Mr. Latimer) asked Mr. Jones had he anything further to add regarding the statements made by Captain Elger. Mr. Jones replied that Captain Elger never complained to him that he did not always attend his vessel personally, in fact the Captain had stated he was perfectly satisfied with the Pilots he had sent to pilot the steamer. He had read Captain Elgers' statements carefully but he still maintained that Mr. Postlethwaite had obtained the pilotage by unfair means. When asked to clarify this statement by the Chairman he replied that in 1908 he asked Mr. Postlethwaite to pilot the steamer from Manchester to Eastham as he was unable to attend to her through having other

129

pressing work (Another example of the "farming out" system). He thought it was very strange, that if Mr. Postlethwaite had not persuaded the Captain for the future pilotage of his vessel, that the Captain should have asked Mr. Postlethwaite to meet the vessel on her next trip into the Canal without informing him that his services would not be required.

Mr. Jones knew Mr. Postlethwaite did not always attend to the pilotage of the "ULEFOS" himself, but sends other Pilots if he has other work to attend to. (Further proof, if proof was needed, that the "farming out " system was rife within the Manchester Pilot Service). He did not think Captain Elger's reason for giving his ship to another pilot was correct, because Captain Elger had told him he was very satisfied with his services. A discussion ensued during which the opinion was expressed that there might be something in what Mr. Jones had stated, but the general opinion was that Captain Elger had given a very satisfactory and straightforward explanation for his action.

It was decided from the evidence placed before the Committee that Mr. Jones had not made out his case against Mr. Postlethwaite that the latter had obtained the pilotage of these three vessels by unfair means, as the Master of the "ULEFOS" had fully disproved this and also the reasons why the Masters of the other vessels transferred the pilotage to Mr. Postlethwaite. The Committee did not think it was necessary to take any further action in the matter. It is difficult to comprehend why with the unsolicited statements made by these two Pilots during this case, proving without a shadow of doubt the "farming out" system was proliferating in the Manchester Ship Canal Pilot Service, the Manchester Pilotage Committee did not take advantage of this golden opportunity to prove they really wanted to stop this odious practice. The Manchester Pilotage Committee had always insisted they would do every thing in their power to stamp out this practice but the two Pilots did not receive a single word of censure or even a caution as to their future conduct. That haunting question can never be answered.

It has already been documented that in normal circumstances the Pilot who had boarded the vessel first claimed the pilotage in the Ship Canal. The Captain merely had to sign the Pilots Note and it was considered sufficiently binding for the Pilot's right to pilot his vessel. No consideration was ever given to the Pilot who may have been waiting without payment two or three tides at Eastham Locks missing other pilotage work whilst doing so. There are always exceptions to the rule in all professions the following incident is just one of those rare exceptions. The Pilotage Committee received a letter from Mr. George Green complaining that he had been engaged by the Captain of the oil steamer S.S. "JOANNIS COULZIS" to pilot the vessel from the river to Eastham Locks and from Eastham to Manchester. On arriving at Eastham Locks the Shipping Agent came aboard with another Pilot, Mr. W Onion who, on the Agent's instructions immediately took charge of the steamer. Although Mr. Green informed the Agent that he had been engaged by the Captain the Agent refused to pay Mr. Green anything for his services.

The Agent had stated that he expected the vessel to have been brought into Eastham Locks by the River Pilot who it appears however left the vessel in the Sloyne, as was the usual custom of some River Pilots, for Mr. Green to pilot her into Eastham Locks and that he had engaged Mr. Onion some days prior to the vessel's arrival to pilot her from Eastham to Manchester and denied that the Captain had hired Mr. Green. The Committee reached the decision that Mr. Green had only piloted the vessel from River to Eastham Locks and such pilotage being outside the jurisdiction of this Committee they could not recognize him as the Ship Canal Pilot for that vessel nor could they collect any pilotage dues that he had earned. The Catch-as-Catch-Can-system for once failed on this occasion. No doubt the presence of the Agent had persuaded the Captain to accept Mr. Onion to pilot the vessel and no doubt Mr. W. Onion had duly paid the appropriate fee to the Agent for the work given to him as was the custom in those far off days.

A further illustration of the unjustness in obtaining pilot work on the Canal is recorded in 1908 when a Pilot was instructed by a Shipping Agent to attend the S.S. "NORD AMERIKA" from Eastham to Manchester. The Pilotage Committee heard that on the ship's arrival at Eastham Locks the awaiting Pilot found that Mr. Herbert Stuart had boarded the vessel in the river and arranged with the Captain for the pilotage. The Pilot stated that he had been waiting at Eastham two tides for this vessel at a cost of lls.6d. (65p).It was ascertained that at the time Mr. Stuart met the "NORD AMERIKA" he was on board his father's tug awaiting the arrival of the S.S. "GRIQUA" which vessel he had been engaged to pilot up the Ship Canal, but when the "NORD AMERIKA" arrived in the river ahead of his own vessel he boarded the "NORD AMERIKA" and obtained the pilotage, at the same time arranging for another Pilot to attend the "GRIQUA" (once again "farming out").

The Pilot further stated that Mr. H. Stuart Snr. must be a very influential man because three years ago he was engaged by Messrs. Watts and Watts Shipping Co. in conjunction with his son to pilot their vessels on the Ship Canal. They made an arrangement with that firm to provide tugs and helmsmen and do the pilotage on the Ship Canal for an undisclosed round sum. They also debarred any other Pilots in the Ship Canal from participating in the piloting of those vessels. The Pilot considered the action of Mr. Herbert Stuart in depriving other Pilots of work through not having the advantage of boarding vessels in the river by the aid of tug boats as grossly unfair. Mr Bowen (Manchester Steamship Owners Representative) agreed it was a great hardship to other Canal Pilots that Mr Stuart should be able through being owners of tug boats to meet vessels in the river and so obtain pilotage on the canal which might otherwise fall to other Pilots who had received instructions from Agents to attend the vessels.

A minute stating " That no licence be granted to any person unless he is prepared to devote the whole of his time to the work of pilotage, unless he be an appropriated Pilot or a Master or

Officer of any vessel navigating the Ship Canal." was discussed and the Committee wondered if the Messrs. Stuarts were complying to the letter of that minute. The Stuarts were tug owners and were engaged in doing work on the River Mersey which also enabled them to deprive other Pilots of their work on the Ship Canal. The Chairman remarked that the question of allowing Canal Pilots to make use of tug boats for the purpose of joining and leaving vessels in the river had previously been before the Committee when it was considered that it was in the interest of the shipowners that they should be allowed to do so and no doubt Mr. H. Stuart would say that it was for this purpose that they made use of the tug boats with which he was connected.

It was revealed that a similar occurrence had taken place when the "NORD AMERIKA" arrived on her last voyage to the Ship Canal concerning the same Pilot Mr. H. Stuart. The Chairman inquired of Mr. Felton (Liverpool Pilots 'Representative) if he knew of anything to prevent their Pilots of doing other work when not engaged in piloting. Mr. Felton replied that the only thing their Pilots were prohibited from doing was that they must not invest any money in any of the Liverpool tugs or Towing Company.

The Chairman felt there was nothing to prevent any of the Ship Canal Pilots owning a boat for the purpose of meeting vessels in the River and soliciting Canal Pilotage work. Unfortunately there were few who were able to afford this, and therefore of course Mr H. Stuart who had some interest in a tug company in Liverpool had no doubt an advantage over other Pilots in being able to so meet vessels in the River and solicit pilotage work. Whilst this method of obtaining pilotage work was not conducive to a harmonious relationship between the Pilots those Pilots obtaining such work by this method were not in contradiction of any of the Manchester Ship Canal Bye Laws, After some discussion it was agreed that the Chairman should arrange to interview Mr. H. Stuart regarding this complaint. The matter was regarded as settled.

The reason the two incidents involving the "ARENDAL" and "NORD AMERIKA" are documented in so much detail is many fold. They show what a truly chaotic state the Manchester Ship Canal Pilot Service had fallen into, undisciplined, uncaring and unjust. It shows the complete lack of camaraderie that should have existed between Pilots, as it did so prevalently in many other pilot services. This camaraderie, sadly, never did exist throughout its entire history. It further shows why some Pilots revelled in the Catch-as-Catch-Can system, but the piratical nature by which some Pilots obtained their work makes one wonder if the Manchester Pilot Service flag would have been more appropriate if it had been replaced by the "Skull and Cross Bones". The lack of co-operation between Pilots was singularly evident even when piloting in the Ship Canal.

A strong complaint was made by the owners of the S.S. "GRAMPUS" that their steamer had been unnecessarily delayed in the Canal between Eastham Locks and Latchford Locks, owing to the S.S. "WINNIE" refusing to allow her to overtake when signalled to for that purpose by the "GRAMPUS" Mr.J.W.Pass the Pilot of the "WINNIE" offered this explanation for his refusal to allow the "GRAMPUS" to pass.

"The Master of the "WINNIE" was desirous of arriving at Manchester Docks that night before dark and for the safety of the ship and all concerned it was not thought safe or seaman-like for the "GRAMPUS" to pass his steamer. Captain Heasley (Canal Superintendent) reported that as these two vessels were of small tonnage not exceeding 700 gross tons, and there was plenty of safe places to pass, larger vessels than these have overtaken one and another in that section of the Canal. There would have been little danger for these steamers to have passed and in doing so would not have delayed the "WINNIE" above five minutes. He considered Mr. Pass had not acted for the best in this refusal to allow another vessel to overtake his vessel, nor had his actions helped in any way towards a spirit of co-operation between Pilots. In an endeavour to assist the unhindered passage of a vessel in the Canal and thus attract trade for the benefit of all

"Ralph Brocklebank". A steel twin screw steam tug built by the Tranmere Bay Development Co., Birkenhead in 1903.

Off: No: 104479. 105'-1" x 22'-7" x 10'-0". (O.A. 110'-0").
172-80 Gross. 64-43 Reg. 83 N. H. P. 500 I. H. P. 11½ Knots.
Engines by John Jones, St Georges Iron Works, Liverpool. New boilers fitted at Lairds in 1922.

Bought from the Shropshire Union in 1922 when that firm closed. First registered at Chester, then Manchester No. 56/1922. Extensively re-fitted in 1936, re-named "Daniel Adamson". Bill of sale dated 29th August, 1972 to the Manchester Ship Canal Services. From 1950 mainly used as a pleasure craft promoting the ship canal. In 1985 it was decided not to renew her passenger certificate. She now rests in the Maritime Boat Museum at Ellesmere Port.

(Courtesy of Captain P. Dunbavand)

concerned every effort should be made to co-operate with other Pilots. Captain Heasley ended by saying he sincerely hoped he would not hear of any similar action of non-co-operation between the Pilots in the future or a more serious view would be taken of the matter. This refusal to allow a vessel to overtake another in the Ship Canal was practised by the majority of Pilots throughout the history of the Manchester Pilot Service.

A more forceful disclosure was that the Master Pilots had over the years quietly and very efficiently taken the control of the pilotage of nearly all vessels, large and small, which regularly transited the Canal and blatantly practised the "farming out" system, with what appeared to be the full support and co-operation of Shipowners and the Manchester Ship Canal Company. Most of the Master Pilots were wealthy men. Messrs. Stuarts for example were not only First Class Pilots in the Ship Canal but were Pilots for Garston Dock, Liverpool and Birkenhead Dock Pilots, Master Riggers, Boatmen (For the purpose of mooring and unmooring vessels at a quay) and tug boat owners. The owning of tug boats was indeed the "Jewel in the Crown". Very often when these tugs were plying for hire on the River Mersey, as was their want those days, they would also solicit Ship Canal pilotage for the Stuarts. If successful in obtaining Canal Pilotage work they would return to shore to pick up one of the Stuarts from whatever boarding stage they had positioned themselves, at that point of time, along the River and transfer them aboard the vessel they had managed to persuade the Master to accept their services.

Other Pilots had outside interests:-

Mr. E. Hankinson - Hotel and Restaurant

Mr. T. Lamey   - Master Rigger

Mr. W. Harvey   - Master Rigger

Mr. J. Cave   - Boatman

Mr. F. Penny   - Ship Chandler

Whilst other Pilots made a very precarious livelihood on their merits as a Ship Canal Pilot only, they were fully qualified and skilful Pilots but, because of the situation that prevailed were not given a fair chance to obtain pilotage work.

The sequel to the "NORD AMERIKA" affair bears out all that has been stated previously in this chapter. The Pilot's (Mr. Stuart) explanation stated that on the night in question he was stationed on the Seacombe Ferry Stage awaiting the arrival of his vessel the S.S. "GIRGUA", as requested by the Ships Agents, when his tug boat the "CONDUCTOR" came to the stage and informed him that the "NORD AMERIKA" was in the River and that the Captain required a Pilot for the Canal. He then went on board and although he mentioned that a Pilot was waiting at Eastham Locks, the Captain stated that unless that Pilot had a letter from the Owners he would refuse his services and would require him (Mr. Stuart) to pilot his vessel up the Canal. On arrival at Eastham Locks a Pilot came on board and presented a letter from the Ship's Agents appointing him Pilot but the Captain said he would not recognize their authority to engage his Pilot and therefore he engaged me to take the vessel to Manchester.

Mr. Stuart admitted he arranged for another Pilot who was at Eastham Lock to attend the "GRIGUA", the original vessel he had been asked to attend. He said that he did not think he had acted unfairly because he had experienced a similar situation and it was a situation that might occur to any Pilot at any time therefore he had made no complaint. It was the situation that prevailed at the time "You win some you lose some". Mr. Latimer pointed out to Mr. Stuart although under the circumstances he was not breaking any of the Company's Bye Laws he thought that Pilots should work in a more give and take spirit with one and another than appeared to have been done in this case and that he should have passed the pilotage of the "GRIGUA" over to the Pilot who was waiting for the "NORD AMERIKA" instead of another Pilot. The Pilotage Committee would expect in similar cases in future that some better arrangements should be made in order to avoid any friction between Pilots and that if this was not done the Committee would have to consider what steps could be taken to alleviate this problem. The Chairman concluded that the Pilotage Committee thought that Mr. Stuart's conduct was very unsatisfactory and they hoped that a further case of a similar character would not be reported to them. It was a forlorn hope for this state of affairs was to continue for another six years.

It is hard to understand how certain Pilots yearned for the Catch-as-Catch-Can system many years after it had ceased to be used. Mr. Joseph Lamey on retiring at the age of 66 years, after nearly 50 years as a Pilot, was quoted in an editorial on his retirement as saying. "I still think the good old days of competition between Pilots "Catch-as-Catch-Can" were undoubtedly the best." He recalled his days as a helmsman when he had to row the Pilot out from New Brighton Pier to a ship in mid river, put him on board then row back, get on his bike and race off to Eastham Locks hoping to meet the same ship to steer her in the Canal. If he did not arrive in time at Eastham Locks the Pilot would have proceeded without him or accepted another helmsman who might have been available at Eastham Locks. He would have received no pay but still it was a great life and a great time."

I complete this chapter with two incidents, both sad in there own way, but showing the utter futility of the Catch-as-Catch-Can system.

The S.S. "JOHANN CUESTES" arrived in the River bound for the Ship Canal, when approaching New Ferry Pier a small "sculling" boat put out from the Pier and boarded a Ship Canal Pilot on the starboard side. Meanwhile a tug boat had simultaneously boarded a Ship Canal Pilot on the port side, both Pilots being totally unaware of each others presence. The two unsuspecting Pilots arrived on the open bridge of the vessel from opposite sides and the Captain and the Liverpool Pilot at first witnessed a heated exchange of words between the Canal Pilots which then broke out into open violence. After a brief but bloodied skirmish they were separated only by the intervention of the Captain and the River Pilot. The two Canal Pilots retired from the bridge of the vessel in an extreme state of distress and in no condition to Pilot a vessel in the Ship Canal. Fortunately a Pilot had already been ordered by the ship's Agents to attend the vessel on its arrival at Eastham Locks two days previously.

Mr James Abram, First Class Pilot since 1899 of 9, Waterloo Road, Runcorn, whilst boarding the coaster "St. MIRREN" in the River on Sunday February 4th 1912, fell between his boarding boat and the coaster and was drowned. Mr Abram was the first and last fatality of a Ship Canal Pilot whilst in the pursuance of his pilotage duties. Mr. John W. Edwards another Canal Pilot had been ordered by the vessel's Agents to attend the "ST. MIRREN" and Pilot her to Manchester. Mr. Edwards had been waiting at Eastham Locks for her arrival for two tides. Despite this tragic accident it did not deter the Ship Canal Pilots from continuing to board vessels in the River.

1922
"Svanholm" GRT.696, L.179', B.28'. This vessel would not steer her own length straight. Chain and Rod steering gear and reverse helm and rudder direction. Top speed 6 knots. Also a one boiler vessel in the canal.

1921
"Granfoss" GRT.1461, L.254', B.39'. Another chain and rod vessel. Always arrived and left the canal with a big list to starboard or port making steering even harder. Top speed 4 knots. Only ran on one boiler in the Canal. Both these vessels still trading to Manchester in 1959.

12.

THE "FARMING OUT" OR "CONTRACTING OUT" SYSTEM

No greater illustration can be given on the working of this infamous and odious practice, beloved of all Master Pilots, than that which was placed before the Pilotage Committee Meeting on Thursday April 10th 1902. The Chairman (Mr.J.Wilson) submitted and read the following communication from Mr. B. Whitehouse and signed by him on behalf of an Association styling itself "MANCHESTER SHIP CANAL PILOTS ASSOCIATION" :-

"On Thursday March 13th the S.S. "PLANET NEPTUNE" on passage from Eastham to Manchester, piloted by Mr. F. Smith ,arrived at Old Quay Lock and tied up for the night. On that same evening the S.S. "SPRING" on passage from Partington to Eastham arrived at Old Quay and also tied up for the night. The following morning Mr. J. Barnes (Pilot) took charge of the "PLANET NEPTUNE" and piloted her to Manchester. Mr. F. Smith piloted the "SPRING" to Eastham. The Pilot originally in charge of the "SPRING" had been sent to Liverpool by Mr. Barnes to pilot the S.S. NORDSTRAND" from Liverpool to Manchester in place of himself.

We wish to know how Mr.F.Smith was paid for his work or if the pilot bills are signed for two separate pilotages for each vessel and if not who draws the pilotage money for work that he has not done? And if this method of work is in accordance with Canal regulations? We think when a Pilot takes charge of a vessel either at Manchester or Eastham he has the right to pilot her through either way without being relieved by any other Pilot as long as he is piloting correctly and is not superseded by the Pilotage Authority. We are also informed that the Hamburg Steamer S.S. "ALSEN" was steered up the Canal on her last voyage from Eastham to Manchester by Mr. J. Kay (Helmsman) and there was no Canal Pilot on board. We have since heard that the Pilotage Bill was signed and the pilotage money drawn although no pilotage services were rendered by any pilot until the steamer arrived at Modewheel Locks Manchester.

We shall be greatly obliged by your views on these matters.

The Chairman stated that on investigation it was found that the Pilotage Bill for the PLANET NEPTUNE had been made out - from Eastham to Manchester - and been presented in the name of Mr. Barnes although he had only piloted the vessel from Old Quay to Manchester likewise the Pilotage Bill for the "SPRING"- from Manchester to Eastham via Partington - had been made out for one pilot only although he too had only piloted the vessel to Old Quay. Mr. Wilson said it appeared that these two Pilots showed a tendency to carry on the system of "Farming Out" pilotage on the Canal - which question had been before the Committee and condemned by them sometime ago - He had given instructions to withhold payment of the pilotage accounts for the three vessels in question pending this matter coming before this Committee for investigation.

The two pilots were asked for their explanation in claiming for pilotage services which they had not performed contrary to No. 11 of the Company's Pilotage Laws. Mr. Barnes replied as follows:-

I arranged for Mr. F. Smith to pilot the "PLANET NEP-TUNE" from Eastham to Old Quay where I knew she was going to tie up for the night. I had a telephone message from the Master of the vessel to join her at Old Quay myself. There was one card signed for the whole distance, there being no extra charges. I paid Mr. Smith one third of the pilotage (£1.8s.4d. or £1.43p) for the whole distance and £1 for his pilotage from River to Eastham Locks a total of £2.4.s.3d. (£2.43p) If this explanation is satisfactory will you kindly forward the remainder of the pilotage fee - £4.5s.0d.(£4.25p) - which was stopped from me.

The other Pilots' explanation ran in similar vein: I arranged with Mr. Smith to pilot the "SPRING" from Old Quay to Eastham leaving the Pilot Bill on board to be completed and signed by the Master on arrival at Eastham. There were no extra charges and I paid Mr. Smith one third of the whole pilotage amounting to 16s.0d. (80p). I boarded the "NORDSTRAND" in the river and arrived in Manchester about noon. If this explanation is satisfactory and meets with your approval kindly forward the amount deducted from my account.

The Chairman announced that the Pilots' explanations had not proved satisfactory and this was the reason they had been summoned to attend before this committee. A conversation had ensued on the statements of the Pilots after which it was decided to hear what the Pilots had further to say on the matter. The Chairman informed them it appeared to the Committee that they had more work on hand than they could themselves perform and that instead of giving the through pilotage (Eastham to Manchester or Manchester to Eastham) of one of these steamers to another Pilot, they had made use of Mr. Smith in taking the "PLANET NEPTUNE" to Old Quay and the "SPRING" to Eastham, in order that they might personally obtain the larger portion of the Pilotage Fees. It was also the Committee's opinion it was a blatant case of "Farming Out" the pilotage on the Canal.

Mr. Barnes stated that he usually piloted the "PLANET NEPTUNE" in the Canal but she had arrived some two days early whilst he was piloting another vessel to Manchester. He had asked Mr. Smith to attend her in his absence. It was whilst lying at Old Quay that the Master telephoned him asking him to take charge of the piloting personally the next morning to complete the passage to Manchester. It was only because of this request that he did so. The reason he had only sent in one Pilotage Bill for the whole pilotage was in order not to make two charges against the owners and so increase the cost of pilotage. He had paid Mr. Smith for the services performed by him which was a correct proportion of the whole pilotage charge and he did not think he was breaking the law in any way.

The second Pilot stated in giving the pilotage of the "SPRING" to Mr. Smith and charging the same on his card and afterwards paying Mr. Smith the correct proportion of the pilotage earnings he also did not think he was doing wrong either. He was well aware of other such cases having taken place on the Canal and nothing had been said about it. He realised, now it had been explained to him, that his actions were against the Bye-Laws and he apologised and said he would not do it again.

There was a lengthy discussion and eventually the Chairman informed the two Pilots that as this was the first case of the kind brought under their notice the Committee had decided not to inflict any punishment for this offence against the Bye-Laws, but they must thoroughly understand that such a case must not be repeated, because if it was, the offender would be more seriously dealt with -The Committee were genuinely concerned about the implications of this complaint and at the conclusion of this case further considered the question of the pilotage of vessels being divided in this way. They viewed it as very undesirable, and ultimately unanimously resolved:-

The Pilotage Committee recommend the adoption of the following order to Manchester Ship Canal Pilots:-

That in all cases where a Pilot has boarded a vessel for the purpose of navigating her along the Canal he shall be the only Pilot entitled to take that vessel to her final destination - subject to the rules and regulations as laid down by the Pilot Committee for the release of a Pilot when on passage-. He shall not delegate any portion of the service to any other pilot on his behalf.

That when a Pilot has been engaged to pilot a vessel from Eastham to Manchester or vice versa or from any point to point in the Ship Canal and for some reason is unable to undertake the work and passes the vessel to some other pilot, that Pilot only shall on his own behalf earn the pilotage charges for his services..

That any pilot found acting contrary to the above resolution shall be liable to have his licence suspended or revoked according to the discretion of the Pilotage Committee.

The Secretary of the Pilotage Committee was instructed to forward a copy of the resolution to every pilot that the same may be generally known by them.

This resolution was easily circumnavigated by the ever devious Master Pilots. They still continued to "Farm Out " pilotage work, but they kept within the limitations of the new resolutions set by the Pilotage Committee. When the Master Pilots "Farmed Out" the work to those Pilots less fortunate in obtaining work - for divers reasons explained in other chapters - they allowed him to complete the full pilotage, thus keeping within the bounds of propriety set by the Pilotage Committee. The main difference was, the pilot of the "Farmed Out" vessel collected his fee it was incumbent on him to pay his employer two thirds of that fee in appreciation of the work given to him. If such a gratuity was not forthcoming the pilot quickly found his source of pilotage working becoming non-existent and the renewal of his Licence placed in jeopardy. The Richard Edwards affair was ample proof of that. Other incidents reflected the pressure the Master Pilots could bring to bear on Pilots, especially Second Class Pilots who were particularly vulnerable, either to bring them under the control of Master Pilots or to force them to leave the service through lack of earnings. The Master Pilots "Farming Out" system could then be maintained..

Mr. J. Lamb (pilot) aged 45 years, after serving as a helmsman for fifteen years was granted a Second Class Licence on September 1st. 1910. His application for the renewal of that licence on September lst. 1911 read as follows:-

"I am the holder of a Second Class Licence for the Manchester Ship Canal and because certain pilots had coveted most of the work I have been unable to obtain pilotage work to enable me to put in the three compulsory passages between Eastham and Manchester and vice versa, during the past year as required by the Bye- Laws for a renewal of my licence. The only pilotage work I have been able to obtain was the S.S."OSCELO" from Eastham to Manchester. However, during the whole of the year I have been regularly navigating the Canal between Eastham and Manchester and vice versa as a helmsman under pilots on vessels of all tonnages - this was a recognised and accepted practice in those days. These services would be about four times a week so you will see that I have been regularly employed up and down the Canal although not in charge as a pilot.

I now request that you will renew my licence for the next year when I hope to get more pilotage work. The Pilotage Committee, under these circumstances agreed to renew his licence. Obviously Mr. Lamb was not among the favoured men of the Master Pilots and one must conclude he did not lay his gifts at the feet of those who could control his livelihood. Every year he had to struggle to make the requisite three transits of the Canal and every year he had to apply for a renewal of his licence under the same circumstances. Eventually he had to give up this unequal struggle when his licence was once again refused, on the usual grounds, on September 1st. 1916. Mr. Lamb then resigned from the service no doubt a very bitter man. The power of the Master Pilots reigned supreme and would continue to do so for a few years yet.

The incident regarding the steering of the S.S."ALSEN" by J. Kay without a pilot on board was suitably dealt with by fining Mr. Kay £1.1s.d, (£1.05p) and withholding the payment for his services. Mr. Charles Cave (pilot) was another story, holding a certificate of competency as Master Mariner he entered the Manchester Pilot Service directly from serving as a Chief Officer in the Lamport and Holt Line, who were regular traders to the Ship Canal. This method of entering the Manchester Pilot Service, without having been a helmsman to a pilot, was not uncommon in those days. These two facts that Mr. Cave had a Master Mariners certificate and had not served under any pilot as a helmsman immediately antagonised the Master Pilots. They had a traditional distrust of educated men especially Master Mariners.

At the age of 40 years Mr. Cave successfully passed his examination for a second class licence on March 29th 1900. In the first year of piloting he quickly became aware of his unpopularity amongst the Master Pilots and the strength of those pilots ability to restrict his pilotage earnings. Mr. Cave's first year's earnings were £58.16s. 8d. (£58.83p). If he had stayed as Chief Officer in Lamport and Holts he would have earned, in that year, £144. Financial circumstances failed to improve dramatically when he became a First Class Pilot in May 1904. Mr. Cave must have been constantly searching for means of additional revenue to compensate his low earnings as a Pilot. In 1901 he perceived there was an urgent need for a Boatman service at Eastham for the purpose of mooring and unmooring vessels when arriving or leaving from Eastham Basin. He realised this was the perfect opportunity to enhance his piloting earnings from an outside source but still be in close contact with the Manchester Pilot Service.

The boating service he proceeded to establish and offer to all vessels in Eastham Basin became very much in demand, much to the chagrin of the Master Pilots, for not having seen this opportunity themselves of enhancing their already substantial earnings. It was well Mr. Cave did establish his boating service for his pilotage earnings for the next six years makes for depressing reading but not wholly unpredictable considering the system of working that prevailed at that time. The Master Pilots really excelled themselves in their treatment of Mr. Cave.

YEAR	EARNINGS	
1906	£60.13s. 7d.	(£60.68p.)
1907	£64. 0s. 7d.	(£68.03p.)
1908	£39.14s. 1d.	(£39.70p.)

1909	£28. 9s. 3d.	(£28.48p.)
1910	£24. 4s. 6d.	(£24.22p.)
1911	9s. 9d.	(48p.)

In the year ending September 1st 1911 Mr. Cave only managed one pilotage service in January and had no other pilotage work for the rest of the year. In 1911 if Mr. Cave had been a Chief Officer with Lamport and Holt he would have earned £216 and had he been promoted to Master - there was every possibility this would have taken place - he would have earned £312. Because of his lack of pilotage, for the first time during his entire piloting on the Ship Canal, he failed to get his requisite three pilotage services between Eastham and Manchester to entitle him to the renewal of his licence.

Mr. Cave presented himself to the Pilotage Committee Meeting in September 1911 to appeal against the refusal of the Committee to renew his licence. The Chairman expressed the opinion that whatever was the decision of the Committee on this matter Mr. Cave was not likely to, lose much judging by the fees he had received over the past six years. Mr. Cave stated that certain other Pilots had their licences renewed although they had not performed the requisite number of services on the Canal. The Chairman pointed out that the circumstances in the two cases in question were quite different to Mr. Cave's. A number of questions were put to Mr. Cave by members of the Committee and it was brought out that he was not dependent on pilotage for a livelihood as he had an established boating service at Eastham Basin. The work was capable of further development and by strict attention to this boating service a very good living could be made from it. It was remarked by a member of the Committee that some pilots had expressed the view that Mr. Cave was not a competent man to be put in charge of a vessel on the Ship Canal and also he was not devoting the whole of his time to piloting as laid down in the Company's Bye-Laws.

1900

Approaching Irwell Park Wharf. Note only one tug attending vessel.
"Mercia". A single screw steam tug built by Westwood, Baillie &
Co. at Poplar, London in 1889 for William Watkins. Bought by the M.
S. C. in April 1895 for £4,000.

Off: No: 966500. 85'-8" x 18'-1" x 10'-7". 94 Gross. 70 N. H. P. 400
H. P.

Registered at Manchester No 3/1895.

In her early days the "Mercia" had a rounded casing from the bridge
deck to the bulwarks on both sides, this was removed some time later.
Sold to S. C. Roberts of Bristol on 17th January, 1935, registration was
transferred to Bristol 15th February 1935. Vessel struck a mine in the
Bristol Channel on the 14th January 1942 and sank, soon becoming
engulfed by the sand.

Registration closed 28th April 1942.

(Courtesy Captain P. Dunbavand)

149

In view of the apparent feeling of the majority of the Committee and certain pilots the Chairman   pressed the pilots' representatives for a personal expression of their feelings on this matter. After a brief discussion Mr. Hindle and Mr. T. Lamey (pilots' representatives) stated they would not oppose any decision reached by the Committee. It was therefore unanimously decided   not to renew Mr. Cave's Ship Canal Licence. The Master Pilots had won again and maintained their avaricious grip on the pilotage in the Canal. Mr. Cave continued to make a living from his boating service and died in 1918 at the age of 65.

One pilot who did manage to beat the "Farming Out" system was Mr. W.H. Roberts Snr. In 1913 he wrote the following letter to the Pilotage Committee:-

" Through not having three pilotage services   complete to Manchester or vice versa I have not this year been notified to apply for the renewal of my second class licence as usually occurs.   I now   therefore take the liberty to apply to the Gentlemen of the Pilotage Committee to allow me to do so. Having had several short pilotage services but only two full length services I of course do not qualify for a renewal of my licence. I hope you will believe me when I tell you this is no fault of my own but is entirely due to the odious system   that is proliferating in the Canal of obtaining work, which you are well aware   of and appear to condone. I refer to the system of "Farming Out".

I am determined to overcome these difficulties. I have performed plenty of steering work and I am fully as conscientious when acting as helmsman as when piloting. I keep myself in close touch with the Canal at all times".

This letter must have touched a raw nerve for the Pilotage Committee immediately renewed Mr. Roberts' licence. Mr. Roberts overcame all manner of problems, directed at him from the Master Pilots, to become a highly respected pilot until he retired on April 30th 1942 after 36 years as a licensed pilot. This was one of the very, very few times the Master Pilots did not get their own way.

What must be the saddest and most unjust incident to be recorded was that of Mr. H. Limb who became another victim of the "Farming Out" system. Mr. Limb joined the helmsmans service in 1905 aged 22 and gained a Second Class Licence on the Canal in 1910. He applied on December 1st 1913 to be examined for a First Class Licence but was refused by the Pilotage Committee on the grounds there was no vacancy for a First Class Pilot in the service at that moment. He re-applied in May 1914 and once again was refused on similar grounds. Mr. Limb complained to the Pilotage Committee most strenuously, that during the period from December when he first applied to May his last application two younger members of the Pilot Service had successfully applied to be examined and had been promoted to First Class Pilots. He thought this was grossly unfair as both these men were younger in age and less senior to him in the Pilot Service. (Authors note. Both the men promoted ahead of Mr. Limb were closely related to the Master Pilots.)

The pilotage interpretation of this seemingly unjust procedure was, to say the least, somewhat puzzling. The Chairman explained when the last two first class licences had become vacant the two pilots in question had applied to replace them. No such application from Mr. Limb had been received. He went on to say that Mr. Limb's application for a first class licence was dated December 1st 1913 and because this application had been refused it could not be considered as an application for any of the two new vacancies that arose.

It does appear to be extremely unfair that Mr. Limb's previous application should not have received more consideration. One would have hardly thought it necessary that a pilot should have to make a fresh application on each occasion a licence became vacant. How much interpretation of this case had been influenced by the Master Pilots, one can only hazard a guess. However out of such adversity some good did emerge. A resolution was unanimously passed which read:-

"That in future, until otherwise decided Second Class Pilots who have made an application for a first class licence and such application having been declined because of there being no vacancies, shall be automatically notified in the event of vacancies subsequently occurring amongst pilots holding first class licences."

Mr. Limb was notified of this resolution and the interpretation the Pilotage Committee had placed on his complaint. They further informed him he would be the first to be notified when the next vacancy occurred The situation never arose for like all good men and true, when King and Country called, Mr. H. Limb volunteered with thousands of others to join the slaughter on the Western Front in 1915. He never returned. He died on active service in France in January 1919 aged 35½ years. Mr. H. Limb was the only Manchester Ship Canal Pilot to make the supreme sacrifice in any of the World Wars.

13.

THE RICHARD EDWARDS'
AFFAIR 1897 - 1907

The intolerant situation of the working system plus the power and influence the Master Pilots of the Ship Canal held over many of their fellow pilots, cannot be better illustrated than the sad affair of Richard Edwards.

Firstly, it was unfortunate that he was the first person to apply for a General Licence who was not related by blood, marriage or friendship to any of the serving Ship Canal pilots. Secondly, he was a candidate of the Liverpool Pilots holding a Canal Licence who had employed him as a helmsman on their ships navigating the canal and thirdly, he held a certificate of competency as a sea-going officer. All these points were of a definite disadvantage to him from the very start of his attempts to obtain a first class General Licence for the following reasons.

The Master Pilots looked upon him as an outsider and/or intruder and one they would be unable to control or influence, therefore making him a potential usurper to their system of making a comfortable living. That he was connected with the Liverpool Pilots when they, the Master Pilots, had already started initial proceedings with the Manchester Pilotage Committee to withdraw all General Licences held by Liverpool pilots, made him even more unacceptable. The holding of a certificate of competency as a sea-going officer must have been the last straw, for the Ship Canal pilots have always, even into the mid 1950s, viewed new applicants with great suspicion and apprehension who held any such qualifications, no doubt fearing that such a person may already be proficient in shiphandling

No tides to Stem

before they had time to be "brain-washed" by them with their own ideas and methods.

On July 14th 1897 Mr Richard Edwards, aged 44 of 29 Gilbert Street, Liverpool, made his first application for a licence to pilot on the Ship Canal, but after a short discussion, the Pilotage Committee resolved that they did not consider Mr R Edwards had had sufficient experience navigating up or down the Canal to enable them to put his name forward as a candidate to the Examining Sub-Committee and therefore his application be not entertained.

An application for a licence was again submitted by Mr Edwards on June 19th 1899, stating that since his last application two years previously he had been regularly employed as a helmsman on the "Clan" line steamers navigating the Canal. It was proposed by Mr Colquitt and seconded by Mr Hill, both Liverpool Pilots, that Mr R Edwards be passed to the Examining Sub-Committee for his examination. An amendment proposed by Capt. Waring and seconded by Capt. Heasley was immediately put forward that Mr Edwards' application be not entertained. Upon a show of hands:

For the amendment - 3

Against the amendment - 3.

As the Chairman declined to vote, the matter was deferred until the next meeting which was held on July 31st 1899 and it was, after further consideration, resolved that the Secretary inform Mr Edwards that there were no vacancies at present, but that when there were, his application would be further considered. The "old brigade" had closed ranks and stood firm once again.

One must admire Mr R Edwards' perseverance in the face of all this adversity and opposition; any lesser man would have given up the quest for a licence after two and a half years. In December of that same year he once again applied for a licence, this time no excuse could be found for not entertaining his application. He was duly examined and successfully passed for a second class licence on January 8th 1900.

154

Because of his reluctance to pay due homage to the "Gang of Four" by way of commission or be a party to any "Contract" or "Farming Out" system, he found piloting work extremely hard to obtain and at times his earnings were a mere pittance. He did however manage to perform the requisite pilotage acts in order that he might duly qualify for a renewal of his licence each year, but this was not always to be.

On June 27th 1901, Mr Richard Edwards now of 46 Windsor Street, Liverpool, applied successfully to be examined for a first class licence. On Wednesday, 7th August 1901, the Examining Sub-Committee reported that they had examined Mr. Richard Edwards, as directed by the Pilotage Committee, but that such an examination had not been satisfactory. They however recommended that Mr Edwards be allowed to come up for further examination in three months time. From this moment on, it was all downhill for Mr Edwards.

Financially, he was now in dire straits, having moved house and home from Gilbert Street, Liverpool, to 27 Nelson Street, Runcorn and back again to Windsor Street, Liverpool, in his desperate search for cheaper accommodation and to lessen the expense of travelling to and from vessels at various points on the canal. At the Pilotage Committee meeting on October 1st 1901, the Secretary reported that Mr Edwards had not taken up his second class licence for the ensuing year 1901-1902. He went on to say that Mr Edwards had written stating that want of means had prevented him taking up his licence on payment of 12/-s. (60p) which amount was now due to him for pilotage and the balance 9/-s.(45p) from the next pilotage fee he earned on the Canal, he would be in a position to pay the renewal fee. From this plea you can readily assess what condition his finances were in and that the Master Pilots' machinations were beginning to take its toll.

A conversation ensued as to what action should be taken in the above case and it was decided to give Mr Edwards a little further latitude, but unless his new licence was taken up by the 12th instant, the same would be cancelled. He was also instructed that the following year he would be expected to take up his licence without any delay, irrespective of his financial status.

Over the next three years little was heard of Mr Edwards. His licence was duly renewed on time each year but on September 1st 1904 the beginning of that licensing year, it was revoked. He had failed to pilot a vessel three times between Manchester and Eastham, or vice-versa, during the piloting licensing year 1903-1904 in accordance with the article in the Canal Pilotage Bye-Laws 1896.

Nevertheless Mr Edwards, now residing at 7 Cranford Street, Rock Ferry, with his never-say-die attitude, applied on October 4th 1904 for a renewal of his second class licence, stating that owing to his being unable to obtain pilotage work he was unable to comply with the Canal Pilotage Bye-Law, but that he had now been promised the pilotage on the Canal by two Liverpool firms and that he hoped in future to be able to put in the required number of ships to entitle him to a renewal of his licence. What he unfortunately grossly underestimated was the power and influence of the Master Pilots' system.

After some consideration of Mr Edwards' case it was resolved that his application be acceded to and he was granted the renewal of his second class licence. I accept it is easy to be critical in hindsight, but I cannot help but make this comment - whilst most of the members of the Pilotage Committee should be commended for their very lenient actions towards Mr Edwards in the matter of the renewing of his licence, surely they must have wondered why this one pilot received so few piloting engagements when other second class pilots were doing comparatively well? Was their conscience troubling them just that little bit, that they accorded Mr Edwards such lenience? They knowing full well the pilotage working system that was rife on the Canal?

Time was running out for Mr Edwards - he had never re-applied to be re-examined for a first class licence, either through lack of pilotage work or he realised the futility of making such an application. On June 29th 1905, the Chairman read a letter from Mr Edwards complaining that a Ship Canal pilot namely

Mr Waterworth, had been requested by the Manager of the Wallasey Ferries to find pilots to take three of their ferry boats from Eastham to Runcorn and back in Whit week, May 8th - May 13th. Mr Waterworth had engaged Edwards to pilot one of the vessels. However on the morning the vessels were to dock into the Canal, to proceed to Runcorn, Mr Waterworth had engaged another pilot for that vessel. Mr Edwards stated he had missed other pilotage work on the Canal in order to keep Mr Waterworth's engagement and now requested the Committee to establish an enquiry with a view to him being paid compensation for the time and work he had lost over the transaction.

The Committee thought the question was one to be settled between the pilots but seeing that there appeared to be some special pilotage arrangement, instructed the Secretary to write to Mr Waterworth and ascertain his statement regarding the matter. This was the first time an example of the Piloting Working System known as "Contracting" or "Farming out" had been brought out into the open and actually put into print. It must have caused quite a stir among certain Committee Members.

The Master Pilots did not have to worry for they did their work well. On August 18th 1905 the Secretary's report to Mr Edwards' complaint was short, sharp and succinct. The Secretary had communicated with Pilot Waterworth who had categorically stated that he did not engage Mr Edwards but had arranged for Pilots, Heath and Peacock to pilot the steamers. The Canal Superintendent Captain Heasley, also reported to the Committee that Mr Waterworth had told him (Heasley) that he informed Edwards that if he required his services he would send him a telegram, and since he had not required him he had not wired him.

The Secretary was instructed to inform Mr Edwards of the result of their enquiry and to stress that the Committee could not take any further action in the matter. I pose the question 'What possible gain could Mr Edwards have thought to achieve in lying about that incident of the Wallasey Ferries?' There was not a glimmer of hope for an appeal in the tone of the reply. The

1899
Sailing Vessel (possibly "Timaru") discharging grain from Australia, Newcastle, New South Wales, to Ellesmere Port via Cape of Good Hope, time taken 17 weeks.

Early 1900's
No. 8 Dock. Vessels double berthed. No other berths available. No.9 Dock had not been completed.

(Courtesy M. S. C. Co.)

158

Master Pilots, having reduced Mr Edwards to almost penury, were now concentrating their efforts on the task of character assassination to enable them to completely destroy the last vestige of credibility that he may have held with the remaining Pilotage Committee members. The Waterworth v. Edwards incident was the first step in that direction.

It never rains but it pours would have been a fitting epitaph for Mr Edwards because on August 31st 1905, his second class licence was again revoked. The Secretary duly wrote to him stating that as Mr Edwards had not piloted vessels three times between Manchester and Eastham or vice versa during the past licensing year, he was in contravention with the relevant Canal Pilotage Bye-Law of 1896. Mr Edwards in a written reply dated September 5th 1905, placed the cause of his failure to comply with that Bye-Law to bad trade, unfair competition and the present system of working on the Canal.

The final paragraph of his letter was the beginning of his last attempt to break the hold on the present working system and therefore save his Licence and consequently his living. It read as follows :

"Trusting your Committee will kindly review my case, I shall only be too glad to give you any further personal particulars of my case and also to prove to the Committee the way the work is obtained. After holding my Licence all these years, to be boycotted out of my living at my age when work is not so easy to obtain and at the same time you are granting Licences to persons who are ignorant of a sea-faring life or have never been in charge of a vessel in their life............"

The Pilotage Committee must be given full credit for the manner in which they dealt with this contentious affair. I feel sure there were sufficient members on the Pilotage Committee who quietly sympathised with Mr Edwards' predicament then and over the past four years. They must have known full well there was something amiss in the pilotage working system on the

Canal for one pilot to obtain so little work and yet seemingly they (the Committee) were powerless to change the system.

The Chairman, Mr Latimer, referred back to the same situation that had arisen on September 1st 1904 regarding the renewal of Mr Edwards' Licence and the Committee's decision to renew that Licence only on Mr Edwards' statement that he had been promised work by two Liverpool firms for the forthcoming year and that because of this work he would be able to put in the required number of pilotage services that would entitle him to a renewal of his Licence under the present Bye-Law.

This had not materialised - in fact Mr Edwards had only performed nine pilotage services on the Canal during the past year and then only between Eastham and Runcorn and in no case had he piloted a steamer right through to Manchester or vice versa. The Chairman had also prepared a statement to show that from September 1st 1901 to September 1st 1905, a period of four years, Mr Edwards had only piloted two vessels between Eastham and Manchester or vice versa, viz:

December 18th 1901 "NORDLYST" Net 277 Eastham to M/Cr
August 10th 1904 "TAUNTON" Net 124 M/Cr to Eastham.

Mr Latimer then asked the Committee that with due regard to the circumstances mentioned above, should they recommend the renewal of his Licence. A discussion took place and considering Mr Edwards' pilotage service record over four years, it was nothing short of amazing that the Committee felt 'that he was an efficient pilot' and recommended the renewal of his Licence. What is more amazing is how Mr Edwards and his family managed to survive on pilotage earnings of £18.18.00p. (£18.90) for one year. The earnings of a second class pilot in 1904-1905 was approximately £108.0d, the discrepancy between the earnings of Mr Edwards and other second class pilots could hardly have passed unnoticed and must again have troubled the conscience of some Committee members.

Mr Edwards' unhappy lot did not improve nor did his pilotage services during the 1905-1906 licensing year. Inevitably, on September 1st 1906 the Secretary of the Pilotage Committee informed him that due to his non-compliance to the relevant Bye-Law, his Licence would not be renewed. The following letter dated September 8th 1906 from Mr Edwards was read to the Committee:

"Dear Sirs

In answer to your intimation of August 30th, I must state I was not the least surprised at your decision, but it comes to this that you are discarding me to put in my place inexperienced men or boys and it is impossible for an honest man on the Ship Canal to earn a living as there is hardly one on the said waterway that does not get his work by giving commission. The fact has been proved to you before. I must say if I had been left alone I would still have had my regulation work and a good deal more, only other pilots gave more commission than I did, therefore, I lost my connections and I have been allowed to starve and lose my home as well as my Licence.

It is a cruel thing to do when it is not my fault, the cause is the pernicious system that you are allowing to exist. After holding a Licence for so many years of honourable service, I am volunteering to come and give evidence before you respecting the same which is carried on to the present day.

Yours truly

Richard Edwards."

This letter was the first time a pilot had committed himself in writing to accuse other pilots of paying commission to obtain work and was prepared to come forth and prove it. What a bomb-shell this must have been to the Committee. It could not be passed over and ignored - that was more than they dare do. After much deliberation it was resolved that Mr Edwards be asked to attend the next Pilotage Committee Meeting when the question of pilots giving commission would be fully gone into.

Mr Richard Edwards
1900-1906

Letters were sent to Mr Edwards requesting him to appear before the Pilotage Committee meeting in November and January 1907 but on both occasions he was unable to attend as he had taken up work in charge of fitting out a vessel in Tralee, West Ireland.   In a letter dated January 4th 1907 from Tralee, he reiterated defiantly 'it is my sole ambition that I should prove to you the longstanding and continued grievance of this wretched commission system that has been the ruin not only of me, but as I must live I took this opportunity of getting this work to keep the wolf from the door'.   It must be remembered that since September 1st 1906 when Mr Edwards' Licence was revoked he had performed no pilotage services on the Canal. He must have been penniless and one can appreciate his desperate search for work in those hard times of the early 1900s.

The Pilotage Committee decided the quickest and best way to convene this meeting with all the principal parties present would be to write to Mr Edwards' to fix his own date.   Because they realised the importance of the question to be discussed, it had to receive early attention and a special Pilotage Committee Meeting was to be called to receive his statements.

At the Pilotage Committee meeting on April 8th 1907, a letter from Mr Edwards in Tralee dated 21st February, was read in which he stated that due to weather conditions and other factors regarding the vessel he was in command of, he was as yet unable to inform the Committee of a convenient date to be able to appear before them.   The Pilotage Committee decided to await further communication from Mr Edwards.

It is interesting to note that at this April Committee Meeting an application for a pilotage Licence was submitted from Mr Edward George Brown of 28 Claude Road, Upton Manor, London. It was proposed by Mr Hindle and seconded by Mr Hill, both Ship Canal Pilots, that the application be not entertained.   The proposal was unanimously passed.   One outsider was already dangerously rocking the boat, another outsider may just turn it over.

The all important meeting with Mr Edwards' and the Pilotage Committee at last took place on July 8 1907 - this was to be Mr

Edwards final appearance before the Committee. The Chairman, Mr Latimer, referred to Mr Edwards' letter of October 18 1906 in which he had stated that the reason he had been unable to pilot vessels three times up or down the length of the Canal in order to entitle him to a renewal of his pilotage licence, was because the work was given to other pilots who he accused of paying a commission on their earnings to ship masters, pilots or ship brokers (agents) clerks, when he had declined to do so. Mr Latimer went on to say that the Committee were now prepared to receive and consider any particulars which Mr Edwards had to place before them in confirmation of the statements he had made. Mr Edwards stated that some years ago when pilotage work had been passed on to him by other pilots on the Canal, under the "Farming out" system, he had been asked to refund a portion of his earnings as commission, but had refused to do so and consequently he had ceased to get further similar work. He went on to state he had done some pilotage work for Messrs. Vogt & Maguire of Liverpool and Messrs Clarke & Grounds of Runcorn, but he alleged in consequence of his refusing to pay a commission to their clerks who arranged for the giving out of their pilotage work, these firms had given the work to other pilots.

Mr Edwards was pressed for more recent and specific cases where he had lost work in consequence of his refusal to pay commissions. He, unfortunately, was unable to give any specific cases at that moment of time, but reiterated that it was well known that commission was still being paid to what he referred to as the "Master Pilots" for pilotage work, passed on by them and also to Ships Brokers (Agents) and their clerks who gave out the pilotage work. He also stated that Pilot Mr Whitehouse was prepared to come before this Committee to confirm all he (Mr Edwards) had said.

After a lengthy discussion the Chairman told Mr Edwards that although the Committee had given him the opportunity of proving the allegations made by him as to the payment of commission and had listened sympathetically to his statements, they felt he had not given any information beyond what the

Committee had before them at the end of 1900, when the question of paying commission to pilots was fully investigated. At that time the Committee had certain information that commission was being paid by pilots to so called "Master Pilots".

Mr Latimer pointed out as a result of that enquiry the practice of paying a commission ceased forthwith and if continued, would result in those doing so losing their licences on the Canal. Since that date no complaints had been made to the Committee re commission except the statements made by Mr Edwards. Mr Latimer then read the relevant Minute dated 30 January 1901 regarding that enquiry. Mr Edwards said he had not heard of that enquiry, but once again insisted that commissions were being paid and that the pilots' representatives on the Committee were well aware of this. He stated that Pilot Mr Hindle, on the committee sitting, had been asked by a certain firm of shipowners to pay them a commission on their pilotage work done by him. Canal Pilot Mr Hindle admitted that a few years ago he had been asked for commission on pilotage work done for a Liverpool firm, but he had refused and has not done their work since. Mr Edwards expressed his regret that he had not prepared any special cases where commission had been paid but he was adamant that he would obtain particulars of several cases where this had been done in recent years and this he would do in order to convince the Committee he had good grounds for making the statements.

Mr Edwards was requested to withdraw from the meeting. The Chairman then asked for the opinions of the Committee regarding the accusation made by Mr Edwards and went on to state that although Mr Edwards had been given every opportunity of obtaining and bringing particulars of commission being paid to the "Master Pilots", he had failed to do so. He thought the matter had been carried no further than their previous enquiry into this question in 1900 and he felt Mr Edwards had not proved his allegations into the paying of commissions. The Committee fully endorsed the Chairman's views and agreed that Mr Edwards had not advanced any proof bearing out his statements regarding commission paid by Ship Canal Pilots.

The subject of the renewal of his licence was tabled and discussed fully by the Committee. Mr Edwards' entire record of pilotage services on the Canal over the past four years was once again reviewed. The Chairman said he did not think it would be a wise course to reissue his licence, as he had practically done no pilotage along the whole length of the Canal over the past four years. He felt it necessary that pilots in charge of vessels when passing up and down the Canal should have constant experience of navigating the whole length of the Canal as otherwise there would be considerable risk of accidents arising, which it was very necessary to avoid in the interests of the Canal Company and Shipowners. The Committee once more fully endorsed the Chairman's remarks. Mr Edwards was recalled into the meeting and the Chairman stated that.

The Committee had carefully considered the statements made by him, but they did not think he had altered the position from what it was in October last, when he wrote stating that he considered it a hardship to lose his licence and that he could prove the reason why he did not get the ships to entitle him to a renewal of the same. The Committee felt that he had not given them this convincing proof of why he was unable to put in three full length passages in order for him to be entitled to a renewal of his licence and they could not, under the circumstances, recommend that his licence should be again renewed. The Chairman concluded by stating to Mr Edwards that the Committee could only deal with facts and if he was able to prove that commission was being paid, the Committee would be prepared to deal with the matter. The meeting was closed. The scene was now set for the final act to be played out to its inevitable conclusion.

It must be admitted that Mr Edwards did himself no favours in the presentation of his case at that last Pilotage Committee Meeting, producing not one shred of evidence that commission was being paid. It was also very noticeable that there is no record of any comments made by Ship Canal Pilots and other influential personages on the Committee during that meeting. They just sat quietly and waited like vultures in a tree, watching the final struggles of a dying animal.

On August 1st 1907, Mr Edwards played his last desperate card in the "game" to get his licence renewed, in the form of a letter to the Pilotage Committee, which read as follows :-

"Dear Sir

In accordance with your wish at the last Pilotage Meeting, I have to report that as a result the news of that meeting has spread throughout the pilot service. It would take little imagination to realise who spread the news and contents of that Pilotage Committee Meeting throughout the length and breadth of the Canal. The warning that any pilot found to be asking for or giving commission for pilotage work would have his licence revoked without hesitation, has made it impossible for me to get any further evidence regarding this grievance. Those pilots I have approached about this matter will not now divulge the individual names in order that I might bring them before you to answer the charge. Therefore, I am left in no better position that I was at your last meeting.

Nevertheless, I would like to bring to your attention a far worse system that is taking place than giving commission, that is the Contract System. This is to contract for certain pilotage work for an arranged fee not in accordance with the Ship Canal Pilotage Tariff Bye Law. The system works as follows - if the pilotage fee for a certain steamer amounts to £7.10.0d (£7.50), the pilot would return one third of this £2.10.0d (£2.50) to the shipowner or broker, thus securing for himself work on certain steamers. I will quote one case in particular : Canal Pilot James Barnes is contracting for some steamers called "HOGLAND" and "HELGE" and all steamers belonging to the same Company. Other pilots are following suit and in a short time there will be a worse monopoly than before. I need scarcely remind you that the Merchant Shipping Act of 1905 covers all these transactions relating to pilotage tariffs and that you have the power to remedy all these evils and give every pilot a fair chance to live.

...Now Sir, I beg to submit for your kind consideration for the renewal of my licence and respectfully apply to be re-examined for a First Class Licence as I have been promised First Class work if I had the licence. I have piloted all classes of vessels up and down without any complaint being made against me. I hope that these statements also my application will meet with your favourable consideration.

Your obedient servant

Richard Edwards"

A copy of a letter dated 20 October 1904 which had been enclosed in Mr Edwards' letter was also read to the meeting. In this letter the owners, August Leffler & Sons of Akriebolag, Sweden, of the "HOGLAND" and "HELGE" offered Mr J Harvey Lamey to personally attend to their vessels in the Canal. It evidently was to have some bearing on the accusations made by Mr Edwards in his letter as to the manner in which Pilot Barnes obtained work on these vessels in February 1907.

A sub-committee was formed to investigate the charges brought by Mr Edwards and for that purpose it was convened on 30 October 1907. The Secretary stated he had given notice on the 24th instant to Messrs Edwards, Lamey and Barnes to attend this meeting but only Mr Barnes was present. A letter from Mr Edwards now in command of a coasting vessel "Fough Ballogh" and docked in Barrow-in-Furness was submitted and read :

"Dear Sir

I beg to state that I have been more than patient over this matter and I have been compelled to take other work for an existence. It is now over six months that my licence has been pending before your Committee and I was unable to wait any longer. I therefore took this position on the Fough-a-Ballagh and will in consequence be unable to comply with your request to attend the Pilotage Committee Meeting at such short notice. If I left my present position at such short notice I should lose it, without any prospects from your worthy Committee but to let me starve whilst others are making a fortune.

My statement re Barnes is only one instance of many but the original letters are in the possession of Pilot James Harvey

Lamey which he will produce on your request. Furthermore, your letter makes no comment on the vital question - the renewal of my licence which was no fault on my part to let it lapse, the real cause being the pernicious systems that exist and they have been made public in the National press. A letter was written to the editor of a major National Daily outlining the working system of pilots on the Canal, but I have been unable to trace which paper it was published in. No notice has been taken of this but they could have been stopped by your Committee long years ago and so give us all a chance to earn a livelihood and not starve.

Yours truly

Richard Edwards"

The secretary also read a letter from Pilot Lamey indicating he was piloting the s.s."Blue Jacket" up to Manchester that morning and may be a little late arriving at the meeting. Later Mr Lamey had sent a telephone message indicating that due to unforeseen delays he would be unable to attend the meeting. The Secretary was asked to inform Mr Lamey that the Committee would no doubt take some notice of his failure to attend this important meeting. Mr Barnes was in attendance - and called into the room. The Chairman explained at some length the reasons for the meeting, stating that Mr Edwards had claimed his inability not to have his licence renewed was attributed to other pilots giving gratuities (commission) in order to receive pilotage work, which he (Mr. Edwards) was not prepared to do and therefore had received very little pilotage work on the Canal.

A further communication had been received from Mr Edwards accusing some pilots of contracting for pilotage work on the Canal at fees contrary to pilot regulations. Mr. Edwards had specifically implicated Pilot Barnes in entering into a contract with Messrs August Heffler & Son for pilotage work and that one-third of the fee had been returned to the owners or brokers. Letters were read to Mr Barnes sent from Messrs August Leffler & Son to Pilot J H Lamey from which it appeared Pilot Lamey was appointed to pilot this firm's steamers from 1904-1907, only to be informed in February 1907 that his services would no longer be required as Pilot Barnes had bound himself to personally attend all their steamers. Pilot Barnes was then asked for his observations on this latter statement.

Pilot Barnes explained that he had performed all the pilotage work on the Canal for that firm since 19 October 1898, including the "HELGE" and the "HOGLAND", but sometime in 1904 he was unable to attend the "HOGLAND" at Eastham and he passed the work on to Pilot J H Lamey. On the passage inward Pilot Lamey had inveigled the Captain to employ him for the outward passage as well. The next time this vessel arrived in the Canal, when he (Barnes) boarded at Eastham Lock, he found Pilot Lamey on board having joined the vessel in the river. The Captain informed him that he had engaged Pilot Lamey as pilot for the canal passage. Mr Barnes stated from that time onwards he did not attend to the "HOGLAND" or "HELGE" again until February 1907, but still retained the contract to pilot other steamers of that firm.

In December of 1906 he had written to August Leffler & Sons, after hearing that Pilot Lamey had made a remark that he was to be appointed for all the firm's steamers, asking if in any way he had forfeited their support by their taking from him the pilotage of the "HOGLAND" and "HELGE" and if it was their intention to take the pilotage of their other steamers from him. Pilot Barnes also revealed that the Captain of the steamers had spoken to the firm very much in his favour with the result that in February 1907 they resumed giving him the whole of the work of piloting their steamers in the Canal.

Pilot Barnes emphatically denied that he had entered into any contract with the firm named, for anything less than the full pilotage tariff and that he made no return of any portion of his pilotage earnings, either to the firm themselves their agents, captains, or anyone else. If he found he was unable to attend any steamers belonging to this firm on its arrival at Eastham, he transferred the pilotage to some other canal pilot and he did not either expect or receive any commission for this. He suggested that the Secretary should write to August Leffler & Sons and ask them direct if any arrangement such as that mentioned by Mr Edwards, existed.

Pilot Barnes was subjected to a very severe cross-examination with regard to the question of making presents to the captains of these steamers or giving perquisites in any form. He strongly denied that he had ever in any way whatever, made any payments out of money earned by him for the pilotage of any steamers in the Canal. From the straight-forward replies given by Pilot Barnes and his general demeanour under severe cross-examination on various points, the sub-committee felt he had not been guilty of making any payments whatsoever and that Mr Edwards' charges had not been proved.

On the morning of October 31st, Pilot J H Lamey called at the Dock Office, the Chairman took advantage of this and convened a sub-committee meeting to question Pilot Lamey on the subject of Mr Edwards' accusations. The Committee consisted of the Chairman and Secretary of Pilotage Committee, Captain Williams, Canal Superintendent and two ship canal pilots, Mr Jones and Mr Lewis. The Chairman asked Pilot Lamey why he had given the letters to Mr Edwards that he had received from August Leffler & Sons and if he had any complaints to make against Pilot Barnes in connection with the piloting work of the "HOGLAND" and "HELGE" and the nature of his complaints. Pilot Lamey stated he had not given the letters to Mr Edwards, that he (Edwards) had obtained them through Pilot Whitehouse who had some personal feeling against Barnes and that by Edwards making his accusations the letters might in some way prejudice Barnes. He had no complaints against Barnes and he had no intention of doing anything further re the piloting of the two vessels in question after he had been advised by Messrs August Leffler & Sons that Barnes was to do the piloting. Pilot Lamey admitted he had transferred the piloting of the "HOGLAND" and "HELGE" to other canal pilots when he was unable to attend them but had never expected or received any commission from the pilots to whom he passed the work, nor had he ever made any payments whatever out of his pilotage earnings to either owners or captains of the vessels in question. The Chairman then asked the two canal pilots on the Committee if to their knowledge any payments were being made by canal pilots to captains, ship brokers or their clerks in order to obtain pilotage work on the Canal. This question and its subsequent answers from the two canal pilots was the final telling blow to any last remaining hope that Mr Edwards would ever be allowed to pilot on the Canal again.

Both Mr Jones and Mr Lewis denied any knowledge of commission being paid and Mr Lewis went on further to state that he did not think anything of the kind had been done for the past six or seven years, certainly nothing of the kind had come to his knowledge during that period. Mr Jones concurred with all Mr Lewis had said. After the long discussion on the various points referred to in the reports, it was unanimously expressed that the Pilotage Committee should not take any further notice of the charges which had been brought forward by Mr Edwards and that the said Mr Edwards, in their opinion, had failed to prove any of the charges referred to in his communications. On 9 November 1907 the final nail was driven into the coffin of Mr Richard Edwards' hopes of ever exposing the pernicious working system that existed on the Ship Canal. It came in the form of the following letter :-

"Dear Sir

Referring to your letter of the 29th to the Pilotage Committee stating that you were unable to attend the meeting of the Sub-Committee which had been appointed to enquire into the charges made by you in your letter of the 1st August last, with regard to commission being paid by pilots out of their pilotage earnings or contracting for pilotage for less than the authorised charges, I am directed to inform you that the Sub-Committee, after interviewing Pilot Barnes and Pilot Lamey and making enquiries from other sources, carefully considered the whole question and from the evidence they have had before them, they have reported to the

Pilotage Committee that they do not consider that you have been able to substantiate the charges made by you that such payments are being made by the Canal Pilots.

With regard to the question of the renewal of your licence to pilot on the Canal, the Committee instruct me to say that seeing you have done no pilotage work on the Canal for the past two years, through your having failed to comply with the requirements of the Board of Directors to pilot vessels three times from Eastham to Manchester or vice-versa during the year ending 1st September 1906, your Licence cannot be renewed.

Yours truly

(signed) J Richardson.

Secretary to Pilotage Committee."

And so ended the Richard Edwards' affair. It had come to its inevitable conclusion and nothing was ever heard of him again. He had tried valiantly but failed miserably as others had done before him, to break the hold of the Master Pilots and establish a fair and equitable working system. Unfortunately he totally underestimated the influence of those pilots who held the reins of power and because of the fear other pilots had that they would too lose work and possibly their Licence also if they were seen to be assisting Mr Edwards in his crusade, all their support and help that was promised to prove his accusations was withheld from him, just when he needed it most.

The Pilotage Committee members who were not connected with the Canal Pilots had acted with great patience and leniency and were absolutely correct in their summing-up of this affair that they must have facts and not unsubstantiated statements in order for them to press charges against pilots. However, I do think some good came out of this sad affair. I feel sure that some members on the Pilotage Committee must have looked deeply into their consciences and realised "there could be no smoke without fire". Whilst some pilots lived by the adage "If you cannot beat the system, join it" - fortunately others much troubled by the Richard Edwards' affair and made of sterner back-bones, took up the cause to carry on the struggle to establish an equitable and fair working system for all pilots. It was to be a long, hard road ahead for them and not a very pleasant one at that, but they were not to be deterred.

On a cold and raw November day in 1908, the police at Weston Point were informed that a body had been observed floating in the Ship Canal in the vicinity of Bridgewater dock. On retrieving the badly decomposed body, it was later identified as that of Richard Edwards, late of Runcorn, who had been reported as missing from home some while ago. Foul play was not suspected. It is ironic that the very Canal he attempted to make his living from, had taken his life from him.

14.

THE LIVERPOOL PILOTS:
CANAL LICENCE SAGA
1896-1919

From the time the Canal Pilots' Association was formed in 1896, there had been friction and dissension between the Liverpool Pilots over their ability to hold a Licence to pilot vessels in the Canal. The Canal pilots were intensely jealous of the Liverpool pilots intrusion into what they considered should be their private domain and rightly so, for much of the main revenue gained from piloting these large ships went as extra benefit to the Liverpool pilots.

In January 1896 forty-three Liverpool pilots held a Canal licence, but by August 1897 that number had been reduced to thirty. A few half-hearted attempts had been made, through the Pilotage Committee, to withdraw their Licences with no success. On 28 September 1899, a letter from Bateson Warr & Wimshurst (Solicitors) was sent to Manchester Pilotage Committee :-

"Dear Sirs

We have been instructed by all the Liverpool pilots whose licences have been improperly refused by the Canal Company, to apply to you formally for the issue of their licences and to give you notice that if the Company still refused to grant them, then the pilots will have no alternative but to enforce their rights under the Merchant Shipping Act. In the latter event, we shall be glad to know to whom we are to send the necessary process."

The truth of the matter was that none of the pilots referred to in the letter had applied for any renewal of their licences and

1896
Old Quay Swing Bridge in Winter.
(Courtesy Mrs W. Yates Collection)

1896
S. S. "Grampus" GRT: 698, L.211', B.28'. Held fast in the ice below
Trafford Road Swing Bridge. Note the open bridge.
(Courtesy Mrs W. Yates Collection)

therefore, they had not actually been refused. At the same time they were not entitled to a renewal, having failed to complete three full length passages of the Canal for the licensing year ending 31 August 1899 as per byelaw.

It was reported that one of the Mersey pilots, Mr Thomas T Boyd of 16 Stanfield Road, Everton, whose Canal licence had not been reissued for the year ending 1 September 1900, had piloted the S.S.Isis from Eastham to Manchester on 19 September and 20 September 1899. A letter had been written to Mr Boyd for any explanation he might wish to give for having piloted the vessel without holding a licence. No reply was received. These matters were left in the hands of the Chairman (Mr Latimer) to take such action as he may think desirable after consultations with the solicitors.

By 1902 the number of Liverpool Mersey pilots holding a Canal licence had been reduced to 15, all of whom were appropriated to Steamship Lines - the other Canal licences held by Liverpool rota pilots had been withdrawn. At the Pilotage Committee Meeting on 2 October 1902, two rather sad letters were submitted and read; one from Mr Whitehouse (pilot) representing the Ship Canal Pilots' Association, asking the Pilotage Committee on their behalf to approach the Liverpool Pilotage Board requesting that they would allow any Manchester Ship Canal licensed pilots to pass an examination for the purpose of being granted a Liverpool Pilotage Licence to enable them to pilot vessels between any of the Liverpool docks and roadsteads south of New Brighton and Eastham docks, so that such pilots may pilot vessels in or out of the Canal without delay or infringement of the Mersey Dock & Harbour Board Laws.

The letter was referred to the Chairman and Deputy Chairman to deal with and report to a further meeting.

The other letter came from the Liverpool pilots service asking for permission for the Liverpool pilots to make applications for full Ship Canal Pilotage Licences and stating that at present only a few appropriated Liverpool pilots held Ship Canal Licences and that on many occasions, ships bound to Manchester had been detained, waiting for Canal pilots, when had the Liverpool pilot been in possession of a Canal Licence, they might have proceeded and saved considerable time and expense. The letter further stated that a great number of the Liverpool pilots would take up a Canal Licence if they were allowed to do so and they would endeavour to forward the interests of both the Ship Canal and the ships as much as lay in their power.

This letter was also referred to the Chairman and Deputy Chairman to consider and report to a future meeting.

These letters did little to help towards a harmonious working relationship between the two services. They only served to accelerate what was already an acrimonious relationship between the two services and displayed for all to see the eccentricity of some of the pilots, to the embarrassment of their colleagues. The Pilotage Committee gave little credence to these letters; they were possibly looked upon as amusement value only, for their "tit-for-tat" content. At the November Pilotage Committee meeting, the Chairman (Mr Latimer) stated he had received a further letter from Mr Whitehouse asking that his previous letter regarding Canal pilots holding a river licence, might be allowed to stand in abeyance. The Committee also decided that no further action would be taken regarding the Liverpool pilots request for a Canal licence. The matter died a natural death and was never raised again at Pilotage Committee.

It was to be another ten years before this contentious subject of appropriated Liverpool pilots holding a Canal licence was raised again at Pilotage Committee, on 6 January 1913. The Chairman referred to the custom which the Pilotage Committee had observed of issuing licences (after examination) to pilots appropriated to Liverpool Steamship Lines, on the request of the steamship owners concerned in order that the Liverpool appropriated pilots could pilot the vessels up and down the Manchester Ship Canal. Mr Latimer stated that a request had been made to the Committee that a Liverpool appropriated pilot should be allowed to present himself for examination for the purpose of obtaining a licence for a particular line of steamers.

It was resolved as there were at present thirteen Liverpool appropriated pilots holding Canal Pilotage Licences, it was considered that the time had arrived when no new licences would be issued to any new Liverpool appropriated pilots. The Committee was empowered to renew at their discretion, the Canal licences held at present by the thirteen Liverpool appropriated pilots. The Canal pilots took up the challenge at a meeting of their Association at Rock Ferry on 22 January 1913. A resolution was passed that the following letter should be written to the Pilotage Committee Chairman :-

"I have been asked to write to you and request you to refuse to renew the licences held by the Liverpool pilots for the Canal at the end of this pilotage year, 31 August 1913. It would be a great benefit to your own pilots and this association consider the pilotage work could be carried on more satisfactorily".

The Chairman replied by referring to the Minute of 6 January 1913, to the effect that no further licences would be issued to Liverpool appropriated pilots. The Pilotage Committee decided that the request of the Ship Canal Pilots' Association not to renew the Liverpool pilots' Canal licences on 31 August 1913, could not be acceded to. The war intervened and any further discussions on this matter was held in abeyance until 1919. At a meeting of the Pilotage Committee held on 3 February 1919, the following letter from a Liverpool appropriated pilot, Mr David Jones, dated 10 January was read:-

"I respectfully wish to inform you that I have to retire as a Mersey pilot on the 14th instant, when I attain the age limit of 65, in accordance with the terms of the licence granted to me by the Mersey Docks and Harbour Board, but at the request of Messrs Cayzer, Irvine and Co, I have arranged to continue piloting the Clan Line Steamers up and down the Manchester Ship Canal as hitherto."

This arrangement by Mr David Jones was given short shrift by the Manchester Pilotage Committee who expressed their opinion that as Mr David Jones had given up his Liverpool Pilotage licence, he could not continue to hold a Ship Canal Pilotage licence as the latter was held by virtue of his being a Liverpool appropriated pilot. The Committee therefore, withdrew the Ship Canal Appropriated licence held by Mr David Jones.

The Pilotage Committee, on 11 August 1919, was informed by the Chairman that one of the conditions of the Ship Canal pilots to the proposed rotary and pooling system, was that licences for the Canal held by pilots from other ports should be cancelled. It had, at last, become patently obvious to all concerned that this obstacle must be removed before any progress could be made towards a new rotary and pooling scheme for pilotage on the Canal.

The Chairman stated that the licences held by the Liverpool Appropriated pilots for the Ship Canal, expired on the following September. The Chairman went on to say that the Board of Directors of the Manchester Ship Canal had been consulted as to the cancellation of these licences and they had agreed that they should not be renewed at the end of the current pilotage year.

It was therefore agreed that the Liverpool Appropriated pilots who held licences for the Ship Canal should be informed of this decision. The pilots in question were as follows :-

R J Pedder	7 Ash Road, Woodhey, Rock Ferry
James Allen	16 Cambridge Road, Liscard
Frank Wilkinson	25 Seabank Road, Liscard
B Llewellin	38 Rossett Road, Crosby, Liverpool
R Littler	14 Chetwynd Street, Bootle, Liverpool
R A Lewis	32 Trinity Road, Bootle, Liverpool
W B Thompson	49 Oxford Road, Bootle, Liverpool
Chas E Vernon	20 Vaughan Road, New Brighton

I do not think for one minute the Pilotage Committee or the Ship Canal pilots realised what a furore the letter to the Liverpool

Appropriated pilots withdrawing their Canal licence would cause. It came from all quarters - ship owners, ship agents/brokers, solicitors and pilots. The following communications were received in August on this now red-hot subject and read to the Pilotage Committee on 2 September 1919:-

1) LETTER FROM F LEYLAND & CO LTD DATED 15 AUGUST 1919

"We are in receipt of your letter of the 14 instant reference P/5 from which we note it is proposed to cancel the Ship Canal Licences at present issued to our Appropriated pilots. We had previous discussions on this question and are still of the opinion that our own men are best qualified for the work. We shall be glad if you will defer the cancellation until we have had an opportunity of discussing the question, as the matter is too important from our point of view to be disposed of at such short notice."

2) LETTER FROM THE LIVERPOOL PILOTS DATED AUGUST 1919

"We the undersigned pilots holding Appropriated Licences for the Manchester Ship Canal, beg to acknowledge the receipt of your letter of the 14 instant informing us of the decision of the Pilotage Committee not to renew the licences which are about to expire. We have received this letter with considerable surprise and are losing no time in seeking advice as to our position. Meanwhile, we beg to state that we shall at the proper time claim renewal of our licences and when we come to deliver them up upon expiry, as you request, we shall do so reserving all our rights and by no means acquiescing in the view which the Pilotage Committee appear to take on this matter.

SIGNED: JAMES ALLAN, FRANK WILKINSON, RICHD A LEWIS, RICHD. LITTLER, W B THOMPSON, C E VERNON."

3) LETTER FROM MESSRS THOS & JNO BROCKLEBANK LTD D/D 23 AUGUST 1919

"We beg to refer to your letter of the 14th instant and to our acknowledgment of the 15th with regard to the special Licences for pilotage of our vessels up and down the Manchester Ship Canal.

We have now had a further opportunity of going into this question and must strongly protest against the decision to cancel the Licence of our pilot Mr F Wilkinson. When these special licences were issued to pilots, it was understood that they would remain in force until such time as they became automatically cancelled by retirement or through misconduct on the part of the pilot. As neither of these causes can be brought to bear upon the licence of our pilot, Mr Wilkinson, we consider the decision arrived at will be equivalent to a "breach of faith" on your part.

As Mr Wilkinson has a particular and special knowledge of all our steamers, we shall be glad to hear that your Committee will decide to revoke the decision arrived at, at their meeting on the 11th instant."

4) LETTER FROM THE UNITED KINGDOM PILOTS' ASSOCIATION DATED 25 AUGUST 1919

"This Association has been informed of the decision of the Manchester Pilotage Committee to refuse renewal of the appropriated licences held by certain of the Liverpool pilots, when same expire at the end of this month.

I need hardly inform you that action of this kind cannot possibly be allowed to go unchallenged, as it threatens the very foundations of the pilots existence. The Manchester pilots themselves will doubtless realise that if a Pilotage Authority is free to deal with Pilots' Licences for no sufficient reason except possibly to benefit the privileged few who remain, they too may sooner or later be subjected to the same treatment themselves.

Your Committee has struck a blow at the very root of all this Association stands for and I hope that on reconsideration of the matter, other counsels may prevail.

Meanwhile, you will understand that notices of appeal must be lodged within the prescribed time, apart from any other steps which this Association may deem it advisable to take."

5) LETTER FROM MESSRS LAMPORT & HOLT LTD DATED 26 AUGUST 1919

"We duly received your letter of the 14 August with reference to Mr Allan and Mr Thompson our appropriated pilots and we strongly protest against your proposal to try and remove these gentlemen from your list of pilots on the Manchester Ship Canal.

Mr Allan has, we understand, had a Canal Pilot's Licence for 24 years and has been doing the pilotage of this firm for 22 years and Mr Thompson has been 14 years a pilot on the Canal and 12 years with us.   As these gentlemen have always done the pilotage of our steamers on the Canal with safety and success, we do not feel we should like to make any change and we can hardly believe that such old servants of the Canal Company as these two gentlemen, can be removed in the arbitrary manner that is proposed".

6) LETTER FROM M S C PILOT J A HINDLE DATED 30 AUGUST 1919

."On the 26th instant, I received a letter from the General Secretary of the UK Pilots' Association enclosing copy of a letter sent to you which protested against your refusal to renew the Appropriated Liverpool Pilots Licences on the waterway.

By return, I wrote to the General Secretary objecting to the action of the UKPA pointing out that these were not licences in the ordinary sense of the word, but simply luxury licences enabling these men to have sugar on their bread and butter (already guaranteed by another Port) at the expense of the

Manchester Canal pilots, that your action had been taken at the earnest solicitations of the Canal Pilots and demanded that the whole matter be laid before the Executive Council and through them before all the branches and said if they endorsed his action then probably all Canal pilots would in a body, leave the UKPA and join some other strong union or federation of unions.

On the 28th instant I received a letter in reply (a copy of which I enclose) quite different in tone from the first letter and can see that the General Secretary realises the justice of our case. I am writing thus to you thinking that you ought to know all that is going on, so that you can form your own opinion and with the knowledge that, given fair treatment, you have all the Canal Pilots support."

7) LETTER REFERRED TO FROM UK PILOTS ASSOCIATION DATED 20 AUGUST 1919

"I have received your letter of yesterday and am sorry that you should regard the matter in that way. I have been careful not to enter into the merits of this particular case and all that this Association is anxious to safeguard is the principle involved, i.e. that a pilot having once received a licence, the Authority granting it should not be in a position to arbitrarily revoke and refuse to renew the same.

I will admit that your letter puts the matter in a new light and I was not in full possession of the facts of this case and I can at once relieve your mind of any fear that this Association is going to interfere when it comes to a question in dispute between the seven Liverpool pilots and the Manchester pilots. If you will refer to my letter to the Pilotage Committee again, you will see that is carefully limited to the principle involved.

As matters now stand, it will come before the Executive of this Association when your letter shall also be brought to their notice and in the meantime, I shall of course not be taking any further action in the matter, having done what I thought to be necessary at the outset, i.e. to take the point which this Association has always been anxious to take in the protection of the body of pilots

1906
Transit sheds at No: 9 Dock. Under construction.
(Courtesy of the M. S. C. Co.)

generally regardless of the interests of any particular section of pilots.

As a matter of fact, I am expecting to see the President of our Association this week and will write you again following our interview."

After consideration of the above correspondence, it was decided that a letter should be sent to the United Kingdom Pilots Association to the effect that the Committee had learned that Mr Hindle, one of the Canal pilots, had fully explained the circumstances connected with pilotage matters at Manchester which were not previously within their knowledge and having regard to this explanation, the Committee did not think it necessary to go further into the matter but that if any further information was required, they would be glad to supply same.

The Chairman stated that six of the Liverpool pilots concerned had made application for their licences to be renewed and had forwarded the fee of £1.1.0.(£1.05).

It was decided that they should be communicated with, pointing out that the Committee did not see their way to vary the decision to renew the licences for the current year and also return the fee of £1.1.0.

The Chairman said he would reply to the communications from the steamship owners above named, pointing out that in view of the fact that the Committee had on foot an amendment of the Manchester Pilotage Scheme whereby the pooling of all earnings will come into operation, they regretted that the licences could not be renewed.

These letters were quite a formidable reaction to the Pilotage Committee's policy not to renew the Liverpool Appropriated Pilots' Canal Licences and one must admire, or even congratulate, the very cool and calm manner in which the Pilotage Committee dealt with them.

On the 5th of September 1919, the Board of Trade, London, received the following letter from Mr A H Evans, Secretary of the Liverpool Pilots' Association :

"On behalf of Mr R Lewis and six other Liverpool pilots who also hold pilot's licences for the Manchester Ship Canal, I beg to send you herewith copy of letter dated 14th ultimo, addressed to Mr Lewis and his colleagues by the Secretary to the Ship Canal Pilotage Committee, intimating the intention of that Committee not to renew the Canal licences held by the Liverpool Pilots referred to. I also enclose copy of the reply sent to the Manchester Pilotage Committee by each of the pilots concerned and copy of a further letter returning the expired licences and making formal application for renewal of same.

Nothing further has been heard from the Pilotage Committee and it is understood that they have deferred the consideration of the matter pending consultation with the Board of Trade. It is, therefore, deemed desirable that the Board of Trade should be put in possession of the facts from the point of view of the pilots concerned , all of whom are members of the Liverpool Pilots Association (of which I am Secretary).

I am informed that originally the whole of the pilotage work on the Ship Canal was performed by Liverpool pilots, but that later it was deemed necessary to license pilots specially for Canal work, leaving however some 30/40 Canal licences held by Liverpool pilots selected by themselves from amongst their number. Subsequently, the Manchester Pilotage Committee, by a series of restrictive resolutions reduced the number of licences held by Liverpool pilots and eventually these were confined to Liverpool pilots attached to Companies trading to Manchester.

When the enquiry under the Pilotage Act 1913 was held in Manchester, the whole question was gone into by the Commissioners and it was understood that, whilst no new licences would be granted to Liverpool pilots for Canal work, those then existing would be renewed from year to year, so long as the holders remained in active service.

I am, therefore, requested by the Liverpool pilots concerned to make formal complaint to the Board of Trade that the Manchester Pilotage Authority has without reasonable cause, failed to renew the Pilotage Licences held by the Liverpool pilots and to ask that the Board of Trade should consider this complaint and if they are of opinion that it is well founded, shall make such order as they think fit for the purpose of redressing the matter. I may point out that if it is within the province of a Pilotage Committee to arbitrarily refuse to renew a pilot's licence without sufficient cause and without compensation, the position of the pilots throughout the Kingdom becomes extremely insecure and would give rise to a strong demand for an amendment of the existing law.

An early reply to this letter would be greatly esteemed".

This was followed by a further letter dated 9 September 1919: "With further reference to my letter of the 5th instant, I now beg to enclose copy of letter from the Secretary to the Manchester Pilotage Committee dated 4th instant (but not received when I last wrote you). You will note that this letter intimates the final decision of the Pilotage Committee not to renew the licences held by the Liverpool Pilots for the Manchester Ship Canal. The matter therefore, becomes urgent as the pilots concerned are unable to do any work on the Canal and are, in consequence, suffering pecuniary loss and I shall be obliged if you can give the matter your immediate consideration. If it would be of any assistance to you, I could arrange for one or more of the pilots concerned to wait upon you in London to discuss the matter."

The Board of Trade immediately sent the following letter to the Chairman of the Manchester Pilotage Committee on 16 September 1919: "I am directed by the Board of Trade to transmit herewith to be laid before the Manchester Pilotage Committee, a copy of two letters dated 5th and 9th September, which have been received from Mr Arthur H Evans, relative to the action of the Committee in declining to renew the pilots licences for the Manchester Ship Canal held by certain Liverpool pilots. The Board will be glad to be favoured with the observations of the Pilotage Committee on these letters".

Mr Latimer replied to the Board of Trade, London, on 8 October 1919, in the usual calm and irrefutable manner that was always his hallmark in all negotiations on pilotage matters and made him such an invaluable servant to the Ship Canal Company: "I regret that some little delay has arisen in my sending you a reply to your letter of the 16th ulto.

With that letter, you forwarded me copy of two letters dated 5th and 9th September which you had received from Mr Arthur H Evans, Secretary of the Liverpool Pilots Association relative to the action of the Manchester Pilotage Committee declining to renew licences for the Manchester Ship Canal held by certain Liverpool pilots.

As you are aware for some time now the pilots who devote all their time to pilotage work in connection with the Port of Manchester have desired to have a pooling system to equalise more nearly than obtains at present, the individual earnings of the pilots.

To this end, they have urged very strongly that the granting of licences to Liverpool pilots who were appropriated only to pilot certain owners' vessels should cease.

I have a meeting with a deputation of the Manchester pilots tomorrow to finally settle I hope the conditions of a pooling system, after which I will communicate with you in order that some necessary amendment may be made in the existing Manchester Pilotage Byelaws.

Notwithstanding the statement made by Mr Evans in his letter of the 5th ultimo, I do not think the Liverpool pilots (nine in number) who held special licences for pilotage on the Canal, have any substantial grounds of grievance.

As regard their living, they are fully secured in that position as Liverpool pilots. The work they did on the Ship Canal was only a side-line with them.

The Manchester Committee in declining to renew the seven licences for the current year, have not I submit, acted in an arbitrary manner, nor can there be any ground for suggestion that because of this particular refusal the position of pilots through-out the Kingdom becomes extremely insecure. If I can afford you any further information on the subject, I shall be glad to do so".

Nothing further transpired in connection with these matters until 12th November, 1919, when a letter from Messrs Bateson, Warr & Wimshurst, solicitors representing Mr F Wilkinson, Liverpool pilot, was sent to Mr Latimer :-

"Mr Wilkinson informs us that he has been a pilot on the Manchester Ship Canal for twentyone years and he is much aggrieved by the decision of the Pilotage Committee. He tells us that in 1913 it was agreed before the Board of Trade Commissioner that there should be no interference with pilots who then held pilots' licences for the Ship Canal Company and he does not consider that the reasons advanced for depriving him of his licence are sufficient. If the decision of the Committee is confirmed by the Board, Mr Wilkinson proposes to move further in the matter. Mr Wilkinson cannot give us a copy of the findings of the Commissioner who sat in Manchester in 1913 and we shall be obliged if you will furnish us with his decision and his findings".

Mr Latimer's reply was succinct and to the point:- "In reply to your letter of the 12 instant, the reason for the withdrawal of the special licence for the Canal recently held by Mr Wilkinson, was that the Manchester Ship Canal Pilots who devote all their time to pilotage in connection with the Port of Manchester, have desired to have a pooling system to equalise more nearly their individual earnings. In this connection they have urged strongly that the granting of licences to Liverpool pilots who were appropriated only to pilot certain owners' vessels should cease.

The Manchester Pilotage Authority do not think that Mr Wilkinson has any substantial grounds for grievance in the withdrawal of his licence. His living is fully secured as a Liverpool pilot and the work he performed on the Canal was only a side line with him.

Referring to the last paragraph of your letter asking for a copy of the findings of the Commissioner who sat in 1913, I find that Mr Greaves-Lord attended that enquiry on your instructions as representing the Liverpool Pilots' Association. No doubt he will be able to supply you with any further information which you may desire to have".

There are no more records of any further correspondence regarding Canal Licences held by Liverpool Appropriated Pilots - therefore, one must conclude that on 1 September 1919 the last of the special licences granted to Liverpool Appropriated Pilots ceased to exist after nearly 25 years. That these licences ended amongst so much acrimony and displeasure was sad and regrettable, the legacy of which continued on for many, many years to come. After all, it was the Liverpool pilots who opened the gateway to Manchester by piloting the first ships on the waterway; they tried manfully to guide the fledgeling Manchester pilots to organise a decent and fair system of pilotage which, at times, must have reduced them to tears at the constant rebuttals from the Manchester pilots. The collection of pilotage fees was based on the Liverpool system and still is.

It must be left as a matter of conjecture how the Manchester Ship Canal Pilot Service would have evolved had the Liverpool Pilot Service been given the pilotage on the Canal as a natural appendage to their district in 1895. Certainly there would have been more discipline, more organisation and above all, more comradeship, but alas this was not to be. One fact does remain indisputable however, not a word of appreciation has ever been given or recorded in the Minutes of the Manchester Pilotage Committee to the Liverpool pilots for a quarter of a century, of dedicated service to the Manchester Ship Canal. It was through their pilotage efforts that the way towards the prosperity and future greatness of the Port of Manchester was opened. I find that omission very hard to understand.

The following is a list of the last Liverpool Pilots to hold a Manchester Ship Canal Licence.

Mr. R.J.Pedder	60	7, Ash Road, Woodhey, Rock Ferry
Mr. David Jones	64	40, Denton Drive, Liscard
Mr. James Allen	60	16, Cambridge Road, Liscard
Mr. Frank Wilkinson	52	22, Seabank Road, Liscard
Mr. Ben Llewellin	58	66, Berkely Street, Liverpool
Mr. Richard Lewis	51	32, Trinity Road, Bootle, Liverpool
Mr. Richard Littler	60	14, Chetwynd Street, Liverpool
Mr. Willam Thompson	49	49, Oxford Road, Bootle, Liverpool
Mr. Charles Vernon	48	20, Vaughan Road, New Brighton

15.

THE FIRST PILOTS CONVENER
Mr. James A. Hindle 1904 - 1924

Mr. Hindle was born on the Wirral at Seacombe in 1859. At the age of 14 years he went to sea in sailing ships, and by 1885 passed all the examinations to attain a Master Mariners Certificate. He became Master in 1894 and at the somewhat advanced age of 41 years, applied for and was successfully examined for a First Class Licence on the Ship Canal in 1904.

He became deeply involved in negotiations at Pilotage Committee level having been voted the pilots' senior representative in November 1904 so soon after his joining the pilot service. His talents must have been seen quite early by the serving pilots. His sole aim was to enhance the Manchester Pilot Service financially and to create an equitable working system ie the rotary and pooling system, and to that end he worked consistently and untiringly. Mr. Hindle's work as a negotiator was not always popular especially with those pilots who wished to retain the "Farming Out" and catch-as-catch-can systems. During his 13 years as a pilots' representative he was twice voted off only to be reinstated to continue his dedicated work.

He accomplished much that he had set out to achieve as can be substantiated in the early chapters of this book, and often against the greatest of opposition from all quarters including his fellow pilots. The long hours piloting coupled with the strain of endless negotiations took its toll and in November 1922 ill health forced him to resign as a pilots' representative. The pilots should have been immensely grateful for the immeasurable contribution which Mr. Hindle had given to the development of the rotary and pooling system and the increase in their financial status, but they were not.

On July 21st. 1924 Mr. Hindle wrote the following letter to the Chairman of the Pilotage Committee:-

"I regret to have to say that at the end of August (the end of the licensing year) I shall not seek a renewal of my Pilotage Licence, not that I am in a position to retire: on the contrary owing to their being no superannuation I shall have to go on exceeding short commons and after 20 years in the Pilot Service I have to apply for a cottage at the Mariners Home, Egremont. I am giving up piloting on the advice of my doctor and that I do not feel able to continue over another winter." [NOTE: Short commons - scanty allowance. Oxford Dictionary)

In September Mr. Hindle applied to be reinstated as a pilot stating that his health was improving although he was not yet fit enough to carry out any pilotage , but felt he would be capable of doing so in the near future. The request was denied on the grounds that he was still to all intent and purposes medically unfit to carry out his duties as a pilot. A further letter from him on October 25th read:-

"I very much regret the decision which the Committee came to over my application for a renewal of my licence if I felt capable of doing the work. After thirty years on the waterway, ten years as Master and twenty years as pilot with a good record, it seems hard that I should be pushed out of the Pilot Service, before I was financially prepared to leave. Had I taken out my licence for 1924-1925 and then found I was unable to work, I should have been entitled to sick pay for six months which would have helped nicely, whereas now although I have worked for the benefit of the pilots and the betterment of the service that is not considered and I am cast aside as though I did not exist. It is a big drop from £600 a year to nothing"

The Pilotage Committee replied that they hoped his health would improve and that they could not hold out any hope at the moment of a Pilotage licence being again issued to him. Mr. Hindle never regained full health for him to resume as a pilot and he died in April 1925 at the age of 66 years. There is no record of any appreciation shown by the Pilot Association for his services to them as a representative for thirteen years. His achievements, often against overwhelming opposition, were never acknowledged.

Eastham Locks Sluiceway. From Left to Right:-
"Eastham Ferry" - Coal barge for bunkering tugs. M. S. C. "Old Trafford", M. S. C. "Mercia",
Dredging Hopper "Bridgewater"

1908

(Courtesy Captain P. Dunbavand)

16.

THE FIRST NAVIGATIONAL LIGHTS

It seems inconceivable that a Canal of 36 miles in length could be constructed without any provision for leading lights or buoyage lights, but this is exactly what occurred when the Manchester Ship Canal was constructed in 1894. This monumental omission was not an oversight, the designers and planners in those days had no reason to doubt that divers industries would be attracted to the banks of this brilliantly conceived Canal and their factories would provide all the lighting that would be necessary. Unfortunately their reasoning was not substantiated and any vessel attempting a transit of the Canal at night had to endure a passage fraught with danger without the assistance of any shore navigational lights

At the January 1898 Pilotage Committee Meeting the first attempt to place a guiding light in the Manchester Ship Canal was made when it was reported that the Canal Company had arranged for a light on an island at the mouth of the River Weaver where it entered into the Canal. The light would consist of three jets of acetylene gas enclosed in globes one over the other and at a considerable height above the water level. This would act as a guide for vessels navigating the Canal at night so that they could easily pick up the channel when passing the Weaver Sluices, a particularly hazardous part of the Canal. An opinion was expressed by the Pilots representatives that the light proposed to be erected would be far too powerful and glaring and it was suggested that in lieu of the three lights there should be fixed two lamps of the ordinary diaptric anchor light showing one red light over a white one. This proposal was accepted and those lights still remain in that position to this day.

In October 1902 the Chairman submitted and read a letter from Captain Waring (Canal Superintendent) to the Pilotage Committee, suggesting the erection of two leading lights for the assistance of vessels navigating the Canal at night to and from Latchford Locks. The first light to be fixed on the south side of the Canal at or near the 24 mile mark so that a vessel leaving Latchford Locks (to Irlam) could steer by this light. Coming down the Canal a vessel had the lights at Latchford locks to steer by. The second light to be fixed on the south side of the Canal at or near the 16 mile mark in line with a tall chimney at Runcorn this for vessels going down the Canal after passing Moore Lane Swing Bridge. Vessels coming up the Canal had Moore Lane Swingbridge lights to steer by. The Pilotage Committee expressed the desire that the proposals for these lights as well as the question generally of providing leading lights on the Canal should be seriously considered. The general feeling of the committee was that the lights in the two positions proposed would be of great service to pilots and captains navigating at night in that part of the Canal and it was further expressed that other points on the Canal where similar leading lights might with advantage be erected. The Pilotage Committee delegated the Canal Superintendents to make a full report on suggested leading lights and report back to the next Pilotage Committee Meeting.

At the November Pilotage Committee Meeting of 1902 Captains Waring, Dudley, and Williams (Canal Superintendents) reported that after a thorough inspection of the proposed siting of the new leading lights they had unanimously come to the conclusion that these lights should be fixed at the proposed places and that such lights showing a white light both back and front should be globular lamps or ordinary signal lamps so that they would act as leading lights to vessels proceeding up and down the Canal. They also suggested places were in their opinion leading lights would be advantageous to night navigation. They especially noted a leading light fixed at or near to

Randles Sluices because whenever the wind was blowing from the north west(the prevailing wind) the dense smoke from the works at Widnes made the Canal very dark at night for a great way between Moore Lane and Wiggs Works and difficult to navigate.

A long conversation on this subject of leading lights followed indicating the general feeling of the Committee to be in favour of the provision of leading lights. The question as to the mode of lighting the lamps at the various points suggested i.e. whether daily or fortnightly and by whom was left for further consideration. After hearing the views of the pilots representatives Messrs. Stuart and Ellis who frequently brought vessels along the Canal during the hours of darkness, it was unanimously resolved that it be a recommendation to the Manchester Ship Canal Company that leading lights be erected on the Canal at the points suggested by this committee. Such lights be fixed temporarily and that some masters of the coasting vessels and pilots together with the Canal Superintendents be invited to pass up and down the Canal at night to inspect the same and express their opinion before the lights were fixed permanently This exercise was carried out and the first leading lights became permanent in January 1903. From this date onwards navigational lights of one sort or another were installed at various points along the Canal until the entire length of the canal on both banks was provided with lights but it look nearly 60 years to complete that task.

During the discussions on the pros and cons of navigational lights as an aid to night navigation a point was raised regarding the lighting at the six swingbridges and it was agreed it would be an advantage to both captains and pilots if a white light was affixed on one of the abutments at each of the swing bridges so as to show opposite to the green light now fixed on the swing bridges. It was thought that this would greatly assist in showing the passage through the bridge more distinctly than at present with only the green light showing when the bridge is open and that pilots and captains would have more confidence in navigating at night if such lights were provided. Such a light was temporarily fixed on some of the swing bridges as a test and after obtaining the opinion of the captains and pilots navigating at night as to their usefulness all swing bridges were permanently fitted with this white light in January 1903.

The fervent hope of the Manchester Ship Canal Company that such new aids to navigation as leading lights and swing bridge lights would persuade the Manchester Pilots to hasten the advent of night navigation to every class of vessel was quickly dispelled. The pilots flatly refused to perform night transits the length of the Canal on large vessels and grimly held on to this established principle even during World War 2. It was not until 1964 that night navigation became an accepted practice for all vessels regardless of tonnage or draft.

17.

THE TAX MAN COMETH 1909

The first intimation that HIS MAJESTYS INSPECTOR OF TAXES, or SURVEYOR OF TAXES, as he was called in those days, was taking a more than passing interest in the earnings of the pilots came about in November 1909. At the Pilotage Committee in November the Chairman submitted and read some correspondence which had passed between the Surveyor of Taxes and himself in which the Income Tax Authorities asked to be furnished with a return for the past three years 1907/8, 1908/9, and 1909/10, showing the names and addresses of all Canal Pilots together with the amounts paid to each pilot. The Chairman stated that as the last communication from the Surveyor of Taxes had only come to hand that morning he had not had time to refer to the section of the Income Tax Act of 1842 relating to the matter, but if the Committee would authorise him to deal with the matter as he might find desirable after he had obtained some further information he would report what he had done to a future meeting. It was unanimously resolved that the matter be left with the Chairman.

At the February Pilotage Committee Meeting 1910 the Chairman stated that he had been in close touch with the Mersey Dock Board, who had been asked to furnish similar returns for the Liverpool Pilots and that Mr. Kirk Burton had now informed him the Liverpool Pilots had decided that they were quite prepared to furnish the returns through the secretary of the Pilots Association and the Dock Board had furnished the information for that purpose. The Chairman further stated that he had mentioned the matter to the Company's Solicitors who were of the opinion that the Company were bound to furnish the returns asked for, and as Mr. Joyce, the Manchester Surveyor of Taxes was pressing him on the matter, he was arranging to call upon Mr. Joyce at an early date and discuss the question with him, but he did not anticipate being able to avoid furnishing the returns asked for.

The pilots' representatives, Messrs. W.Jones and W. Hindle, on the committee were asked if they had any observations they wished to make. They expressed the opinion that the returns would have to be furnished and that it would be for the pilots through their Association after hearing from the Income Tax Authority to take up with them with a view of obtaining as large a reduction as possible from each pilots' assessment in connection with the expenses which they had incurred in carrying out their pilotage duties. The matter was left in the hands of the Chairman to deal with as he might think desirable after the interview with Mr. Joyce.

At the August Pilotage Committee Meeting it was reported that after numerous meetings with the Surveyor of Taxes and the pilots representatives a compromise had at last been arrived at to the effect that 30% of a pilot's gross earnings (excluding any choice/appropriation fees) would be allowed for expenses incurred whilst carrying out Pilotage duties. In 1913 this percentage was reduced to 25% and remained at this figure until 1939. The Manchester Ship Canal complied with the request of the Surveyor of Taxes to supply him each year with the earnings of all the individual pilots.

The following arrangements were negotiated in 1939 with the H.M. Inspector of Taxes.

MANCHESTER SHIP CANAL PILOTS -

ALLOWABLE EXPENSES

This is to confirm that I am prepared to agree expenses allowances for the pilots on the following basis:-

1. A fixed annual allowance of £40 to cover the cost of Uniform, Cap and Badge, Oilskins, Tide Table, Pilot Flag, Pilot Licence, Watch and business use of telephone.

2. An allowance of 20% "POOL" earnings (excluding reimbursed travelling expenses and choice/appropriated retaining fees) to cover travelling expenses, meals and all other allowable expenses (including capital allowances where a claim may be competent).

This arrangement held good for another 44 years despite many attempts by various Inspectors of Taxes to substantially alter it but in 1982 another investigation was instigated by the Inspector of Taxes and the following reports were concluded and they remain in force to this day.

MANCHESTER SHIP CANAL PILOTS ASSOCIATION
PRO FORMA EARNINGS CALCULATIONS FOR TAX
PURPOSES

Fees per Payslips
(inclusive of balance of attendance allowance)   10, 000.00
Add   any choice fees   300.00   10, 300.00
Less: 18.5% of Fees   1, 905.50
Deduct Travelling Expenses
reimbursed   300.00   1, 605.50
     8, 694.50

N.B. You may claim any Accountants fees and
     U.K.P.A. Subscriptions as well.

18.

FORMING A ROTARY SYSTEM
1913 - 1914

After the heartbreaking rebuff in 1901 by the Ship Canal Company and certain pilots to attempt to equalise pilots' earnings by way of a rotary system, very little was heard during the next twelve years at Pilotage Committee level of any further attempts to introduce a new system of working for the pilots. That was not to say negotiations and meetings for a rotary system did not continue to be promoted and pursued within the pilot service; far from it. · A hard core of dedicated pilots continued to pursue unselfishly the complicated and extremely difficult task of persuading all pilots to accept a rotary system.

The plight of certain pilots earnings was illustrated once again when a resolution was placed before the Pilotage Committee on February 7th 1900 - it read as follows :-

"That second-class pilots should be allowed to pilot vessels on the Canal of a larger tonnage than 600 net tons to which they are at present restricted. This will enable them to get more experience of handling large vessels and to enable them to get more work - thus relieving the penury of their present financial situation." A general discussion on this resolution took place and eventually it was recommended that on and after 1 March 1900, second-class pilots would be allowed to pilot vessels up to and including 800 net tons.

On April 10 1904, the following petition from the pilots holding Second-Class Licences was read out to the Pilotage Committee :

"Dear Sir

We the undersigned 2nd Class Pilots, beg to petition the Canal Company with a view to the said pilots being allowed to pilot vessels of a larger tonnage than 800 net tons. It is almost impossible for a 2nd Class Canal Pilot to make a living owing to, 1) the majority of ships using the Canal at the present time, being over 800 net tons; and 2) the present system of pilotage working. It cannot be denied or concealed that we, from circumstances beyond our control, are reduced to the lowest ebb of poverty and distress. We, therefore, beg that you will place this matter before your committee, asking them to raise the tonnage for 2nd class pilots to 1,000 net tons in an attempt to alleviate our financial situation.

We are, Yours respectfully,

R. IDDON, CHAS LOVE, HERBERT STUART, JOHN W KEATH, HENRY HILL."

The Pilotage committee recommended that on and after the 1 May 1904, all Second Class Ship Canal Pilots shall be allowed to pilot vessels up to and including 1,000 net tons. There is no record of any discussion on a change of working system.

A new scheme for the establishment of a working system for pilots was submitted by the Pilots Association representative, Mr Hindle, to the Pilotage Committee Chairman on 18 March 1913. Mr Hindle pointed out that the Pilots Association had already appointed a deputation of five members to wait upon the Chairman in order to discuss the scheme. After some consideration, it was decided that the appropriate course would be for the matter to be first discussed at a meeting of the Pilotage Committee when the representatives of the Steamship Owners would be present. The Chairman would arrange for all members of the Committee to be supplied with a copy of the new scheme.

This was the classic first move in any negotiations with the Canal Company, which inevitably were protracted and hard fought. These negotiations were not going to be any different from those negotiations in the past, only that the Canal Company must have realised the patience of the pilots was fast coming to an end. Nevertheless, the Canal Company were still determined to fight a long rear-guard action to try and preserve the Master Pilots' system that had served them so well over the past years.

At the April meeting of the Pilotage Committee, the Pilots' representative Mr Hindle, explained the views of his association and stated out of the 33 licensed pilots, 28 were in the association. Of these 28 members, 23 were in favour of an alteration of the present system of pilotage and the majority had approved the proposed system. From these figures it can be seen that nearly one-third of the pilots were not in favour of a new working system and those who approved were not unanimous in their approval of the new scheme. "Divided we fall" and the Canal Company was not slow to exploit this heaven-sent opportunity.

The Chairman pointed out that the Canal Company was the Pilotage Authority for the Port of Manchester and therefore, was empowered under the Pilotage Act 1913 to submit to the Board of Trade a revised scheme of pilotage if A REVISED SCHEME WAS CONSIDERED NECESSARY. To enable the Company to prepare a suitable scheme it was desirable that ALL pilots should co-operate with the Company's officials.

Mr Hindle further explained that abuses had developed under the present system; e.g. there was inequality of earnings; there were cases of employment of one First-class pilot by another First-class pilot. These were both matters of serious complaint by some of the pilots and it was to remedy such abuses that the proposed scheme had been prepared. The Pilotage Committee Chairman said that in order to ascertain the views of all pilots concerned regarding the aforementioned abuses and the new scheme proposed, he would send a copy of the scheme to each pilot and ask for his comments and observations thereon. The committee agreed to this procedure.

The Pilots' representative expressed the Association's willingness to co-operate with the Company and for that purpose, had deputed himself and four other pilots - Messrs Green, Marke A, Peacock and Baxter, to meet with the Chairman. Mr Browning said he would arrange an early meeting to take place and would ask Captain Williams to be present.

The results of the letter sent to all Pilots regarding the proposed scheme of pilotage, was read out at the May Pilotage Committee meeting.

The following was a summary of the results.

Pilots entirely in favour...23

Pilots in agreement but who require Runcorn work to be dealt with separately...3

Pilots in agreement with the exception of the clause relating to four pilots being always stationed at Eastham.......................................1

Pilots who have not replied...6

33

The Chairman also reported he had met the deputation of pilots and had discussed with them the details of the proposed scheme. Several suggestions had been put forward but nothing definite had resulted from them and he now awaited further discussions with the pilots on this matter. The pilots' representative stated the pilots had nothing to add to the views and suggestions already expressed. They still supported the scheme which had been submitted and if no agreement could be reached with the Canal Company and the Steamship Owners, they were of the opinion the matter should go before the Board of Trade. Mr Hindle pointed out the pilots did not desire this course of action but would prefer a mutual settlement between the interested parties.

Mr Browning informed the pilots that the Canal Company was to give notice to the Board of Trade that as the Pilotage Authority for the district they proposed to submit a new scheme, it was in accordance with Sec 4 - Sub Sec 4 of the Pilotage Act 1913. If such a new scheme could be made acceptable to the Steamship Owners and the pilots, the Board of Trade were not likely to intervene. Before he discussed the scheme with the Steamship Owners, he was awaiting an official communication from the pilots or a further meeting with the pilots' representative to explain their views on the proposed modifications of the new scheme which had been suggested at the previous meeting.

There appears to have been no further conclusive meetings regarding the new working system - each party being unwilling to bend to the suggestions of the other party, until October when the Chairman of the Pilotage referred to the requirement of the Pilotage Act, that a scheme of pilotage should be submitted to the commissioners of the Board of Trade not later thanDecember 6th. He said it was of vital importance that an early discussion should take place between all the interested parties in order that a basis of a suitable scheme might be prepared and presented to the commissioners by December 6th. Eventually a draft pilotage order for a new scheme of pilotage working was agreed upon and duly forwarded to the Commissioners of the Board of Trade. On 9 February 1914, the Chairman reported at the Pilotage Committee that a letter dated 26 January had been received from the Assistant Secretary to the Board of Trade (Harbour Dept.), stating that they proposed to appoint the Hon. T H W Pelham CB, Sanford D Cole Esq and Captain W J W Barnard RN as Commissioners under the Pilotage Act 1913 to hold a public enquiry at Manchester for the purpose of considering the Draft Pilotage Order and of reporting to the Board of Trade thereon. The date was fixed for Tuesday, 24 February at 10.30a.m.

One must question if someone in the Canal Company influenced the Board of Trade to hold a Public Enquiry in Manchester - the attempt to establish a new scheme of pilotage was already twelve months on and an enquiry could only further prolong its implementation. If that was so, how successful that person was, for unbeknown to him, war clouds were gathering on the horizon. Time was not and never had been on the pilots' side.

The Public Enquiry was duly held at the Chartered Accountants Hall, 60 Spring Gardens, Manchester and conducted in the
most impeccable manner. The Commissioners returned back to
London to deliberate over their findings no doubt in their own
good time.

On 4 August 1914 time ran out for the pilots. War was
declared on Germany and with it, all hope of a rotary system for
the Manchester pilots until hostilities ceased.

1910
Pomona Docks
*The end of the Manchester Ship Canal. The long warehouse at the
top of the picture eventually became the Arthur Guiness Terminal. The
other docks were mainly for stone from the quarries of North Wales.*
(Courtesy of the M. S. C. Co.)

19.

THE GREEN CONNECTION
1894-1977

Since the Manchester Ship Canal was opened in 1894 until 1977 there had always been a Green piloting vessels along its 35 miles.   This family of pilots was no less controversial or colourful that the other piloting families on the Ship Canal, but by far the most colourful character of all the family was Captain George Green.   It was he who commenced the 83 year tradition of the Green's piloting on the Manchester Ship Canal;   he had a lifetime of wonderful memories and notable achievements. Captain Green commenced his nautical career in deep-sea sailing ships in 1863, at the unbelievable age of nine years;   and by the time he had reached the age of fifteen he had joined a Liverpool Tug, the "COMMODORE", working in the River Mersey.

Eight years later he became Master and it was while he was Master of the "COMMODORE" that he was involved in a very thrilling incident.   This particular incident inspired the artist J Witham to commemorate it in an oil painting entitled "Follow the Leader".   This well known painting is hung in the Liverpool Walker Art Gallery.   The occasion was as follows :-

On the night of 8 February 1881 during a severe WNW gale, distress signals were observed being sent up in an area off Formby Point and four Liverpool tugs, including the one commanded by Captain Green, responded to those signals without hesitation.   They had a terrible time endeavouring to reach Formby Point - it was a bitterly cold and dark winters night and the weather conditions were described in a contemporary account as "atrocious, the constant heavy rain turned to sleet reducing visibility even more through the flying spume, the raging seas continually swept over the tugs from stem to stern and at times deluged the open flying bridge where Captain Green stood at the helm to command his vessel".

They pressed on regardless of the stormy elements and eventually reached the place from whence the distress signals had been sent up. There they found the three masted cargo vessel "IMPORTER" in extreme difficulties. By seamanship and shiphandling of the very highest order, Captain Green was able to place a towing line aboard the stricken vessel. After much manoeuvring and continued assistance from Captain Green, the remaining three tug-boats successfully placed their lines on board the "IMPORTER".

The extreme weather conditions had made it impossible to embark any Liverpool Pilot on the inward bound vessels who were all displaying the signal for a pilot. The Pilot boat, the sailing schooner NO:2, the "LEADER" built in 1856, Master, Captain William Jones, signalled to the vessels to form a procession behind the "LEADER" and he led them down the Queens Channel into the relative calm of the port - thus inspiring the oil painting. The four tugs and their salvaged vessel "IMPORTER" sailed right through the procession of vessels and they too gained the calmness of the river. The four tugs were awarded £6,000 salvage money, of which Captain Green's tug "COMMODORE" received the largest percentage.

In November 1895, Captain Green of 40 Russell Road, Rock Ferry, applied for a First Class Manchester Ship Canal Pilot's Licence. He had been recommended - in the custom of the day - by Captain R Williams (Canal Superintendent) Mr Adam Cartwright (No: 1 Manchester Ship Canal Pilot) and Mr Jos. Stuart (No: 2 Manchester Ship Canal Pilot). He was duly examined and found satisfactory but he was only granted a First Class Licence if he was prepared to devote the whole of his time to pilotage on the Canal, as per Bye-Law; otherwise a Certificate would not be granted if he continued his present command of the tug "COMMODORE". He resigned as Master of the tug.

During Captain Green's 34 years as a First Class Pilot he piloted thousands of ships on the Manchester Ship Canal, during which time he never incurred a single accident report; truly a remarkable record. In November 1919 he was appointed Appropriated Pilot for the Cunard White Star Line and had the notable honour of being introduced to the President of the United States, Woodrow Wilson, after he had piloted the Cunard tender "MAGNETIC" to Manchester in 1921. Another notable first occurred when as senior No. 1 Pilot he was chosen to pilot the Royal Naval cruiser HMS BRISTOL on the occasion of the Royal Navy's first official visit to be made to Manchester.

At the time of their diamond wedding in 1931, Captain and Mrs Green received a congratulatory message from King George V and Queen Mary. The message is one of the family's most precious treasures. It was not the last time that Royalty acknowledged the Green family. Captain Green was a lifetime total abstainer and non-smoker. He retired in August 1929 aged 75 years. (NB: There was no fixed age for retirement from the Pilot Service in those days.) He lived for another 20 years and when he died in 1949 aged 95 years, his obituary read: "The recent death of Captain George Green at his daughter's home in Blundellsands, Liverpool, has meant the loss of a well known and kindly personality, as well as the district's oldest resident, after a career of more than sixty years on the River Mersey and the Manchester Ship Canal".

Captain Green's age of 95 has not been surpassed by any pilot in the Manchester Ship Canal Pilot Service. He did not die without issue; he had two sons to carry on the piloting tradition, Mr Matthew Green born in 1887 and Mr Robert Green born in 1890. Mr Matthew Green had gained sea experience on his father's tug the "COMMODORE" and became a steersman on the Ship Canal at the age of 19 years in 1906. He obtained his Second Class Licence in 1913 and in 1914 he volunteered to join the Army and enlisted in the Royal Engineers. He did not return immediately to the Manchester Pilot Service after the end of hostilities in 1919 as the other pilots did - they had been promised by Pilotage Committee a renewal of their Pilot's Licence on returning from the war - instead he sought alternative employment in a Harbour Authority in British Colombia, Canada. In February 1920 he returned to England a very disillusioned man and immediately applied to be re-instated as a Second Class Pilot. It was not to be an easy return to the Pilot Service. Firstly, there were no vacancies for additional pilots and Pilotage Committee had rightly assumed he had left the Service when not applying to be re-instated immediately after the war. Secondly and more importantly, one must never forget that family feuds were still very much to the fore and much was done by other families to prevent his return. Eventually after much pleading and lobbying and many heart rending letters, for Mr M Green was indeed a most persuasive and compulsive letter writer, he was granted the renewal of his Second Class Licence in September 1920.

He successfully gained his First Class Licence in 1923 and was appointed Appropriated Pilot for the Liverpool firm of T & J Harrisons, a position he held until his retirement in August 1954. Mr Matthew Green was one of only two pilots whose house was destroyed by enemy air raids in the 1939-1945 war. The other pilot was Mr N Colvin.

Mr Robert Green first started as a steersman for his father at the age of 18 years in 1908 in those dark days of "catch-as-catch-can" and "farming out" systems so prevalent at that time. He became a Second Class Pilot in 1916 and four years later passed the examination for a First Class Licence. For thirty years from 1926-1956 he was the Appropriated Pilot for the British Tanker Company. Mr Robert Green holds the record for having had the longest service in the Manchester Ship Canal Pilots/Helmsmans Service, a total of 48 years. No pilot has ever surpassed that. He had the notable distinction of being the only person connected with the Manchester Ship Canal Company to be awarded the Queen's Coronation Medal. This was the second.time Royalty had deemed to recognise the family. The Greens are the only family in the Manchester Pilot Service to receive any Royal accolade. Mr Robert Green retired in August 1956 at the age of 66 years.

The family link with the pilot service did not end there. A third generation of Greens entered the Manchester Pilot Service as helmsman. His eldest son, Robert T Green, became a helmsman in 1935 and obtained a Second Class Licence in 1949 .

He gained his First Class Licence in 1953 at the age of 41 years. On the retirement of his father from the British Tanker Company in 1956, he was appointed to replace him as their Appropriate Pilot. When they ceased trading to the Manchester Ship Canal, he was appointed Appropriate Pilot to the Shell International Marine Limited in March 1959 and remained one of their choice pilots until his retirement in August 1977 at the age of 65 years.

Mr Robert T Green will always be best remembered for his forceful contribution to the Manchester Pilots Association as their representative at Pilotage Committee and at National level during the emergence of the Manchester Pilot Service as a force in the late 1940's and 1950's. He was solely instrumental for three major changes in the Manchester Pilot Service that did so much to alleviate the injustices imposed on the pilot service over the years. Firstly, he orchestrated the abolition of the Eastham Pilot Station against the most strident opposition from everyone connected with shipping in the Manchester Ship Canal. He even had to suffer the scepticism from some of his own colleagues that it could never be enforced. Secondly, he instigated the Board of Trade Enquiry in August 1956 which gave pilots so many extra benefits and thirdly, he promoted the relief at Latchford system, one of the greatest and most beneficial changes in the history of the Manchester Ship Canal Pilot Service.

During his years as the representative of the Manchester Pilots Association, he worked unstintingly for the betterment of the Pilots Service and much of his work became the source for future improvements in the service by other representatives. The sad comment is that for all the hard work he did - and it was a great amount - for the Manchester Pilot Service, it was never truly appreciated or acknowledged by the members of the Manchester Ship Canal Pilot Service. He died in 1986.

The youngest son, Mr Alan G Green, who died so tragically young, is fully documented in another chapter of this book regarding his career in the Manchester Ship Canal Pilot Service.

So ended the era of the Greens which lasted 83 unbroken years - a quite remarkable record from quite a remarkable family. There is still a connection in piloting in the Green family, Mr Robert T Green's eldest son, Alan Green, is a First Class Liverpool Pilot. A fourth generation of pilots in the North West.

1906-1954
Mr Matthew Green

19.

THE WORKING SYSTEM : 1914-1918
THE ADMIRALTY TRANSPORT
SCANDAL : 1914 - 1916

With the outbreak of war, the Ship Canal Company appeared to take over the overall running of the Pilot Service in a very high handed manner and to such an extent that they granted three new pilot licences without consultation with the Pilots' Association. This provoked a swift response from the pilots in the form of a solicitors letter to the Ship Canal Company from Messrs Weightman Pedder & Co on behalf of the Pilots' Association. It read as follows :-

"Our clients the Manchester Ship Canal Pilots Association, inform us that since the enquiry before the Board of Trade Commissioners which took place on the 24 February last, the Pilotage Committee have added to the number of pilots by granting a certificate to Mr Matthew Green and have also accepted the application of Mr W H Roberts and have fixed a date for his examination with the view to advancing him from the second to the first class and have also accepted the application of Mr John Unwin for a Pilotage certificate and have fixed a date for his examination.

The Association instruct us to remind you that for some time past, your Committee have objected to increase the number of pilots or to give first class certificates to those at present holding second class certificates, with a view to these matters being

"Ballymoney" GRT. 1342, L.240'. B.38'.
The Pilots bread and butter work.
(Courtesy World Ship Society)

British and continental vessel "Cormorant", GRT: 1595, L210, B36
To keep expenses to a minimum only one tug was employed in the canal.
(Courtesy Mrs W. Yates Collection)

postponed until the New Pilotage Order and the new Byelaws under it should have come into operation.

The Association instruct us to protest against any addition being made in the number of pilots or any advance being made from one class to another until the new Pilotage Order and Byelaws have come into operation and also, until consideration has been given to the suggestions contained in the scheme which was enclosed in our letter of the 4 December last.

The Association whom we represent, is desirous of making the Pilotage service on the Canal as effective as possible and satisfactory to all parties concerned and with this view, they beg that their suggestions shall be taken into early consideration and they will be glad to send a deputation of their number to wait upon the Pilotage Committee to discuss any points on the scheme which require elucidation or call for explanation."

A letter was also sent to the Ship Canal Company from the Harbour Department of the Board of Trade, enclosing a copy of the above letter and asking for the remarks of the Ship Canal Company thereon. The Ship Canal Company's reply was short and to the point :- "That the Pilotage Committee were dealing currently with ALL pilotage matters as they arose, including the appointment of new pilots and irrespective of the draft order which was now under the consideration of the Board of Trade". This reply was to be sent to the solicitors and the Harbour Department of the Board of Trade. The matter was closed and never came up for discussion again.

The declaration of war did not in any way alleviate the constant struggle of certain pilots to make a satisfactory living, nor did it stop the war between the pilots in their fight for financial security. On 17 November 1914, the following letter was read out at Pilotage Committee which had been received from the Secretary of the Manchester Pilots :-

"Dear Sir

At our meeting held at Rock Ferry on the 19 October, I was instructed to write you regarding the more equal employment of pilots on the Canal. As you, no doubt, are aware Sir, the present war is responsible for several of the pilots being practically thrown out of employment and we would be pleased if you could see your way clear to do something for us in the way of a more equal distribution of the work on the Canal, as our present system of working is very unsatisfactory at a time like this when other Trade Organisations are doing their best to equalise the work amongst their members or employees.

We hope that you will be able to do something for us in this situation.

Thanking you in anticipation,

J A HINDLE."

The Canal Company coolly and aloofly pointed out to the representatives of the pilots at that meeting that they had no power to frame and put in operation a scheme for the equalization of employment on the Canal. The matter was deemed to be satisfactorily concluded. The main cause for the inequality of work was mainly due to the appointment by the Admiralty of Commander Acheson RN as District Naval Transport Officer. He had experienced delays in the pilotage of Admiralty Transport vessels and had considered it advisable to have ONE pilot (Mr R S Southwood) who would be responsible to him for the prompt and efficient navigation of Admiralty vessels over the Ship Canal. This system was granted to Commander Acheson by the Ship Canal Company.

No one pilot could possibly cope with all the Admiralty Transport Vessels. It, therefore, naturally followed that the pilot so appointed would "farm-out" to his favourite pilot - all he was unable to attend to - no doubt, on a commission basis. This was just the illegal system the pilots had fought so hard against since the inception of their service and caused so much bitterness between pilots, even to the exclusion of one such pilot from the service, (see Richard Edwards affair). Unbelievably, this system was being accepted and condoned by the Ship Canal Company who, in the past, had often denied such a system ever existed and always promising stringent action to stamp out any such malpractice should it come to their notice. This system was probably granted with a wry smile, a shrug of the shoulders and a topical expression of that era "c'est-la-guerre", which covered a multitude of sins.

At the Pilotage Committee meeting in June 1915, the above sentiments were expressed in a letter from the Secretary of the Pilots' Association and read as follows :-

"Dear Sir

At a meeting of the Manchester Ship Canal Pilots Association, I was instructed to point out to you that the pilots feel very much against the appointment of one pilot to do the whole of the Admiralty work. This has led to the worst case of "farming out" that has yet taken place on the Canal. We would suggest that a list of pilots be placed before the Admiralty, each pilot being given a ship in turn (Author's note: i.e. a small version of a rotary system) and in the event of any pilot not giving satisfaction to the Commander, then let his name be struck off the Admiralty list.

We would be very pleased to have your views on this matter.

Your obedient servant

J A HINDLE."

The Chairman of the Pilotage Committee, Mr Latimer, explained that the appointment of Mr R S Southwood as pilot for the Admiralty ships, had been arranged by Commander Acheson who was in complete control of the Admiralty work for the Ship Canal. The appointment of Mr R S Southwood had been made after the names of several pilots had been submitted to the Commander for his consideration. The two pilots' representatives Messrs Hindle and Green, expressed their disapproval of the appointment, quoting instances of vessels which they had expected to pilot but which Mr R Southwood had taken over under the Admiralty Commissions, thereby losing a substantial amount of earnings. They also criticized the fact that

Mr R Southwood should not be in a position to order his fellow pilots to take-over vessels to which he could not attend.

In reply to this latter point, the Chairman used the rather subtle and clever play on words by stating that Mr Southwood could not give such an order to another pilot - his instruction was that if unable to attend to a vessel he must "ASK" another pilot to do the work for him.   There was no difference in "ASKING" one of your cohorts or "ORDERING" one of your cohorts, so far as pilots were concerned - all they were concerned about was earning money and they would board any vessel whether "ASKED" or "ORDERED".

The Chairman summed the matter up quite succinctly by saying the Committee was favourable to the appointment and as the letter from the Association had only been acknowledged by himself, it was left with the pilots' representatives to convey the Pilotage Committee's views to the other pilots. The matter was considered closed and it would be nearly 12 months before it would be raised again.

That moment occurred at the Pilotage Committee on 1 May 1916, when the Chairman, Mr Latimer, reported that a letter had been received from the Board of Trade (Harbour Dept), enclosing a copy of a letter from Pilot G Young addressed to them regarding the pilotage of Admiralty vessels on the Manchester Ship Canal and asking for the observations of the Ship Canal Company thereon.   The gist of Mr G Young's letter was his complaint that one pilot had been appointed to look after Admiralty work with the power to appoint other pilots to undertake work he was unable to do. This, he alleged, was a grave injustice to pilots, as shipowners, whose vessels were on Admiralty Charter (and most were), could not give their work to the pilots who were accustomed to it before the war.

The Canal Company's observations on this matter to the Board of Trade was to neatly "pass the buck" on to Commander Acheson RN.   They replied stating that the appointment of one pilot for the Admiralty work was solely the responsibility of the District Naval Transport Officer, a certain Commander Acheson RN. and had nothing to do with their administration of pilotage work.

The pilots' representative, Mr Hindle, explained that he had, on behalf of the Pilots Association, sent a letter to the Director of Naval Transports and to Mr Graham Thomson of the Board of Trade, reiterating that the pilots were dissatisfied with the work being centred on one pilot and Mr R Southwood being in a position to pass work on to other pilots. They would not object to receiving instructions for pilotage from the Canal Company officials and stated that this was the proper method for distributing the work. He concluded by saying that certain pilots, himself included, would refuse to accept work given out by Mr R Southwood in the future.

The Chairman once again came to the rescue of the Pilotage Committee with a superb explanation to completely subdue the Pilots' representatives. He explained to them that the Company's officials could not undertake to arrange the pilotage of Admiralty vessels, as the Admiralty representative (Commander Acheson RN) was practically the owner of the ships for the time being (the duration of the war). He was, therefore, in the same position as other Steamship Owners who made their own arrangements as to the pilotage of their vessels - (appointing appropriated pilots).

In this respect, the principle of distributing the Admiralty pilotage work was identical with that which had been obtained at Manchester since the opening of the Canal. There was no answer to that statement; what a brilliant man Mr Latimer was - he must have been worth his weight in gold to the Canal Company in his dealings with the pilots. The Committee decided it could not take any action in this matter but did agree to approach Commander Acheson RN for his views on this contentious issue.

The threat of certain pilots to refuse to accept orders from Mr R Southwood for his surplus Admiralty work must have caused the Pilotage Committee some disquiet and for them to pause for awhile for a complete re-think on this matter. At the June Pilotage Committee meeting, the Chairman said that he had recently had a discussion with the District Naval Transport Officer, Commander Acheson RN, on the subject of pilotage for the Admiralty work. Commander Acheson RN had, after a lengthy discussion, stated he desired that the distribution of the Admiralty pilotage should be in the hands of the Canal Company officials. The calling on the pilots for admiralty vessels would, therefore, be done in future by the Company's Dockmaster. The pilots' representative, Mr Hindle, expressed his opinion that such an arrangement would meet the wishes of the majority of the pilots.

Thus, the "Admiralty Transport System" finally came to an end, but not until nearly 2 years had passed and there was a "sting in the tail" with its conclusions. It was decided in Pilotage Committee that a list of pilots' names who were considered suitable to pilot the Admiralty Transports, should be presented to the Admiralty District Transport Officer, Commander Acheson, for his approval. When the approval was confirmed, the chosen pilots were formed into a mini-rota system for the exclusive purpose of Admiralty work. How these pilots came to be chosen as "suitable" is not recorded and remains a mystery to this day, but it would not take a lot of imagination to realise an "old pals" act had been instigated.

Therefore, with this system, those pilots who were not in favour with their colleagues and would not co-operate with the Canal Company, were still effectively prevented from making a decent living - a classic case of 'out of the frying pan into the fire'.

This was evidenced in a letter read out to the Pilotage Committee on 4 December 1916.

"Dear Sir

With reference to the piloting of Admiralty vessels, I should be pleased if you would let me know why I am not included in the list of Admiralty Pilots. As you are no doubt aware, there is little other pilotage work, other than the Admiralty vessels and I am sure I have as much right to earn a living out of them as other pilots. Will you kindly go into this matter and advise me as soon as possible and much oblige,

C. Young."

It should be remembered that it was Mr C Young's letter to the Board of Trade (Harbour Dept) that explained fully the iniquitous system that existed with regard to the Admiralty vessels, which eventually started the move to changing that system.

The Pilotage Committee decided that the Chairman should see Mr Young personally and explain to him the reason for his non-inclusion in the list of pilots for Admiralty vessels and not to discuss this matter any further in Committee. This was unanimously agreed. It is interesting to note that no pilot who had objected to the original system for Admiralty vessels was included in the list of pilots for Admiralty work.

On 5 May 1917, a further letter was read out to the Pilotage Committee from Mr Young, complaining he had received no acknowledgement to his letter of 4 December 1916 and that his working situation was still the same. The Chairman explained that an opportunity had not presented itself to see Mr Young, but he would endeavour to arrange an early date to do so. It seems incredible that in 6 months "an opportunity had not presented itself to see Mr Young".

The Committee again decided to leave the matter in the Chairman's hands to deal with it on the lines they had suggested way back in December. There are no further records of any such meeting taking place and Mr. Young was never included on the list of Admiralty Pilots.

On the 1st August 1917 the Pilotage Committee passed a further resolution stating that when a vessel was working as a Government Transport the choice pilot of the line to which the vessel belonged was not entitled to pilot the vessel. Whilst 'the vessel was engaged as a Government Transport such vessels should take the pilot from the rota of Admiralty Pilots as arranged by the Company's Dockmaster. This very effectively blocked all attempts of pilots not included on the Admiralty List from increasing their earnings by excluding them from the larger vessels transiting the Ship Canal.

21.

PILOTAGE TARIFF : 1915 - 1916

Between the years 1904 - 1917 there was no increase in pilotage rates, although during that period certain anomalies arose from piloting vessels between berths on the Canal and other piloting duties that had not been foreseen when the original schedule of charges was instituted in 1895. This necessitated the following additional rates to be implemented.

EXTRA SERVICES:

1a) For a vessel requiring the services of a pilot when moving from point to point in the docks at Manchester or between Manchester and Barton or at Partington, the following charges according to the net register tonnage of the vessel shall be payable in respect of the services rendered:-

For a vessel-

			£	s	d	
Not exceeding 300 tons				5.	0.	(35p)
Exceeding 300 tons but not exceeding 600 tons			10.	6.	(52½p)
" 600 tons " 1,200 tons			1.	0. 0.	(£1.00)
' 1,200 tons "			1.	10. 6.	(£1.52½)

b)   When for the convenience of the owner a vessel is moved at Eastham from the locks to the dolphins or sheer legs, or vice versa, or between the sheer legs and the dolphins, the

following charges according to the net register tonnage of the vessel shall be payable in respect of each such service :-
For a vessel-

	£	s.	d.
Not exceeding 1,000 tons		5.	0.
Exceeding 1,000 tons		10.	6. (52½p)

c) When for the convenience of the owners of a vessel on her passage up or down the Canal calls at Partington, Acton Grange, Runcorn, Ellesmere Port, or other place for bunkering or for any other purpose and proceeds on her journey within four hours thereafter a charge shall be made by the Pilot of 5/- (25p) for berthing - but when detained for a day or part of a day in excess of four hours a charge of 10/- (50p) per day or part thereof be made for berthing and detention provided that such charge of 10/- (50p) per day does not as a total charge exceed one half of the initial fees.

d) When a pilot is ordered to attend upon a vessel about to sail and the vessel is not ready to sail within two hours of the time at which the pilot is ordered, a detention fee of 5/- (25p) shall be payable, provided that no fee shall be payable if the vessel is delayed by stress of weather.

e) When a vessel inward bound for a point below Mode Wheel Locks is brought to the Manchester Docks for the purpose of swinging, the pilotage service shall be deemed to be completed when the vessel has arrived at Manchester. The pilotage of the vessel back to any point on the Ship Canal shall be treated as a separate service in respect of which the fees payable for moving a vessel from point to point in the Canal shall be charged.

f) When a vessel outward bound is brought to the Manchester Docks from a point below Mode Wheel Locks for the purpose of swinging, the pilotage service to the Manchester Docks shall be chargeable at the same rate as that prescribed for moving the vessel from point to point in the Ship Canal and the pilotage service from Manchester shall be charged as a separate service.

g) When an inward bound vessel is brought to the Sluiceway below Mode Wheel Locks for the purpose of swinging before proceeding to a berth between the said Locks and Barton Aqueduct, or an outward bound vessel is brought from any berth above Barton Aqueduct for the purpose of swinging in the Sluiceway below the said Locks before proceeding on her voyage, a fee of 5/- (25p) shall be payable in addition to the scheduled pilotage dues for a vessel entering or leaving and navigating the Ship Canal under pilotage.

h) Where a pilot has been ordered from Runcorn or Liverpool to Manchester to attend a vessel and, on attending, is not then required, and has to return home, a fee of 7/6d.(37-p) shall be payable to the individual pilot concerned.

At the pilotage committee meeting on October 11th 1915, a letter from the secretary of the Canal Pilots Association (Pilot J A Hindle) asking for their assistance to obtain a 40% War Bonus on the present Tariff Rate for pilotage on the Canal, was received :

"Dear Sir

The association would like to call your attention to the fact that the present tariff is over 20 years old and while the pay of other men all over the country has been increased, the pay of the Canal pilots is still the same. During the last 18 months the Government admit that the cost of living has gone up 40% and the Canal pilots consider they are fully entitled to a similar increase, more especially as the profits made by Ship Owners during the war are so great that the Government are arranging to take part away from them. Another way of looking at this matter is that a great proportion of the pilotage fees are paid by vessels of Foreign Nationality who also are making huge profits and surely it would be better if they paid increased Pilotage fees and thus enable us to retain a portion of their profits in this country.

Your obedient servant

J A Hindle. "

What at first appeared on paper to be a straightforward claim for a War Bonus, already nationally granted to all walks of life in the United Kingdom, was to become a twelve-month struggle for the pilots to be granted a War Bonus of any percentage. True to form, from the very onset of these negotiations the Canal Company used every means to prolong any increase in the pilotage rates, but it must be fair to state that the intransigence of some pilots added to the delay of progress for this increase, not inconsiderably.

The Chairman (Mr Latimer) pointed out to the committee that in the first place an increase in the pilotage fees could only be sanctioned by the Board of Directors but subject to that reservation the matter could be discussed in order to ascertain the views of the parties concerned.

The Chairman said that the war allowances recently granted by the Canal Company had been made to workers whose rate of pay was very low, whereas some of the pilots earnings were at a high rate. Furthermore, the request was for an increase of 40% on earnings whilst the increase in prices only touched the portion of the earnings required to meet living expenses.

The Chairman said he had mentioned the matter to Mr Baddeley and Mr Bowen, representatives of the Manchester Steamship Owners Association, on the Pilotage Committee, and he did not think the Shipowners would object to meet the position in the case of pilots with low earnings - the pilots who had not yet been persuaded to work for the "Gang of Four". He suggested that the matter might be discussed at a meeting between the parties interested and asked Pilot Hindle to call a meeting of the Pilots Association so that two representatives could be appointed to meet representatives of the Steamship Owners Association and himself.

The Chairman then put forward a suggestion that there might perhaps be a certain percentage increase sanctioned by the Canal Company in the pilotage fees and that the increased earning from such percentage might be put into a fund out of which the lower paid pilots might have their earnings supplemented by a percentage monthly to a rate not exceeding a maximum say £250 to £300 per year.

Pilot Hindle agreed with the Chairman's remarks concerning the ability of the more highly paid pilots to meet the increased cost of living and said that he thought the Chairman's suggestion was one which would commend itself to the majority of the pilots. He said he would call a meeting of his association at an early date for discussion and he hoped to have appointed at such meeting, two members to meet the Chairman and the shipowner's representatives to discuss the matter and arrive at a recommendation for submission to the Chairman after the meeting of the Association had taken place.

During further discussion it was suggested that the pilots earning less than £300 per year should be regarded as entitled to receive a proportion of the percentage fund. In order to arrive at the annual income the earnings for both pilotage work and steering during say the period of 18 months from the 1 April 1914 to 30 September 1915 should be taken. Thus ended the first discussions on this contentious subject.

At a meeting of the Pilotage Committee on Monday, 6 December 1915, the Chairman reported that Pilot Hindle (Secretary of the Manchester Ship Canal Pilots Association) had informed him by letter dated 8 November that "Messrs Baxter and Hindle were elected as representatives regarding the War Bonus for pilots". The Manchester Steamship Owners Association had also appointed three representatives to discuss the matter on their behalf, viz: Mr G Lowen (Chairman of the Association), Mr A E Bowen and Mr T Baddeley. The Chairman further stated that before the War Bonus claim had been settled by an order in Council, he had taken the advice of the Company's solicitors as to whether they could be varied except by an order in Council. The opinion of the Company's solicitor was that the pilotage rates could only be so varied. It therefore appeared likely that there would be difficulty in obtaining the consent of the Board of

Trade to an increase in pilotage fees applicable to pilots earning more than, say, £300 per year.

Pilot Hindle said that there was a difference of opinion amongst the pilots themselves, as some of the pilots earning fees in excess of £300 per annum objected to increased fees being collected in respect of steamers piloted by them from which they would obtain no benefit. The outright unwillingness of certain pilots to help their less fortunate colleagues and the total lack of any camaraderie whatsoever in the Pilots Service, even in times of war, is indeed hard to believe but sadly it is totally true and that this trait still exists even unto today, is still even sadder. Without the consent of such pilots it was difficult to take the matter further.

After discussion it was arranged that Pilot Hindle should again approach the pilots referred to and endeavour to obtain their consent to additional fees being charged and applied for the benefit of the pilots earning less than £300 per annum.

Pilot Hindle said he would report the result of his further enquiries to the Chairman.

Nothing further was heard or done after that 6 December meeting, for nearly five months but on 28 April 1916, the following letter was written by what must have been a very angry and frustrated secretary of the Pilots Association :

"Dear Sirs

As nothing has so far been done with regards to the War Bonus claim for the pilots and standards are getting progressively worse, I shall be glad if you will allow further discussion at the Pilotage Committee Meeting on Monday 1 May regarding this very pressing and important matter. I would like to point out that the Canal Pilots are the only group of men who have not received a substantial increase of pay since the beginning of the war and with Income Tax raised to 2/3d. (llp), in the pound, along with the very low purchasing power of the sovereign, it has become increasingly difficult for some of the pilots to remain financially stable. I agree that certain pilots have benefited by the war and of course, they are not entitled to an increase, but there are others who have lost directly through the actions of a certain petty Government official who has taken part of their work away from them and given it to others. (See Chapter on Admiralty Transport Scandal). You must admit that these pilots are entitled to some form of compensation.

Yours faithfully

J A Hindle."

Accordingly, at the May Pilotage Committee meeting, the letter was submitted and read. The Chairman then asked the Secretary of the Pilots Association if he had any suggestions to make as to how a scheme for War Allowances could be arranged. It has always been generally accepted in negotiations, especially regarding monetary matters, that it certainly strengthens one's hand immeasurably if you know what the other party are asking for and how they intend to go about getting it. This enables one to arrange one's own strategy for discussion and assess the strength of the opposition, giving you much more room to manoeuvre in negotiations. This ploy was constantly used by the Canal Company over the ages and these negotiations proved no exception.

In his reply to the Chairman, Mr Hindle said the matter had recently been discussed amongst the pilots at Association level but they had not been able to come to a decision for a scheme, as the difference of opinion which had previously thwarted them, i.e. the participation in the War Allowance of the more highly paid pilots, had again arisen. There were six senior pilots who objected to an additional percentage being added to the pilotage fees of their vessels, unless they were allowed to participate in the War Allowance, a classic case of "much wants more".

Mr Hindle went on to say that all the other pilots were agreeable to a scheme whereby a percentage should be added to the pilotage fees, such percentage to be divided amongst the pilots whose earnings at the present time were below £30 per

1920
Trafford Park Wharf.
A busy day with 8 grain barges in tow for overside discharging of grain from floating grain elevator.
This wharf mainly received grain and timber.

(Courtesy of the M. S. C. Co.)

236

month, but not to bring any pilots earnings up to more than his average monthly earnings for the year 1913 and not, in any case, to exceed a total of £30 per month.

The Chairman requested Mr Hindle to submit full particulars of the scheme proposed by the pilots and also give the names of those in favour of and against the scheme. It might perhaps then be possible for some steps to be taken in this matter, provided that the majority of the pilots (75%) were in favour of the scheme.

This was indeed a very guarded statement from the Chairman - it gave nothing away nor did it promise anything tangible. The interesting point in the statement was the request for the names of pilots for and against the scheme, rather a clever move. All through the history of the Canal Pilot Service various pilots have always feared the wrath of the Canal Company and have constantly refused to back or sign any scheme document they thought might incur disfavour on themselves from the Canal Company - thus jeopardizing their chance of becoming an Appropriated Pilot or to be given the benefit of the doubt in an accident report.

A letter dated 16 May 1916 received from the Secretary of the Pilots Association was read to the Pilotage Committee on Monday, 5 June 1916 :

"Dear Sir

We, the undersigned pilots on the Manchester Ship Canal, would take it as a great favour if you could see your way to arranging a War Allowance to be collected from all vessels taking pilots on the Canal and to be distributed to all pilots, as we consider that under the existing circumstances we are justly entitled to a substantial increase of pay.

Yours faithfully

J A HINDLE	J G BAXTER	W PEACOCK
RICHARD LLOYD	J W EDWARDS	J BARNES
WILLIAM LAMEY	J W LAMB	THOS. LAMEY
CHARLES YOUNG	ALFRED YATES	G DAVIDSON
A E POSTLEWAITE	J W HEATH	J H LAMEY
G GREEN	J INGLESFIELD	E HAWKINSON
G CARTWRIGHT	W MARTEN	R SOUTHWOOD

and J D SHAW."

Mr Hindle informed the pilotage committee that he had been unable to meet two pilots viz: W Southwood and W Onion, but he understood they were in sympathy with the request. Regrettably, no progress had been made towards getting all the pilots to agree to a scheme whereby the extra percentage collected would only be distributed to those pilots earning below a certain figure (£360 per annum), Mr Hindle then returned the ball into the Canal Company's court by suggesting that the Chairman should address a letter to all pilots embodying a proposed scheme on the lines discussed. This would result, he thought, in an expression of opinion showing that 75% or more of the pilots were in agreement with such a scheme.

The Chairman reiterated that it would be necessary to approach the Board of Trade for their approval to an increased charge in pilotage rates. He also expressed grave doubts as to whether the Board of Trade would agree to increased pilotage fees for the purpose of granting a War Allowance to pilots earning £360 per annum or £270 per annum net, allowing for pilots expenses of 25%. The matter was left with the Chairman for further consideration.

The first breakthrough came on 7 August 1916 when it was announced at the Pilotage Committee that the Manchester Steamship Owners Association had signified their willingness to pay an additional 10% only on pilotage rates during the period of the war, for the purpose of providing a War Allowance for pilots. This was a far cry from the 40% originally claimed. The 40% was a really a highly unrealistic percentage to claim and I am in no doubt that the pilots of those days appreciated the fact and were under no illusions they would receive their claim in its entirety, but at least it was what one might call "the thin edge of the wedge" and something tangible the pilots could work on.

The suggested scheme for the division of the additional percentage to be collected was on the basis that pilots earning above a certain amount per month should receive no allowance, but that pilots earning below a certain amount should be given an allowance graduated so that the lowest earning pilots would receive the largest measure of relief. Complicated, but at last headway was being made. The amount of £30 per month was suggested above which pilots should not receive War Allowance. The Chairman stated he had seen the seven largest earning pilots, i.e. T Lamey, W Lamey, J H Lamey, W Southwood, R Southwood, G Cartwright and A Yates. From those names it is easy to see how the "Families" were slowly beginning to control all pilotage work.

When it was explained the suggested method of distribution, surprisingly all had signified their willingness to agree.

The Chairman was to draft a letter outlining a scheme for the distribution of the increased percentage and sent this letter to the Secretary of the Pilots Association in order that Mr Hindle could submit the proposals to his Association for their approval. On the 28 August 1916, the Canal Company advertised that they intended to apply to the Board of Trade to confirm a Pilotage Bye-Law made by the Company to increase by 10% all pilotage rates for the duration of the war. A period of 14 days must elapse to receive any objections before application to the Board of Trade for confirmation.

The confirmation of the Bye-Law to increase the pilotage rates by 10% was duly given by the Board of Trade on 19 September 1916 and the increase would be implemented as from 1 October

1916 ten days short of twelve months from when these negotiations began.

At the Pilotage Committee Meeting on 24 September 1916, the Chairman outlined the proposed scheme for the distribution of the War Allowance to pilots and the matter was generally discussed. It was agreed that copies of the scheme should be distributed to all the pilots concerned.

THE MANCHESTER SHIP CANAL COMPANY SCHEME FOR DISTRIBUTION OF WAR ALLOWANCE TO PILOTS.

By Byelaw dated 25 August 1916, approved by the Board of Trade   19 September 1916, an increase of 10% in the pilotage rates was authorised operating from 1 October 1916 during the period of the War. Until the Pilotage Authority otherwise determine the amount which may be realised from the above-named 10% increase in Pilotage rates the amounts will be distributed month by month in the following manner :-

First Class Pilots: The 10% collected on the fees in respect of vessels piloted by First Class Pilots to be put into a common fund for distribution as follows :

Nine-tenths of the amount collected to be distributed as follows: amongst those pilots whose earnings in each month fall below the sum of £35.

Scale of Allowances
To pilots whose earnings exceed £35 in each month   Nil
To pilots whose earnings fall below £35 in each month :
To the three lowest earning pilots   Three-tenths
To the next four pilots on the earning scale   Three-tenths
To the remaining pilots whose earnings fall
below £35 in each month   Three-tenths.

The amount allowed to each pilot to be such however as not to bring his total receipts for each month to a sum not exceeding £35 e.g. should a pilot's earnings amount to £33.10. 0d., the additional amount to be allowed to him is not to exceed £1.10. 0d.

The War Allowance to any pilot in any month is not to exceed 50% of his earnings excluding War Allowance. Any balance remaining after giving effect to the above conditions to be carried to a "Suspense" Account to be dealt with as mentioned below.

One-tenth of the amount collected on vessels piloted by First Class Pilots to be carried to the "Suspense" Account mentioned above. The distribution of the "Suspense" Account to be decided later by the Pilotage Committee and the Pilots' Association.

The Pilots Association in arriving at a decision as to the distribution of the "Suspense" Account to be bound in the event of disagreement by the votes of 75% of the First Class Pilots.

Second Class Pilots: Each Second Class Pilot is to receive the 10% collected on the fees in respect of vessels piloted by him, e.g. if the earnings of a pilot be £8 in any one month, he will receive an extra allowance of 16/- (80p).

Appropriated Pilots: Each Appropriated Pilot is to receive the 10% collected on the fees in respect of vessels piloted by him e.g. if the earnings of a pilot be £4 in any one month he will receive an extra allowance of 8/- (40p).

NOTE: It is expected that each pilot will continue to perform approximately month by month the same amount of pilotage as in the past. Should it be thought that the granting of a War Allowance leads any pilot to reduce the volume of his work, the amount of such pilots War Allowance may be reconsidered by the Pilotage Authority at any time.

An amendment in the division of the 10% collected on behalf of First Class Pilots had been discussed with a deputation of pilots and had been agreed upon on 28 October 1916:

1) To the three lowest earning pilots : 25% Not three-tenths
2) To the next four pilots on the   30% Not three-tenths
   earning scale :
3) To the remaining pilots whose earnings
   fall below £35 per month.   45% Not three-tenths
                                       of nine-tenths of
                                       the additional
                                       10% collected.

T. S. "San Casto" GRT. 2526, L.306', B.51'.
Eagle oil tanker approaching Latchford Locks outward bound from
Modewheel oil berth. This vessel was a regular trader to the canal. Very
difficult to pilot being underpowered, poor steering gear and twin
propellers.

(Courtesy of Mr D. Bell, Lockmaster.)

EVENTS ON THE MANCHESTER SHIP CANAL

July	1899 There were 20 Public Houses registered in Runcorn.
Sept	1903 There were 87 Public Houses registered in Runcorn.
13 July	1905 The new dock (No:9) at Manchester opened by King Edward Vll.
27 July	1907 A porpoise was caught in the canal at Eastham. It was shot by a lock gateman. It weighed 40lbs.
13 Oct	1909 The deepening of Manchester Swinging Basin to 28' completed.
20 Oct	Pilots were paid today with paper money, 10/-(50p) and £1 notes, for the first time.
21 Mar	1921 Commenced deepening the canal from Eastham-Stanlow from 28'6" to 30'00", width 100'.
	1922 No: 1 Oil Dock at Stanlow opened.
31 Oct	1929 Eastham Ferry Stage for sale. It was established in 1509.
	1933 No: 4 Oil Dock at Stanlow opened.

22.

THE SUSPENSE/SURPLUS ACCOUNT 1916-1923

The Suspense Account had its beginnings in the 1914-1919 war, when in October 1916 a war allowance of an additional 10% on all Pilotage Tariff was granted to First Class Pilots only. Second Class Pilots were not included, they were classed as Helmsmen. How would that have stood up in todays (1994) job discrimination tribunal I wonder ?. The four senior second class Pilots had volunteered for *"King and Country"*. The war allowance increased to 25% in October 1917 and to 50% in 1919. Four conditions had to be met regarding the granting of the war allowance.

1. No pilot would personally receive the war allowance if his individual earnings exceeded £35 per month. This was increased to £40 per month in October 1917.

2. A pilot's individual earnings must not exceed £35 per month when a recipient of the war allowance.

3. All excess revenue from the war allowance to be placed in an account, to be called the Suspense Account.

4. The Suspense Account would be equally divided between all First Class Pilots every six months.

The first recorded division was in June 1919 when 25 Pilots received £26.1s.2d. (£26.06) from the Suspense Account and in December the same year the share was increased to £33. There was a certain amount of dissent among pilots, especially those pilots in the high earning bracket - over £40 per month. The very thought that the 50% war allowance on their earnings was being used to help other pilots financially less fortunate than themselves, went very much against the grain of their longstanding selfish principles. On the 5th. May 1919 the Chairman (Mr. W. Browning) of the Pilotage Committee reported that a letter had been received from the Pilots Association which read as follows.

"At a general meeting of the Association 18 First Class Pilots voted for the immediate equal division of the amount standing to the credit of the Suspense Account and I shall be glad to hear that you agree to make the division with the April monthly payment. The Pilots cannot come to a unanimous decision as to the proposed division of the War Bonus so as to do away with the Suspense Account, I therefore presume it will have to continue". A further two First Class Pilots agreed to the proposed division of the Suspense Account thus making 20 out of a total of 21 who had agreed.

With the introduction of the Pooling System in January 1920 the pilots chose to be paid a fixed monthly income viz; A First Class Pilot £35 per month Second Class Pilot £25 per month and any excess tariff to be placed in a new account to be called the Surplus Savings Account. The division of this account was to be implemented every quarter instead of half yearly and all pilots participated in the distribution. The Second Class Pilots would receive 30% of a First Class Share. A balance of £500 was retained in the account to meet any contingencies or emergencies. This was a system the Liverpool Pilots had already put into practice and continued to do so until 1990.

This left the little matter of distributing the residue from the old Suspense Account. The Pilots had been vacillating for some months over this subject and on January 25th 1920 the following letter was read to the Pilotage Committee:-

"The Pilots Association request the Pilotage Committee to move in the matter of dividing the surplus money held over from the old War Allowance. The disposal of this Suspense Account is to be settled by the will of 75% of the First Class Pilots).

Would it not be possible for the secretary of the Pilotage Committee to send voting cards to all Pilots? It was agreed that a letter reading:-

"Whether the money should be left in the Suspense Account or whether it should be divided equally amongst the First Class Pilots", should accompany the voting card. The result of the vote was as follows:-

In favour of equal distribution   In favour of leaving in / suspense"

15   1

1 voted "Immaterial"
1 did not vote.

It was therefore decided that the Suspense Account be equally divided amongst the First Class Pilots and the Suspense Account was finally closed.

The first division of the new Surplus Earnings Account is recorded for the quarter July-August-September and was as follows:

All First Class Pilots.	£48.2s.0d. (£48.10)
All Second Class Pilots	£36. ls.8d. (£36.08)
The total sum divided was	£1,266.3s.6d (£1,266.17)

The forethought of the pilot's representatives in establishing a contingency fund in the form of £500 being retained in the Surplus Earnings Account at all times, proved its invaluable worth, far sooner than any pilots anticipated. On May 9th. 1921 the Chairman stated at the Pilotage Committee that the earnings for the month of April had not reached the figure necessary to provide for the usual payments of £39 for the First Class Pilots and £30 for the Second Class Pilots; therefore £80.17s.11d.

(£80.90) had had to be drawn from the Surplus Earnings Account to make up the deficit. The forecast for the month of May having regard to the coal strike was that earnings would again fall short of the target figure.

It was a particularly depressing time for the Ship Canal and the North West of England in general. In 1920 the annual tonnage using the Ship Canal was 4,387,363 tons, in 1921 it fell alarmingly to 3,293,670 tons, a difference of 1,093,693 tons. It was the lowest annual tonnage since 1901 when 2,943,393 tons was recorded. The pilots' quarterly earnings from the Surplus Account naturally reflected this loss of tonnage. From the heady days of September 1920 when First Class Pilots received £48.2sOd. (£48.10) and Second Class £31.1s.8d. (£36.07) their share was dramatically reduced in September 1921 to £18.7s.3d. (£18. 36) and £13.15s.0d. (£13.75) respectively.

The tonnage in the Canal never dropped so drastically again. In fact a decade was to pass before another decrease in the annual tonnage was recorded. In March 1923 the pilots approved the formation of a new Contingency Fund of £200. In April 1923 the pilots reverted to their original system of payment whereby all pilotage earnings was proportionally distributed between First and Second Class Pilots every month. A small percentage was from time to time placed in the Contingency Fund to maintain a balance of £200. The final quarter distribution amongst the pilots on April 12th 1923 was as follows:-

First Class share   £69.6s.0d. (£69.30)
Second Class share   £48.10s.0d (£48.50)

23.

FORMING A ROTARY SYSTEM
1917 - 1919

While the British Generals continued to orchestrate the annihilation of the flower of British manhood in the bloodstained trenches and fields of Flanders in a seemingly never ending war, the pilot war of attrition for over twenty years against the Canal Company carried on. Their impatience with the unjust working system and unequal financial earnings, coupled with the escalating cost of living (Income Tax had almost doubled since 1914 to 5/-d (25p) in the pound), was once more surfacing and making itself felt to the Canal Company.

At the Pilotage Committee of April 9th 1917, the Chairman (Mr Latimer) must have either been forewarned or had had a premonition that the pilots' disquiet over the working system was again to become a major cause for discussion. He, therefore, pre-empted any attempt of the pilots' representatives to put before the Pilotage Committee a scheme of their own, by taking the unprecedented step of presenting to that meeting a tentative outline of a proposed scheme of pilotage on the Ship Canal which he had prepared himself.

It read as follows :-

1) The establishment of a rotational system with the proviso that appropriated pilots might be appointed.

2) Pilots' earnings to be pooled and distributed on a scale to be arranged.

3) The establishment of a superannuation fund.

A copy of the scheme was handed to each member of the committee and the pilots' representatives, Messrs Hindle and W Onion were requested to bring same before the notice of all their fellow pilots to enable each pilot, should they so wish, to make their observations.

At the following Pilotage Committee in May, a number of pilots' comments were placed before the committee and discussed. This revealed one insurmountable problem to the new scheme proposed by the Chairman, that there must be an increase in tariff in conjunction with any new scheme for pilotage.

The pilots' representative, Mr Hindle, stated that the consent of the HIGHER PAID pilots (those pilots on Admiralty work) to a new scheme, would only be given subject to an increase in the tariff being arranged. The Chairman intimated that he had received two letters from senior pilots W Lamey and G Cartwright, to the same effect.

As it appeared no progress was going to be made at this pilotage meeting, it was decided that the new scheme for pilotage should be left to a sub-committee consisting of the Chairman and Vice-Chairman of the Pilotage Committee; Captain Williams, Canal Superintendent; and the two pilots' representatives. The sub-committee's comments could then be placed before the shipowner's representatives who, in turn, would duly place these findings before the Steamship Owners' Association. This was a laborious and time-wasting exercise, so beloved and so often practised by the Ship Canal Company in the past and would be continued to be practised in any negotiations in the future. It never failed to slow down any contentious legislation to an almost halt; it would have tried the patience of Job, never mind the frustrated pilots. This was indeed procrastination of the highest order and the Ship Canal Company were masters of that art.

The sub-committee duly met and reported their findings and conclusions to the June Pilotage Committee, but the main bone of contention remained that the majority of the pilots opposed any new scheme of pilotage unless it carried with it an increase in tariff. As there did not seem to be the slightest likelihood of the proposed new scheme of pilotage being accepted by the pilots, the Shipowners' representatives on the committee declared that they would not now submit the matter to the meeting of their association in August as previously agreed. The Chairman said he could see no compatible basis for a satisfactory conclusion to these discussions and therefore, he could not see any further continuance on this matter being fruitful. He closed the meeting but intimated to the pilots' representatives that if the pilots were desirous of appointing a deputation to wait upon him to discuss this matter again, sometime in the future, he was ready and willing to arrange a convenient date to meet them.

No further developments on this matter occurred until over twelve months later when at the Pilotage Committee Meeting on 1 July 1918, a certain Mr Beckett, who had become the Secretary of the Manchester Pilots' Association, submitted the following proposal :

"That a Rotary System for the pilotage of ships should be adopted and that the earnings of pilots should be pooled and distributed in proportions to be agreed between the first and second class pilots."

The Committee decided, because of the complexity of the matter, the Chairman should meet a deputation of the pilots to discuss the matter fully. This meeting was held on 11 July 1918 when a full and frank discussion took place. Unfortunately, the continuing intransigence of the Chairman to increase the tariff in conjunction with the new scheme of the Pilotage could not be overcome. Mr Beckett brought the meeting to a close by stating:

"With regard to the Rotary system of working and the equalisation of earnings, whilst these were urgent points, it was felt in the light of these present discussions that at this time no active steps could be taken to bring them to a satisfactory conclusion".

On the 13 July 1918, the Secretary of the Pilots' Association, Mr Beckett, sent the following letter to all pilots :-

" INCREASE OF TARIFF : ROTARY SYSTEM EQUALIZATION OF EARNINGS

I beg to inform you that the deputation of pilots appointed to meet Mr Latimer and representatives of the Shipowners, attended at Manchester yesterday.

1) Mr Latimer expressed sympathy with the claims of the pilots but pointed out that it was impossible to get the Board of Trade to allow an increase of tariff, or make any alterations in the present system until after the termination of the war.

2) He also stated that the Pilotage Committee had considered the matter and had come to the conclusion that taking the work into consideration, there were too many pilots engaged upon the Canal and that the work could easily be carried out if a reduction of five or six pilots were made.

3) He also pointed out that the necessity for all men at the present time being fully engaged on work of National importance warranted him in suggesting that at least five or six of the pilots who are doing little or no work should look out for work of National importance, other than acting as pilots on the Ship Canal.

4) He promised that any pilots who accepted this suggestion would not lose their pilotage licences but that it would be reissued to them if they were in a fit condition, so far as health etc, is concerned, upon application to the Canal authorities.

Before taking any further steps in the matter, he stated that the Committee had decided to give the pilots an opportunity of agreeing amongst themselves as to the five or six pilots who should take up work of National importance and I understand from him that one or two pilots had already applied to the Committee for such leave.

I shall be glad if the pilots who have already applied and any pilot who is willing to take the step desired, will kindly communicate with me without delay and at any rate before Wednesday next, the 17th instant, which date a general meeting will be held to consider the whole scheme."

The two paragraphs numbered 3 and 4 made rather grim and chilling reading; the phrase "look out for work of National importance". Did that mean going "over the top" at Ypres or Nimy Ridge? Did the phrase "if they were in a fit condition" mean they had not been gassed, had both arms and legs or were not suffering from shell-shock? Times were hard but the men from the Ship Canal Company were equally hard.

Incredible as it may seem, the pilots agreed to this method of increasing their earnings, even knowing the terrible consequence of sending their younger colleagues to almost certain death or mutilation in France. As stated before the pilots had no conscience, just greed; they too were hard men when it came to discussing their hard cash. At the Pilotage Meeting on 21 August 1918, the Chairman referred to the suggestion from the Pilots' Association that six of the youngest pilots should be taken off the list, three of them to be transferred to helmsmen's work to replace three helmsmen to be taken off the list and said that the matter had been considered by Mr Latimer who thought it would be a mistake to allow six of the youngest pilots to be taken off the list as there was some prospect of an improvement in traffic owing to the increasing number of steamers which were passing and likely to pass along the waterway. Mr Latimer was of the opinion that it would be sufficient if three pilots in addition to Mr W Lamey, who had already been taken off the list, were allowed to go; such three pilots to be transferred to the helmsmen's list to be available for pilotage in case they were required at short notice. This would allow three helmsmen to be to be released for National Service.

As regards the suggestion of the Pilots' Association for the licences to be taken away from the Liverpool Appropriated

Pilots for the period of the war, the Chairman said that Mr Latimer was of the opinion that the time was not opportune for this to be done.

After consideration of the matter it was

Proposed By: Mr Baddeley   Seconded By: Mr Southwood Pilot.

Resolved : That the suggestion of the Pilots' Association for a reduction in the number of pilots and the taking away of the Liverpool Appropriated Licences for the period of the war should be deferred for discussion at the next meeting of the Committee.

This was a very cynical, but totally predictable proposal to "allow three helmsmen to be released for National Service" with all the horrors that went with it.   I do not think it came as a great surprise to anyone at that meeting - helmsmen had never been treated as an equal or even humanely; they were always considered expendable and have been ever since; even into the late 1980's.

The continuing failure and frustration to make any advancement towards a Rotary System left the pilots with no alternative but to by-pass the Ship Canal Company and plead their case direct to the Board of Trade (Harbour Division), London, in the fervent hope of a more conciliatory and sympathetic hearing. Consequently, the following letter dated 24 February 1919, signed by 18 pilots, was sent to the Board of Trade :-

"Dear Sir

We, the undersigned 1st and 2nd class Licensed pilots on the Manchester Ship Canal, having failed in our endeavour to obtain from the Ship Canal Company an equitable and just system of pilotage on the waterway, earnestly appeal to the Board of Trade to assist us in our efforts to equalise work and earnings. Pilotage on the Canal is at present not compulsory and each pilot obtains what work he can from Shipowners, Ship Brokers, Freight Clerks, etc. This, as you must understand, leads to abuse which

1952
A levelling tide at Eastham. The River Mersey flows into the ship
Canal if a tide is over 29'6". Large vessels in River and in the Canal
must wait until the tide ceases to run. Note near top of left side of picture
the Q. E. II oil dock being built

1953
Opening day of the Q. E. II oil dock at Eastham

is so prevalent in this pilotage. At present, there are 21 first class and 4 second class pilots working and 2 first class and 2 second class pilots with HM Forces, a total of 29 pilots; all holding Licences for the Canal. We maintain this is more than ample, but if the Pilotage system were altered to a Rotary System, coupled with a pooling of earnings, there would not be an extravagant but a decent living for all pilots. There is no Superannuation Fund attached to the earnings of pilots - therefore, if a pilot is unable to save enough during his period of active service to make provision for his old age, then nothing remains but the Poor Law Institutions for him. We beg the question, "What chance have the pilots to provide for old age under the present unjust and unequal Pilotage Working System?.

The majority of the pilots have been urging the Ship Canal Company for the last eighteen or nineteen years to alter the working system to a Rotary system and pooling the earnings, but hitherto without effect, though the Canal Company have had to admit that the Admiralty Vessels (Chartered and requisitioned) which have been worked on a rotary since shortly after the war broke out, has been an unqualified success. Under these circumstances, we appeal to you for earnest consideration with a view to remedy the defects of the present Pilotage System.

Shortly after the war broke out, the Canal Company obtained powers to collect a 10% War Allowance, afterwards increased to 25% and last year was again increased to 50% on all Pilotage Fees collected by the Canal Company, ostensibly to assist the pilots, but owing to an unfair system of pilotage, coupled with an unjust mode of distribution of the Bonus, it has failed lamentably in its object. For whereas it would appear as though it were intended to benefit the pilots who had suffered through the war, the contrary is the case; for it benefits, by the present mode of distribution, those who have suffered the least, i.e. the more a pilot earns, the greater his War Allowance.

We state as a fact that pilots whose earnings mount up to £40 or £50 per month receive more War Allowance than pilots who, through no fault of their own, only manage to earn £5 or £6 per month. This alone will show you the hardship under which such low paid pilots are labouring. You can easily ascertain this for yourself by calling upon the Canal Company to furnish a return of the earnings of the different pilots and the War Allowance given to the same since the 50% bonus was first collected.

You will no doubt be surprised to hear that some of our first class pilots are only earning £2.15.0.(£2.75) per week, including War Allowance. From this amount there has to be deducted travelling expenses, telephone, etc, equalling 25% of this figure, leaving very little to keep their homes together, while others again equally licensed, are earning £10 per week and more; and this does not include War Allowance. This is all due to the present iniquitous working system practised on the Manchester Ship Canal. Taking everything into consideration, we trust you will see by the foregoing that a radical alteration is most urgently needed. We have repeatedly stated our case to the Ship Canal Company and asked for a new system, but perhaps because we have been orderly and not threatened them in any way the only reply we have received is that it is impossible to make any alteration in the system during the war, because the Board of Trade would not approve of it. We, therefore, place our case before you.

Your obedient servant

J BECKETT AND 18 PILOTS."

It does not take a great deal of thought to realise why the pilots took this action in writing such a full and frank letter to the Board of Trade. It was very significant that out of the 25 pilots licensed and working, only 18 signed the letter - the seven non-signatories were all engaged on Admiralty Work. They were the pilots who constantly earned £40/£50 per month, sometimes even in excess of those figures - they were not in the least concerned about the plight of their colleagues' finances. One thing was for certain, they did not wish for a change of a working system and the style of life it brought with it - not in a hundred years.

The pilots' letter of complaint to the Board of Trade brought a swift response from all parties. Firstly, the Board sent a copy of the pilots' letter to the Ship Canal Company requesting their comments on this letter. Secondly, at the Pilotage Committee Meeting on 7 April 1919, Mr Latimer's letter in reply to the request from the Board of Trade for their comments, was read out to the meeting. In it he stated that this was the first information he had received that any communication had been made to them from the pilots in connection with the following matters, viz:

a) Unfair system of pilotage; and

b) Unjust mode of distribution of the War Allowance.

The subject of a different system of pilotage engagement and payment, also the distribution of the War Allowance has been under consideration by the pilots and the Pilotage Committee for some time. As regards (a) the Company are quite willing to put in force a rotary and pooling system and to that end, schemes have been under consideration - the last occasion being on 11 July 1918. Mr Latimer quoted the relevant minute (see Pilotage Earnings 1918-1919) and Mr Beckett's statement (see earlier in this chapter) closing the meeting. Since then nothing further has been heard by the Company from the pilots on the matter.

As to (b), the Pilotage Committee have been waiting for some time, for an expression of opinion by the pilots as to what they desire shall be done in respect of an altered method of distributing the War Allowance. The Company have no objection to alter the system, provided the pilots can agree amongst themselves as to a suitable rearrangement. The existing scheme of distribution was approved by the pilots before it was put into operation.

Mr Latimer again quoted the relevant minutes of 4 November 1918 and 2 December 1918 (see Pilotage Earnings 1918-1919). He concluded his letter by saying that the Board of Trade will see from the foregoing that the Pilotage Committee are awaiting an assurance from all the pilots that the proposed method of distribution is agreeable to them. When this assurance is received, the

Company are quite willing to adopt the pilots' proposals. He also informed the Board of Trade that he was sending a copy of this letter to Mr Beckett, Secretary of the Ship Canal Pilots' Association, telling him that any responsibility for delay in dealing with either of the points, entirely rests with the pilots themselves and not with the Canal Company. Further developments were now awaited.

At last developments did seem to be gaining momentum in the right direction for the pilots. The representatives had prepared themselves thoroughly for a final effort to try and change their odious existence under the present working system. They seem to have sensed a wind of change blowing through the corridors of the Ship Canal Company and the Board of Trade; and the pilots accordingly were getting their act together.

The Secretary of the Manchester Pilots' Association immediately convened a meeting of his committee for the purpose of acquainting the pilots' representatives with the contents of the letter sent by the Ship Canal Company to the Board of Trade and to ascertain what action was now to be taken to keep on the offensive. It was unanimously agreed that another letter should be sent to the Board of Trade, London, refuting some of the aspects of that letter and giving a more in-depth report on other points made by the Ship Canal Company. The letter read as follows :-

"Whilst admitting that the Canal Company's letter on the face of it is correct, there are a lot of matters underlying the facts which have not been dealt with in it and in this, letter I will testify the stand taken up by the pilots in the matter.

As to the pooling system - on the 11 March 1912, the pilots put forward a scheme to the Canal Company accompanied by a request for an increased tariff. With reference to the tariff, the rates now in existence were created at the opening of the Canal in 1894 - the largest ship at that time going through the Canal was about 1500 tons nett and the ships have been increased in size to 5 - 7000 tons nett, without any increase in tariff.   The scheme was acknowledged by the Canal Company on the 2 April 1912 and it was promised attention.

A request was also made that the Licences on the Canal held by Liverpool Pilots should be withdrawn. A number of Liverpool Pilots hold Licences for Canal work and in addition to their work at Liverpool where they receive the full pay of Liverpool pilots, earn additional pay on the Manchester Ship Canal.

Nothing having been done, the pilots on the 11 November 1913, wrote to the Canal Company pressing for a reply to their demands and stating that otherwise they would be reluctantly compelled to appeal to the Commissioners to hold an enquiry.

A deputation from the pilots was afterwards received by the Canal Company but without result and finally a full enquiry was held but the war intervening, no alteration in the system or increase in tariff has taken place. You will have full reports of the enquiry and I think that you will agree that in truth the pilots fully justified their claims for an alteration. Again, in 1917, a scheme based on the scheme put forward by the pilots was sent out by the Canal Company duly considered by the pilots to a point when only two or three questions of difference were outstanding but as there was no idea of the Canal Company agreeing to an increase of tariff for which the pilots asked, the following resolution was passed by the pilots on 15 May 1917.

> 'The Amended Canal Company Scheme was then read over and a long discussion ensued but as the representatives at Manchester pointed out that Mr Latimer was against any increase of tariff, it was agreed that further discussion was useless and the Secretary was instructed to write to Mr Latimer and inform him that this Association could not consider the Scheme without an increase in tariff.'

The matter then dropped for a time and the tariff question was partly met by the payment of War Bonus.

Again in May 1918, the pilots put forward an application for a rotary and pooling system accompanied by an increase of tariff and the Canal Company asked for a deputation to wait upon them.

A strong deputation attended and in his remarks Mr Latimer stated that it was impossible to get the Board of Trade to sanction any increase in the tariff charged by the Canal Company or to make any alteration in the system of working and it was after hearing this statement, that I made the remarks attributed to me in his letter.

In making these remarks, I only referred to the fact of your objection to any alteration putting a veto on our claims at the time, but it was then understood that on the termination of the war, immediate steps would be taken to obtain satisfaction, as the pilots since 1912, have been thoroughly dissatisfied with the way in which matters have been arranged by the Canal Company.

The pilots beg to point out, however, that notwithstanding the statement by Mr Latimer that the Board would not allow them to raise the tariff in the Canal, the tariffs have been raised in respect of other matters for instance; the payment to the tugs which have been raised 300 per cent.

On the last occasion, when the pilots claim for an increased tariff and a rotary and pooling system was put forward it was met by Mr Latimer with a statement that there were too many pilots in the Canal and I enclose herewith copy of a Circular which I issued to the pilots on the subject.

Three of the pilots accepted the offer and found other work of National importance but are now back on the Canal.

With reference to the War Bonus, the pilots have been told on all occasions that that is simply a war bonus and not a permanent increase in pay.

As to a question of its distribution, a majority of the pilots have agreed to a system of its distribution, but on this being submitted to Mr Latimer he stated that it was necessary for "all" the pilots to agree - 7 pilots out of 25 have not agreed and the division is at present being made on the first scheme arranged.

However, this matter of the distribution of the War Bonus is not a pressing one, but the pilots now put forward a petition to you under the following heads :-

(1)   An increase of the tariff to meet present conditions on the Manchester Ship Canal and to provide such a rate of pay that a rotary and pooling system can be brought into operation.

(2)   The Liverpool Licensed pilots to be withdrawn from the Canal.

(3) More equitable representation of the pilots on the Manchester Pilotage Committee.   At present it consists of Mr Latimer, Chairman; Mr Brown, Vice Chairman; two Manchester Steamship Owners representatives; four Ship Canal Superintendents; one Secretary and two pilots. Mr Latimer the Chairman, is also Managing Director of the Canal Company.

From this letter you will see that since 1912 the pilots have been asking for a Rotary and Pooling system accompanied by a revision of a Pilotage tariff and on their part are quite willing to adopt same subject to receiving reasonable remuneration for their services, accompanied if possible with a pension scheme on their retirement. Should you desire any further information in explanation on the subject, the pilots are quite willing to send a deputation to London to see you and place their views before you if you will kindly grant them that favour.

PS: Since writing the above, a past Secretary has brought me a letter from you dated 24.6.13 promising the pilots an opportunity of making representations on a Scheme that the Canal Company had promised to submit to you; in reply to a letter addressed to you by the pilots asking for your intervention."

On 11 April 1919, Mr Garnham Roper of the Board of Trade, London, sent a letter to Mr Latimer enclosing a copy of the second letter he had received from Mr Beckett, Secretary of the Pilots' Association. He concluded this brief note by saying : "I shall be glad if you can make it convenient to call on me when you are in London with a view to discussing the matter - letting me know beforehand the day and hour when you can call".

From this moment onwards, the progress towards a rotary system began to "gather way". The speed at which the negotiations developed was almost supersonic after nearly 20 years of procrastination and internal strife that had beset all past negotiations between the Ship Canal Company and the Manchester Pilots. On 1 May 1919, the following letter was sent by Mr Latimer to Mr Garnham Roper :-

"Re your letter of 11 April, I regret I was not able to call in and see you respecting the above named subject. I have read with interest the letters which have passed with Mr Beckett, Secretary of the Pilots' Association and I think perhaps I can get a move forward with the Association, - if my doing so directly with the pilots would fall in with any views you may have formed in connection with this matter. Oh the other hand, if you think it would be better that I should have first a discussion with you, then I shall be glad to call on you in two weeks' time when next I am in London."

Mr Latimer knew he had to work fast if he was to keep control of the negotiations with the Manchester Pilots regarding any new tariff and working system. His sole control and manipulations at such negotiations was of tantamount importance to the Ship Canal Company and their shareholders. Mr Latimer must have read the minds of the Board of Trade, for they had little or no enthusiasm for individual internal struggles in far away Manchester. Proof of this came in a swift reply to Mr Latimer's letter dated 3 May :-

"I am much obliged to you for your letter of 1 May on the subject of the Ship Canal Pilots and think that it would be better for you to discuss the situation with the pilots as you propose, leaving over the question of a discussion here. I will therefore inform the pilots that you propose to communicate with them direct".

24.

UNLICENSED PILOTS
SECTION 30 (5) OF THE PILOTAGE ACT 1913

IF ANY PERSON OTHER THAN THE MASTER OR A SEAMAN BEING A BONAFIDE ONE OF THE CREW OF THE SHIP, IS ON THE BRIDGE OF A SHIP OR IN ANY OTHER POSITION (WHETHER ABOARD SHIP OR ELSE-WHERE) FROM WHICH THE SHIP IS NAVIGATED, THAT PERSON SHALL FOR THE PURPOSE OF THIS SECTION, BE DEEMED TO BE PILOTING THE SHIP UNLESS THE CONTRARY IS PROVED.

So reads the pilotage act, very succinctly and very clear, but in those early days of the Manchester Ship Canal, piloting became almost piratical, especially amongst pilots themselves. Many unqualified individuals of dubious sea-going background attempted to seek employment as a pilot on the Ship Canal, outside the jurisdiction of the licensing authority of the Manchester Pilotage Committee. Indeed many barge masters and some older (in age only) helmsmen were not averse to offering their services to captains of small coasting vessels, at quite a substantial reduction in the pilot fee. It was not unusual for them to make a charge of one fee for piloting a vessel inward and outward of the Ship Canal. The Mersey Pilots too, would find multiple excuses for being unable to disembark from a vessel at Eastham - levelling tides, high wind, no Canal Pilot on the lock at Eastham etc. etc, and pleading most conscientiously they did not wish to incur unnecessary expense due to the delay of the said vessel arriving on her discharge berth.

The first such incident of piloting without a Licence was heard at the Pilotage Committee on Friday December 23rd 1898 when the secretary submitted a letter which he had received from a Canal Pilot Mr. Stringer stating that a River Pilot Mr. R. Smith, who was not licensed to pilot on the Canal, had piloted the barquentine "ELIZABERTHA" from Eastham Locks to Runcorn on Sunday the 11th December. Captain Heasly (Canal Superintendent) had made extensive enquiries but could not find any corroboration of Mr. Stringer's statement that the Liverpool Pilot gave any instructions whilst proceeding along the Canal. It appeared that Mr. Smith was unable to land at Eastham Locks due to the levelling tide and therefore had to accompany the vessel to Runcorn. Mr. Smith denied that he had given any orders or had taken any part in the navigation of the vessel whilst in the Canal. Mr. Hill a member of the Committee also stated that he was on the Pier Head when the vessel was entering Runcorn Docks and that he did not hear or see Mr. Smith take any part in the piloting of the vessel. A statement from the Master of the steam tug "CHARLES GALLOWAY"- who had been assigned to accompany the "ELIZABERTHA" to Runcorn - that immediately after passing through the Locks at Eastham the Liverpool Pilot left the wheel of the "ELIZABERTHA" and did not go to it again during the passage up the Canal, the Pilot simply strode up and down the quarter deck. The Captain of the tug went on to say he could not bring up his vessel in the Lock at Eastham due to the 'Level' running.

NOTE:- When certain tidal conditions prevail at High Water at Eastham Locks the height of the River rises and exceeds the height of the water in the Ship Canal, thereby forcing the Lock gates to open, making the River and the Canal one continuous stretch of water. This usually occurs one hour before High Water until one hour after High Water. The current running through the locks can vary between two and ten knots depending on weather conditions and the height of the tide.

All the reports were at variance with Mr. Stringer's report and it appeared that he had made a complaint without having any grounds to do so. As Mr. Stringer was in attendance the Chairman called him to the meeting. Mr. Stringer stated he had based his complaint on a conversation he had with the tug master and one of the Bridgewater Piermaster's on the Runcorn Docks but he had not seen Mr. Smith piloting the vessel himself. The Chairman administed a severe reprimand to Mr. Stringer for giving the Committee so much trouble when there was no occasion for doing so and that he would be fined £1.1s0d (£1.05) for making an unfounded charge. The fine was to be paid within 14 days or his piloting licence would be withdrawn.

It was not until 1930 before another incident of unlicensed piloting came to the notice of the Pilotage Committee when Mr. Browning (Chairman) stated that there was a case of the vessel "ALLANWATER" entering Eastham Locks with a man on the bridge who was presumably acting as a pilot to the ship. The man in question Mr. A Kirby, was an Upper Mersey Pilot, and was not licensed to pilot vessels in the Ship Canal. Mr. A Kirby had long been suspected of unlicensed piloting on the Ship Canal, but no Canal Pilot had been prepared to lodge a formal complaint on the subject. This incident was the first time an official statement had been made against the Upper Mersey Pilot, and it was not to be the last time by far. The secretary of the Pilotage then read to the meeting a letter from the secretary of the Manchester Ship Canal Association.

I am instructed to report to you that on Wednesday 10th December the vessel "ALLANWATER" entered Eastham Locks on the Level, having on the bridge a person (namely Mr. A. Kirby) who was not the Master nor a member of the crew of the ship and was apparently acting as pilot of the ship. Mr. R. Green (Pilot) who was on the Lock at Eastham drew the attention of the Lockmaster to the presence on the vessel's bridge of Mr. Kirby and the Head Gateman hailed the Master of the vessel and informed him that he had an unauthorised man on the bridge but received no reply. The shipping control clerk on enquiring the draft of the vessel was answered by Mr. Kirby. I understand that the vessel proceeded to Runcorn apparently in charge of Mr. Kirby. The matter was reported at once to Captain Perry (Harbour Master Eastham).

I am asked that the Pilotage Committee will enquire into this matter with a view to a prosecution being instituted against Mr. Kirby and the Master of the vessel under Section 30(5) of the Pilotage Act.

Captain Perry reported that he boarded the vessel on arrival at Weston Point Docks and interviewed the Master and Mr. Kirby. The Master stated he was in charge of the vessel when she entered Eastham and the vessel remained in his charge until she docked at Weston Point. Mr. Kirby stated that he had boarded the "ALLANWATER" on the previous day to pilot her to Weston Point Dock via the upper reaches of the River but owing to fog the vessel was turned back and anchored, which necessitated him remaining on board. When the Master decided to proceed to Weston Point via Eastham Locks he - Mr. Kirby - was there in the capacity of a passenger and had no active part in the piloting of the vessel. Further, he was well aware that he was not allowed to pilot vessels on the Ship Canal and would never attempt to do so.

Captain Perry informed Mr. Kirby that if, at any future date, he was on board a vessel under similar circumstances he must not remain on the bridge as his presence might lead to misunderstanding and consequently, trouble. Mr. Kirby promised to act on this advice. The Pilotage Committee's opinion was that Mr. Kirby had rendered himself to prosecution under Section 30(5) of the Pilotage Act 1913, but in this case it was decided that a warning letter should be addressed to him and the Master of the vessel concerned. The matter was considered resolved.

In June 1932, Mr. A. Kirby was once again involved in allegations of unlicensed piloting aboard the vessel S.S. "IPSWICH TRADER" from Eastham to Runcorn. The secretary of the Pilots Association lodged the complaint at the Pilotage

Committee meeting and requested the secretary of the committee (Mr. Eyre) to write to the owner of the "IPSWICH TRADER" asking him for and explanation of the Master's actions in employing Mr. Kirby to pilot his vessel on the Canal, in contravention of the said Pilotage Act. The Pilotage Committee received a reply from the owner enclosing a copy of the following letter the owner had received from the Master:-

"In answer to your letter of the 31st ultimo with regard to Mr Kirby being on board the "IPSWICH TRADER" going to Weston Point. He was sent by our Mr. Morris with our orders, as it was doubtful if we were to go up the River or the Ship Canal on account of the tide. Mr. Kirby was not the pilot at all and I spoke to the Dock Master about it on the telephone from Liverpool and told him the same. I have been in the Ship Canal many times when I was Master of the S.S. "JAMES TANNANT". Mr. Kirby did not touch the wheel, telegraph or give orders at any time.

The pilots' representatives intimated that in their opinion Mr. Kirby had ample opportunity of leaving the vessel before she entered the Canal when he knew he was not required to pilot her in the upper reaches of the River to Weston Mersey Lock. The explanation given of his presence on board and particularly in the wheelhouse, contrary to the provisions of the Pilotage Act was far from satisfactory. The Committee decided to postpone further consideration until statements had been obtained of the evidence against Mr. Kirby.

At the July Pilotage Committee Meeting the Chairman read to the Committee two letters which had been received from the Secretary of the Pilots Association, requesting action should be taken by the authority against Mr. Kirby. He also read a letter from Mr. J. Lee (pilot) who had offered his services to the Captain of the "IPSWICH TRADER" on the occasion under notice and was refused. Two reports were read from lockmen who were on duty at Weston Mersey Lock when the vessel passed, who had observed Mr. Kirby on the bridge of the vessel.

The Chairman stated it was the intention of the authority to prosecute under the relevant Pilotage Act, subject to the Committee agreeing. After further discussion it was agreed that as this was not the first case of a like nature which had been brought against Mr. Kirby the prosecution against him should proceed.

The Authority's case was duly placed in the hands of their solicitors Grundy, Kershaw, Samson and Co. The hearing was to take place in the Liverpool City Police Court on Friday August 12th 1932. The case against Mr. A. Kirby was duly heard , the Manchester Ship Canal Co proved conclusively the presence of Mr. Kirby on the bridge of the "IPSWICH TRADER". The Defendant had failed to prove that he had not piloted the vessel and the Deputy Stipendiary fined Mr. Kirby £5.0s.0d. (£5.00) with £10.10s.0d. (£10.50) costs.

Having regard to the fact that Mr. Kirby had been successfully convicted under the Pilotage Act, the Master of the vessel by employing an unlicensed pilot had rendered himself liable to prosecution for an offence under the same section of the Pilotage Act . The Pilotage Committee decided that the attention of the owners of the "IPSWICH TRADER" be drawn to the case at the same time intimating that as the Master had not been previously warned the Committee did not propose to take any further action. The sequel to the successful prosecution of Mr. Kirby, was the owner of the "IPSWICH TRADER", somewhat surprising attitude, to the letter sent to him from the Chairman of Pilotage Committee pointing out to him that although the Master had rendered himself liable to prosecution the Committee proposed to take no further action to which the owner responded as follows.

"I beg to assure you that whatever the Captain of the ship did, was entirely without my instructions and as a matter of fact I do not think the man Kirby was engaged to pilot the ship, as such a small vessel requires no pilot, other than what the Captain can do by himself. The Captain had navigated the Canal on previous occasions and is capable of his own pilotage. I must state the man Kirby was never paid any pilotage fees and I think the conviction was unjustifiable.

It would have been reasonable to assume that the severity of the fine handed down by the Court would have curtailed the practice of unlicensed piloting - the fine would have equalled a month's pay for an Upper Mersey Pilot or a Chief Officer of a large coasting vessel. Strangely, it still continued, albeit very sparsely and in a more surreptitious manner by taking extra care they were not seen by Ship Canal Pilots or employees in a position on board a vessel that would constitute they were piloting the vessel under the Pilotage Act 30(5) 1913. Certainly one would have expected Mr. Kirby to have learnt the error of his ways from his very expensive experience with the "IPSWICH TRADER". Sadly to report he did not.

A complaint from Mr. T. Lamey (pilot) stated that when the vessel S.S. "LENNY" proceeded into Eastham Locks outward bound for the River he observed on her bridge Mr. A. Kirby and also heard him give at least one direction concerning the handling of the vessel. The Pilotage Committee were reminded that Mr. Kirby was fined in respect of a similar charge nine years ago, but as this was the first complaint which had been received since that occasion, it was decided not to take proceedings. It was agreed, however, that any future similar complaint would leave the Authority no option but to take legal action once again and Mr. Kirby should be notified by the Chairman of this decision. Mr. Kirby was an extremely fortunate man to escape with just an admonition considering his previous record. This was the last record of unlicensed pilotage.

The Ship Canal Pilots were assailed from all sides in their early years by persons attempting to obtain their pilotage work. The Manchester Ship Canal Co had started issuing Licences to Masters and Mates of vessels who were regular traders. Upper Mersey Pilots encroached on their territory and there was another form of obtaining pilotage on the Ship Canal that occasionally occurred. The incident regarding the piloting of the S.S. "TANKE" in 1903, amply illustrates the form it took.

"A Ship Canal Pilot had been appointed by the Agents of the S.S. "TANKE" to meet her in the river and pilot her up the Canal. The vessel was due on the 8th. August and he attended in the River until the 11th when she at last arrived. He boarded and offered his services to the Master but they were refused, the Master stating that he had engaged a Canal Pilot in Liverpool Bay from the Liverpool Pilot boat. The Liverpool Pilot was not to take charge until off New Ferry as he had already a River Pilot on board. It was always understood Liverpool Pilots do not usually solicit Ship Canal pilotage in Liverpool Bay unless they are also the pilot in charge for the river.

The Chairman of the Pilotage Committee (Mr. E. Latimer) wrote to the Liverpool Pilot stating that it had been alleged he solicited and obtained the Manchester Ship Canal Pilotage before the vessel arrived in the river. The Agents of the "TANKE" had engaged a Ship Canal Pilot to take the vessel from Eastham to Manchester and the Manchester Pilot in question, complains. bitterly of the very unfair manner in which he considers the Ship Canal Pilotage was secured by you.

It is thoroughly understood at the time Ship Canal Licences were granted to River Pilots that they were only to be used in continuation of the river pilotage or when they were stationed at Eastham Locks looking for canal work. The Chairman asked him to report in writing under what circumstances he undertook the pilotage of the "TANKE". The Liverpool Pilot's reply was read to the Pilotage Committee Meeting in which he stated he was the pilot of a vessel from Liverpool Docks to the Bar Light Ship and arrived on board the pilot boat about noon. A few minutes later I went aboard the "TANKE" for a passage back to Liverpool, not for the express purpose of securing the Ship Canal Pilotage as I have been led to believe the Manchester Pilotage Committee are under that impression.

I had been on board the vessel for some considerable time before the Ship Canal Pilotage was mentioned, the Liverpool Pilot in charge of the vessel explained to the Master that I held a Ship Canal Licence and could take his vessel to Manchester. The Master thereupon decided to engage me for the Ship Canal pilotage. The River Pilot landed in the Custom Launch at the Liverpool stage, when I remained on board and concluded the pilotage to Manchester.

On the reading of the reply Mr. Felton (Liverpool Pilots' Representative) stated that as the representative of the Liverpool Pilots holding Ship Canal licences he took great exception to that part of Mr. Latimers' letter which states:-

Ship Canal Licences granted to Liverpool Pilots were only to be used by them in continuation of the River Pilotage or when they were stationed at Eastham Locks looking for canal work .

Mr. Felton contended that no restriction was placed upon the General Licences when issued to the pilots holding River Licences and that therefore they were quite within their rights in accepting any pilotage work that was offered to them under any conditions. He further stated that he was borne out in his contention by Messrs. Backhouse and Colquitt, two Liverpool Pilots who had served on this very committee in the early days of its inception. Mr. Felton expressed a view that his colleagues thought from the recent actions of this committee that they were desirous of getting rid of the Liverpool Pilots on the Canal. He specially mentioned that they thought the rule calling for a pilot to navigate the whole length of the canal three times in one year before being entitled to a renewal of his Licence was unnecessary as he contended that any pilot, who was worth his salt, and had navigated the canal some six times or so would have sufficient knowledge to navigate a vessel up or down the canal at any time after.

Mr. Latimer replied that although there did not appear to be anything recorded in the minutes of this committee as to any conditions being placed on the River Pilots when issued with a

Ship Canal Licence, it was certainly the expressed opinion of the majority of the members of this committee - most of whom had been members since its formation - that these restrictions were abided by, and that had caused him to make the remark in his letter to the Liverpool Pilot which Mr. Felton now took exception to. The Chairman pointed out to Mr. Felton that whilst the pilot in question had not broken any bye-laws, he felt the Liverpool Pilot had unfairly manipulated the regulations to his advantage. The Liverpool Pilots had an assured living on the river, whilst many of the Canal Pilots' livelihoods depended solely on the pilotage in the canal. The Chairman concluded that he hoped Mr. Felton would express the feelings of this Committee at the next meeting of his Association. Mr. Felton replied he would certainly convey the feelings of this Committee to his colleagues.

25.

FORMING A ROTARY SYSTEM : 1919
THE FINAL FRONTIER

The Board of Trade, London, duly notified the pilots that Mr Latimer would be responsible for any negotiations on their demands and that he would arrange for a meeting with Mr Beckett (Secretary of the Pilots' Association) with a deputation of pilots as early as possible. This meeting was convened on 26 June 1919, when a full statement of the proposals for a rotary and pooling system of pilotage was placed before the Chairman of the Pilotage Committee, Mr Latimer. It read as follows :-

1)   1) Increase in tariff
       2) Rotary and pooling system
       3) Cancellation of Licences held by pilots
          from other ports
       4) Pension on retirement
       5) More equitable representation on the Manchester Pilotage Committee.

2)   THE ROTARY SYSTEM   The pilotage service on the canal to consist of not more than 28 pilots.   The qualifications for a second class pilot shall be (with the exception of helmsmen at present engaged) at least two years' sea service in some capacity on deck;   at least five years' steering under a general Licenced Pilot on the canal and not to be under 25 years of age.

One half the number of pilots to work down from Manchester each month and the other half to work up from Eastham to Manchester.

A station at Eastham at which six pilots shall always be in attendance.

Six hours notice to be received for any pilots wanted. Notice to be given between 9 a.m. and 6 p.m.

A telephone to be placed in a hut at Eastham.

Other pilots required for vessels entering Eastham or moving from other points on the canal, i.e. Manchester, Partington, Runcorn to be ordered by rotation. Second class pilots to take turns (as far as the limits of their Licences will permit) with first class pilots.

No separate arrangements to be made in respect of so-called Runcorn pilots who must take their turn with other pilots as necessary.

Helmsmen shall be registered by the Canal Company after approval by the Pilots' Association who will before giving that approval have an opportunity of testing applicants for the position of helmsmen through their members on the canal.

A nominal charge of 10/6d(52p) p.a. shall be made for the registration of same to go to Pilots' Superannuation Fund. On a vacancy occurring in the pilotage service, the helmsman having the longest service shall be allowed to come up for examination should he so desire; if not then the next in seniority of service and so on.

One firm of shipowners or ships agents to be entitled to one appropriated pilot.

Such pilot as far as possible to perform pilotage work in respect of such shipowners' vessels to the exclusion of unappropriated pilots.

No shipowners or ships' agent to be entitled to more than one choice pilot and no pilot to be appropriated to more than one company.

3) CANCELLATION OF LICENCES HELD BY PILOTS FROM OTHER PORTS

The Manchester Ship Canal Pilots demand the immediate cancellation of the licences held by pilots holding licences at other ports and docking in the canal.

4) MORE EQUITABLE REPRESENTATION ON THE MANCHESTER PILOTAGE

The pilots asked for four representatives on the Pilotage Committee.

All the demands made by the pilots were thoroughly discussed and Mr Latimer closed the meeting by stating he would report same to the Directors of the Company for their consideration and comments.

At the Pilotage Committee meeting on 7 July 1919, the full account of the pilots' demands were placed before them. Mr Latimer stated that in order that a co-ordination scheme could be created, he would arrange with the deputation that Mr Beckett and two pilots should discuss details with Mr Browning (Vice-Chairman) and two Canal Superintendents, Captains Acraman and Adamson. A meeting would be arranged as early as possible and the further negotiations reported to the Pilotage Committee at their next meeting.

Closely interwoven with all the pilots' negotiations relating to an equitable working system, the subject of a new tariff and the manner in which the monies should be distributed, had always been considered as an inherent part of any new reorganization. This insistence was to cause some delay in implementing the new proposed scheme of pilotage. Two months of intense negotiations between the pilots and the Pilotage Committee culminated in the Chairman, Mr Latimer, putting forward an application to the Board of Trade to amend the Manchester Pilotage Byelaws, under their terms and conditions, dated 14 October 1918.

The standard procedure for such an alteration in a Pilotage Byelaw was for it to be published in a national newspaper and if there were no objections received within a period of one calendar month, the said byelaw would automatically become law. One objection was received by the Board of Trade to the proposal for a new scheme of pilotage, in a letter sent by the one person who had worked nearly all his pilotage life for fair shares for all pilots; no less than such a personage was Mr J A Hindle. What a shock and a blow this must have been to all concerned, especially the pilots.

The whole scheme of reorganized pilotage in Manchester was once again suspended.

A letter was received from the Board of Trade addressed to the Chairman of the Pilotage Committee dated 29 October 1919 and read to the Pilotage Committee meeting on 4 November 1919 :

"Dear Sir

I am directed by the Board of Trade to transmit the accompanying copy of a letter which they have received from Mr J A Hindle objecting on behalf of the majority of the members of the Manchester Branch of the United Kingdom Pilots' Association to the proposed byelaw relating to the pooling of earnings and the increase of the pilotage rates at Manchester and I am to state that the Board will be glad to receive the observations of the Manchester Pilotage Committee in the matter as soon as possible."

The letter signed by Mr J A Hindle dated 27 October, referred to in the Board of Trade's letter, read as follows :-

"Dear Sir

I note the Manchester Ship Canal Company intend to ask for confirmation of a byelaw to supersede Byelaws Nos. 15 and 16 approved and confirmed by an order in Council dated 21 November 1895 and subsequently amended by the Pilotage Byelaw confirmed by the Board of Trade on 14 October 1918.

I am instructed by a majority of the members of the Manchester Branch of the United Kingdom Pilots' Association to most emphatically protest against the first clause relating to the distribution of the pilotage rates. We think it would be most unjust to the pilots to leave the distribution of the rates to the Pilotage Authority, to, as the proposed byelaw states, 'divide in such manner as the Pilotage Authority may from time to time determine'. We cannot consent to this and would much prefer that the byelaw shall clearly declare how and when the rates are to be divided.

For many years now, the Manchester pilots have been endeavouring to obtain the consent of the Directors of the Manchester Ship Canal Company to a rotary and pooling system of pilotage so that the pilots would have an equal share of the work and proceeds. It is now promised, but nothing is said in the proposed byelaw to this effect - we would like this done.

As regards the proposed new initial fee, some time ago a list of initial fees proposed by the pilots sent to the Managing Director for his approval, but was not accepted; the list of initial fees placed in the new byelaw was sent by him to the pilots sixteen days ago and at a hurriedly convened meeting of the pilots at which only eleven out of twenty five were present, the proposed fees were accepted by eight to three against.

We think this should not be taken as final - a referendum of all the pilots should be taken. It is quite impossible to get all the men to a meeting as the work on the canal must be carried on; time should also be given to the men to consider what the smaller tariff means considering the high cost of living and travelling expenses; this has not been done and hence our objection which please note."

One must feel for Mr Hindle; he had long felt how bitter it was over the past years to meet disappointment, disenchantment and delays again and again. What a truism it is to state that "deeds deferred make the heart lose hope", even now his buoyant calculations of an early settlement for a rotary system were cruelly crushed once again - the more heart-rending by his very own violation. His personal reaction must have been extremely painful, but he fought on for the undeniable right he so worthily championed, that every pilot in the Manchester Service should be equal in all things appertaining to their profession.

The Chairman of the Pilotage Committee reiterated that due to the above letter, the whole scheme had been suspended. Before the scheme could be proceeded with, the objection would have to be withdrawn by Mr Hindle and the pilots concerned with it. Failing that, it was probable the Board of Trade would once more hold a Public Enquiry into the circumstances. The pilots' representatives knew full well what a frustrating and procrastinating experience a Public Enquiry with the Board of Trade could be and after a long discussion, Mr Hindle agreed he would explain to the pilots generally the views of the Pilotage Committee and the steps which had been taken to get the new scheme into operation. Mr Hindle thought, in the light of the alternatives, e.g. Board of Trade Enquiry, the pilots might agree to the objection being withdrawn.

The Chairman said a useful purpose might be served if a letter was sent to Mr Beckett suggesting that the whole of the pilots, or as many of them as could attend, might meet him on Monday 10 November, with a view to clearing up any misunderstanding which might have arisen with the pilots. This proposal was unanimously agreed.

Accordingly, sixteen pilots met with Mr Latimer on the 10 November 1919. What heart-searching there must have been done by the pilots' representatives, one can only surmise, but a lot of midnight oil was burned during those following days after 4 November. As a result of the November 10th meeting, the objection to the byelaw for the new proposed scheme of pilotage which had been sent to the Board of Trade was withdrawn by Mr Hindle on behalf of the pilots.

This last hurdle successfully cleared, it only remained for the Board of Trade to notify their approval of the byelaw to the Pilotage Committee, which they did on 21 November 1919. Immediately a meeting was arranged for Monday, 24 November, between Captains Acraman and Adamson, Canal Superintendents' and the representatives of the pilots, Messrs Hindle and Postlethwaite, when the following memorandum of arrangements were drawn up to implement the long awaited Pilotage Rotary System.

1) Two pilot stations to be provided - Manchester and Eastham.

2) Three pilots to be in attendance at Manchester and four at Eastham.

3) The rota to be started as per alphabetical list and pilots to maintain their relative positions on the rota.

4) In calling pilots, the priority to be given to Manchester, i.e. when pilots are called for Manchester and Eastham, the first of the rota to go to Manchester.

5) Pilots who are nearly on turn must keep in touch for their orders either at Manchester or Eastham by telephone.

6) If vessels loading at Partington can be completed within eight hours, the pilot to remain and complete the journey.

7) Shifting at Manchester above Barton Bridge and at Eastham not to count a turn but to be done by the pilots on duty.

8) Each pilot to report as soon as his service had been completed and immediately send his Pilotage Card to the Dock Office.

9) Pilots stationed at Eastham will be required to be on duty during the time the locks are working, i.e. four hours before to four hours after Liverpool High Water.

10) Any point not covered by these provisional rules will be dealt with as it arises by the newly appointed Pilotage Clerk, Mr R Bennion.

11)   CHOICE PILOTS :-

Pilots   Applicants

Jas Barnes   )   Anglo-American Oil Co.
)   Felber Jucker & Co.

Thos.Lamey   )   F Leyland & Co.
)   J Leete & Sons

J T Baxter   )   Manchester Liners Ltd.
Geo Cartwright)

Geo Green   Cunard Steamship Co.

R Southwood   Marwood & Robertsons

W D Southwood   Prince Line Ltd.

It was decided that no pilot should be alloted to more than one firm of shipowners and it was thought that as regards the applications of Messrs Leete & Sons and Messrs Felber Jucker & Co, whose steamers were of a less tonnage than 1,000 tons, they should be informed that although the Committee had not come to any decision, it was not likely that they would agree to appoint Choice Pilots for vessels less than 1,000 tons.

As it was probable that further applications for Choice Pilots would be made, the matter was postponed until the next meeting of the Committee. It was agreed that in the meantime where Choice Pilots had been asked for their services, they should be made available accordingly as far as circumstances would permit.

The date for the introduction of the new Pilotage Rotary System was set for 1 December 1919, exactly 23 years, 8 months and 22 days, after the first Rotary System was muted in 1896. It had been a long, hard and often bitter struggle that pitted father against son, families against families and pilots against pilots. Such were the bitter memories that it soured relationships within the pilot service for the next 40 years. Some pilots refused to work willingly within the new Rotary System until their dying day, ever longing for the old "catch as catch can" system and "farming out" ships. They could not or would not be convinced that a rotary system and pooling of earnings would give them far more benefits.

While it is happy to record that a fair and equitable system of pilotage had, at long last, been achieved by the Manchester Pilot Service, it must also be said it was sad that the internecine attitudes of those pilots would always disrupt the future of the Manchester Pilot Service.

APPENDICES

(10 & 11 GEO. 5.)   Pilotage Orders Confirmation   (CH.cili)

(No.1) Act, 1920

CHAPTER   ciii

An act to confirm certain Pilotage Orders made by the Board of Trade under the Pilotage Act 1913 relating to the Pilotage Districts of Liverpool and Manchester.

(4th. August 1920)

Manchester

MANCHESTER   PILOTAGE   ORDER

Pilotage   1. The limits of the Manchester Pilotage District
District. (hereinafter called "the Pilotage District") shall
be the Manchester Ship Canal (as constructed under the Manchester
Ship Canal Act 1885) and the subsequent Acts relating to the
said canal from its eastern termination at or near Woden Street
footbridge in the city of Manchester to the outer sill of the
river entrance at Eastham Locks.

Pilotage   2. The Pilotage Authority for the Pilotage District
Authority. shall be the Manchester Ship Canal Company (hereinafter
called"the Authority"

Pilotage   3. Pilotage shall not be compulsory in the Pilotage
not com-   District.
pulsory.

Pilotage   4. - (1) There shall be constituted a Pilotage Committee
Committee, of the Authority (in this order referred to as "the
Committee") consisting of members appointed by the Authority
and of represntatives of shipowners and pilots(hereinafter referred
to as "shipowners representatives" and "pilots representatives
respectively) as follows:--
                (a) Such number of persons not exceeding five appointed
                    by the Authority as the Authority think fit of
                    whom at the time of appointment at least two
                    shall be directors of the Manchester Ship Canal.

                (b) The shipowners representatives appointed by the
                    Manchester Steamship Owners Association.

                (c) Two pilots representatives elected in manner
                    hereinafter provided by the pilots licensed for
                    the Pilotage District (hereinafter referred to
as the "licensed pilots") from among persons who are either or
have been licensed pilots for the Pilotage District..

                (d) The members of the committee shall be appointed
and elected repectively at the time and in the manner in the
schedule hereto provided.

                (e) Any persons who were on the first day of November
1919 members of the Pilotage Committee for the Pilotage District
shall until the thirty-first day of October 1920 be the committee
as though they had been appointed or elected under this order.

281

2

Powers of
Pilotage
Committee. 5. The Authority may delegate to the Committee any of their powers or duties under the Pilotage Act 1913.The decisions of the Committee on questions so delegated shall not require confirmation by the Authority but the Committee shall report their proceedings to the Authority.

Proceedings
of Committee. 6.-(1) The Chairman if present shall preside at every meeting of the Committee. If the chairman is absent at ant meeting such other member as the members then present choose shall preside.

(2) Every question at a meeting of the Committee shall be decided by a majority of votes of the members of the Committee present and voting on that question and in the case of equality of votes the person presiding at the meeting shall have a second or casting vote.

(3) The quorum of the Committee shall be four present and qualified to take part in the proceedings unless tthe Authority otherwise direct..

(4) No member of the Committee shall take part in any proceedings of the Committee relating to any question affecting himself personally.

(5) Subject to the provisions of this order the Committee may regulate their own proceeduré.

(6) No act or proceeding of the Committee shall be invalid on account of any vacancy in their body or on account of the appointment or election of any member having been defective

Period of
office. 7. Members of the Committee shall hold office from the date of their appointment or election respectively until such time as their successors may be appointed or elected respectively.

Retiring
members. 8. Members of the Committee going out of office may be re-appointed or reelected respectively.

Sperate
accounts. 9. Seperate accounts shall be kept by the Authority of all moneys received and expended by them in connection with the Pilot Service..

Repeal date
of commen-
cement. 10..Section twenty-two of the Manchester Ship Canal Act 1894 shall cease to have effect and shall for the purposes of section 59 of the Pilotage Act 1913 be deemed to be superseded..

Shorttitle. 11.This order may be cited as the Manchester Pilotage order 1920.

12. This order shall come into force on the day when the Act confirming this order is passed.

S C H E D U L E.

With respect to the appointment and election of the Committee the following provisions shall have effect (that is to say):-
1. The persons to be appointed by the Authority as members of the Committee and shipowners representatives respectively shall be appointed at the first meeting of the Authority and the Manchester Steamship Owners Association respectively held after the commencement of this order and in the month of October in every year thereafter.

3

2. For the purpose of electing Pilots representatives the secretary of the Committee shall on the First day of October 1920 and in every year thereafter send out by registered letter to all the Pilots of the first and second class a circular announcing an election and enclosing a list of persons qualified under the order to be pilots representatives, a voting card and a stamped addressed envelope in which the card when filled in is to be returned to himself.At the expiration of twenty one days from the issue of the said circular the said secretary shall check and count the voting cards returned to him and the two persons who have received the greatest number of votes and are otherwise qualified under this order shall be the pilots representatives for the ensuing year. The said secretary shall thereupon send out by registered letter to all pilots of the first and second class a further circular announcing the result of the election and an election of substitute representatives for which latter purposes a proceedure shall be adopted similar to the proceedure for the election of pilots representatives.Provided always that it shall be lawful for the Authority at any time with the consent of the Board of Trade to substitute a different proceedure for the election of pilots representatives or substitute representatives

3.A substitute representative shall be entitled to attend and vote at any meeting of the Commmittee in the place of any pilots representatives who may be unable to attend.

4.The members of the Committee shall come into office on the first day of November in the year of which they are appointed and elected respectively and shall remain in office until the following thirty first day of October and shall then go out of office but they may be re-appointed or re-elected as the case may be.

5. In the case there is a failure in any year to elect any pilots representatives or substitute representatives the Board of Trade may appoint any duly qualified person to fill the vacancy and the person so appointed shall hold office as though he had been dulyelected.

6.- (1) In the case of any vacancy occurring in the members of the Committee appointed by the Authority or among the shipowners representatives otherwise than by offluxtion of time the Authority and the Manchester Steamship Owners Association respectively may(subject in the case of the Authority to the provisions of sub-section 1(a) of section 4 of this order) appoint a person to fill the vacancy.
   (2) In the case of any vacancy occuring among the pilots representatives or substitute representatives otherwise than by offluxtion of time the vacancy shall be filled in the same manner as is provided for the annual election of pilots representatives or substitute representatives.
   (3) A person appointed or elected under either of the two proceeding subsections shall remain a member of the Committee or a pilots substitute representative as the case may be so long only as a person for whom he is substituted would have remained a member or substitute respectively.

7. The costs charges and expenses of any preliminary and incidental to elections of pilots representatives and substitute representives shall be paid by the Authority out of the pilot fund or account of the Pilotage District.

No tides to Stem

GENERAL INFORMATION

The entrance to the Ship Canal at Eastham is 25 miles from the bar at the mouth of the river Mersey, and the access is from the sea via the lower estuary.

The access channel has been excavated to a depth of 13 feet below Liverpool Bay Datum. The available depth of water is announced from time to time.

The Ship Canal is 35½ miles in length, and the principal docks are at Manchester.

The Ship Canal between Eastham and Ince Oil Berth has been excavated to a depth of 30 feet and from Ince Oil Berth to Manchester, including the large docks at Manchester, to 28 feet.

The general constructed bottom width of the Canal at the depth of 28 feet is 120 feet, with the following exceptions :—

(a) At the curve at the Weaver Outfall the excavated width is 180 feet. At the bend at Runcorn, below the Runcorn Railway Bridge, the excavated width is 175 feet. Between the Runcorn Railway Bridge and Runcorn (Old Quay) Lock, the excavated width is 150 feet.

(b) For a part of the length between Latchford Locks and Partington Coaling Basin—*i.e.*, from Warburton Bridge to the upper end of Millbank Wharf (about three quarters of a mile in all), the excavated width is at present only 90 feet.

There are two parallel locks at Eastham which are open to estuary level whenever the tide rises more than 26 feet 2 inches above Liverpool Bay Datum. When the tide is below this level, access and egress are obtained by locking. The large lock is 600 feet by 80 feet, the other lock is 350 feet by 50 feet. Width of the Ship Canal at Eastham Locks, 315 feet.

The lower sill of the large lock at Eastham is 13 feet below Liverpool Bay Datum, the upper sill of the large lock is 30 feet below water level.

High water at Eastham—12 minutes after Liverpool.

High water at Runcorn—40 minutes after Liverpool.

Queen Elizabeth II Dock.—The dock, which was officially opened in January, 1954, is adjacent to the locks at Eastham and is approached from the Mersey through its own entrance lock. This lock is 807 feet long by 100 feet wide. The dock has four berths, each capable of accommodating a tanker of 30,000 tons and upwards and is directly connected to the refinery at Stanlow by 6 miles of pipeline. The dock has a depth of 40 feet of water

Eastham Lay-bye.—West Berth, 1,560 feet ; East Berth, 650 feet.

Equipment is available for removing and replacing the tops of masts and funnels.

Bowaters Mersey Paper Mills Ltd., Paper Works—Wharf alongside works available for ocean-going vessels. Equipped for handling wood pulp, minerals, etc. Length of berths, 1,100 feet.

Ellesmere Port.—The docks are leased to the Ship Canal Company by the British Transport Commission.

The equipment of the Docks and wharves includes quay sheds, electrically-equipped grain warehouse (capacity 20,000 tons) and other warehouses, coal tips, etc.

Additional wharfage accommodation with quay sheds, one 10 ton and ten 50 cwt. electric cranes.

The deep water wharf (2,250 feet) is laid out for two double-unit coal conveyors each capable of handling 800 tons an hour. The coal wagons are assembled on sidings at the back of the plant, where arrangements allow for a speedy exchange of empty and full wagons. Full wagons pass on to the tipping tables where hydraulic tippers empty them. Wagons can be tipped from either end so that turn-tables are unnecessary. The coal is then carried on conveyor bands by way of a telescopic arm with a radial movement of 30 degrees and may be raised or lowered to accommodate them to the largest vessel using the Canal or to a barge with a foot or two of freeboard. The maximum tipping height of the plant is 85 feet

No tides to Stem

and the reach over the quayside 50 feet. The conveyors can be concentrated on the forward or after hatchways, or operate at two points up to a distance apart of 260 feet without moving the vessel. The plant is electrically driven and one double unit is already installed. This method of loading coal allows the handling of general cargo to go on at the same time between the ship and the transit sheds and rail and road conveyance.

The Manchester Ship Canal Company performs the work of loading and discharging vessels and other labour services at the Port.

Ellesmere Port is the terminus of the Shropshire Union Canal, which navigation extends to Autherley Junction, near Wolverhampton and, by junctions with other canals, gives access to north and south Staffordshire, the Midlands and the South.

The London, Midland Region and Western Region of the British Railways have direct rail communications with the Port.

The Ship Canal Company has a large area of land at Ellesmere Port which has deep water frontage and railway communication. This land is available for development for traffic purposes and sites for works.

Stuart Wharf : (South Side).—Berth 390 feet long. Tying up place for vessels.

Manchester Dry Docks Co., Ltd., Works and Floating Pontoon Dock.—The pontoon is 300 feet in length, 58 feet in width, with 16 feet of water on the blocks, which are 4 feet in height, available for vessels up to 4,000 tons burden.

Stanlow Wharf : (South Side).—Berth 590 feet long : (Cement Co.). Tying up place for small vessels.

Assoc. Ethyl Wharf, 600 ft. long; depth of water, 30 ft.

I.C.I. (Dyestuffs) Wharf : (South side).—Berth 300 feet long. Tying up place for small vessels.

Esso Petroleum Co's. Barge Wharf : (South side).—Berth 100 feet long. For loading and discharging of Petroleum Barges.

Stanlow Oil Docks.—The Canal Company has constructed docks on the River Mersey side of the Ship Canal where cargoes of petroleum spirit and other dangerous fluids flashing below 73° Fahr., also petroleum, lubricating and other oils are discharged. Coasting vessels can also be loaded at a separate berth within the docks. Two subways have been provided with pipes and all other facilities for carrying the oil underneath the Ship Canal into tank installations which have been erected by oil importing companies on the south side.

Vessels up to 530 feet B.P., can be turned in the basin at the entrance to the oil docks.

Stanlow Lay-Bye.—Wharf with berth 600 feet long, where vessels discharge oil and obtain supplies of fuel oil.

Ince Oil Berth.—Berth 600 feet long with wharf 300 feet long where vessels discharge oil and supplies of fuel can be obtained

Tying-up Berth, Ince.—1,230 feet long. Berths for large vessels.

Weston Mersey Lock Wall : (West side).—Berth 1,000 feet long. Tying up place for vessels.

Weston Mersey Lock.—600 feet by 45 feet. Access from the River Mersey to the Ship Canal for the passage of traffic across the Ship Canal between the estuary and the Weston Point Docks of the River Weaver Navigation Trustees, also between the estuary and Runcorn Docks and the Bridgewater Canal.

I.C.I., Ltd., Salt Division, Weston Point Works.—Berthage accommodation for vessels up to 500 feet long.

Runcorn Lay-Bye.—This lay-bye abuts on the Manchester Ship Canal a Runcorn, immediately below Runcorn Docks. It is 1,260 ft. in length with an excavated depth of 26 ft. of water alongside.

No tides to Stem

Runcorn Docks.—Owned by the Manchester Ship Canal Company ; include the Tidal, Alfred, Fenton, Arnold, Francis and Old Docks ; covering an area of 70 acres (water space 16 acres), storage ground covering 77 acres. Road transport facilities. Tidal dock entrances : width, 50 feet ; depth, up to 14 ft. 6 in. Levels of Alfred and Fenton Docks are maintained at a depth of about 16 feet. Quayage, 2,500 yards. The docks are equipped with steam, hydraulic, mobile and floating cranes and derricks. There is a graving dock for the repair of small craft.

Petrochemicals, Ltd. Fenton Dock, Runcorn.—Berthing accommodation for sea-going tankers loading low-flash carbons, including Toluene, Xylene, etc. from tanks installed by Petrochemicals Ltd. Access to the installation by road.

Bridgewater Canal.—Entrance to navigation running inland from junction with Ship Canal at Runcorn Docks.

Runcorn Railway Viaduct.—Carrying the London, Midland Region Railway over the River Mersey and Ship Canal. Headway 76 feet above high water spring tides.

Widnes Transporter Bridge.—For the transportation of the Public and -vehicles between Runcorn and Widnes.

Old Quay Lock Wall : (North side).—Berth 1,500 feet long. Tying up place for vessels.

Old Quay Lock, Runcorn.—250 ft. by 45ft.—Access from River Mersey to che Ship Canal for barge traffic.

Old Quay Swing Bridge,· Runcorn.—Span, 120 feet.

I.C.I. (General Chemicals) Ltd. Wharves.—Two wharves at Old Quay, Runcorn, are respectively 386 feet and 690 feet long with berths excavated to a depth of 26 feet and 22 feet.

Chemical & Metallurgical Corporation Barge Wharf : (North side).—Length 100 feet.

Moore Lane Lay-bye—720 feet long.—Tying-up berth for large vessels.

Moore Lane Swing Bridge.—Span 120 feet.

Acton Grange Wharf.—(National Coal Board.), Acton Grange, near Warrington, berth 300 feet long, excavated to a depth 20 feet.

Acton Grange Viaduct.—(Railway viaduct), span ·264 feet. London, Midland Region and Western Region main line.

Chester Road Swing Bridge.—Span, 120 feet.

Warrington Wharf—where vessels can be loaded and discharged, 300 feet long (berth, 350 feet long) excavated to a depth of 20 feet. The equipment includes a movable hydraulic transporter with a capacity of 30 cwts., and a steam crane with a capacity of 5 tons.

Walton Lock : (North side).—Length 150 feet, Breadth 30 feet, connecting the Canal and River Mersey.

Northwich Road Swing Bridge.—Span, 120 feet.

Twenty Steps Lock—85 feet by 19 feet 6 inches.—Access from the River Mersey above Warrington.

Latchford High Level Bridge (Cantilever).—Centre span, 206 feet.

Knutsford Road Swing Bridge.—Span, 120 feet.

Latchford Viaduct (Railway Viaduct).—Span, 250 feet. London, Midland Region, Warrington and Manchester, Liverpool and Stockport.

Latchford Lower Lay-bye.—Length 600 feet.

Latchford Locks.—Large lock, 600 feet by 65 feet ; small lock, 350 feet by 45 feet. Width of Ship Canal at the locks, 290 feet. Latchford Railway Station is about three-quarters of a mile from Latchford Locks.

Latchford Upper Lay-bye.—Length 520 feet.

Thelwall Ferry (Public).—¼ mile above Latchford Locks.

Warburton High Level Bridge (Cantilever). Centre span, 206 feet

Cadishead Ferry (Public).—¼ mile below Cadishead Railway Viaduct.

Cadishead Viaduct (Railway Viaduct).—Span, 137 feet. London, Midland Region, Stockport and Liverpool.

Partington Coaling Basin and Lay-bye.—Water space, 6½ acres ; 24 miles of railway sidings. There are six tips fitted with hydraulic machinery and each tip has a capacity of 300 tons per hour. There is direct railway communication with all the coalfields of the Kingdom. Partington is the nearest point of shipment for the Lancashire, Derbyshire and Staffordshire coalfields.

Partington Ferry (Private).—Operating in Partington Basin.

Lancashire Steel Corporation Ltd. (Partington Steel and Iron Works).—Connected by the Ship Canal Company's railways with the Manchester Docks and with the London, Midland Region of the British Railways.

Irlam Ore Wharf.—Alongside the works of the Lancashire Steel Corporation Ltd., available for ocean-going vessels and equipped for the handling of ore, minerals, etc., length of berth, 600 feet.

Irlam Viaduct (Railway Viaduct) Span, 119 feet 6 inches. London, Midland Region, Manchester and Liverpool.

Irlam Wharf (C.W.S.).—Berth, 275 feet long, excavated to a depth of 20 feet. The Co-operative Wholesale Society's soap and candle works and margarine factory are connected with the London, Midland Region of the British Railways at Irlam and Glazebrook and with the Manchester Docks by means of the Ship Canal Company's railways.

Irlam Lower Lay-bye.—Length 600 feet.

Irlam Locks.—Large lock, 600 feet by 65 feet ; small lock, 350 feet by 45 feet, Width of Ship Canal at the locks, 370 feet.

Irlam Upper Lay-bye.—Length 520 feet.

Irlam Ferry (Public).—¼ mile above Irlam Locks.

Hulmes Bridge Ferry (Public).—¾ mile below Barton Locks.

Barton Locks.—Large Lock 600 feet by 65 feet ; small lock 350 feet by 45 feet. Width of Ship Canal at the locks 330 feet.

Barton Upper Lay-bye.—Length 485 feet.

Barton (Road) Swing Bridge.—Span, 90 feet.

Barton Aqueduct.—(Carrying the Bridgewater Canal over the Ship Canal)—235 feet long, 6 feet deep, 18 feet wide.

Barton Oil Berth.—For the discharge of oil in bulk to the tanks of Shell-Mex & B.P. Ltd. ; The Regent Oil Co. Ltd. ; Gulf Oil (Great Britain) Ltd ; Manchester Oil Refineries Ltd., and Lubricants Producers Ltd. Vessels can obtain supplies of fuel oil at this point. Length 508 feet.

Irwell Park Lay-bye—600 feet long ; tying-up berth for large vessels.

Irwell Park Wharf, Eccles—The ports main bulk discharging depot. Recently underwent extensive reconstruction. Length 1100 ft. Equipped with latest type of electric grab cranes for discharge of sulphur, ores and other bulk cargoes. Direct discharge to road and rail.

Eccles Oil Wharf and Barge Berth.—For the discharge and loading out of oil in bulk to the tanks of Shell-Mex & B.P. Ltd. Vessels can obtain supplies of fuel oil at this point. Length 600 feet.

A. Guinness, Son & Co. Ltd., Wharf: (South side).—Berth 700 feet. Tying up place for vessels.

Thomas Hedley & Co. Ltd.—Factory for the manufacture of soap, with overhead pipeline across the Ship Canal at a height of 90 feet above normal water level for conveyance to factory of oil discharged in bulk from vessels berthed at Weaste Oil Wharf.

Weaste Oil Wharf.—For the discharge of oil in bulk to the tanks of Berry Wiggins & Co. Ltd. and others. Length 557 feet.

Weaste Coaling Crane Wharf : (North side).—Berth 380 feet long. Tying up place for vessels.

Weaste Lay-bye—600 feet long.—Tying-up berth for large vessels.

Weaste Wharf, connected with the Salford Sewage Works at Mode Wheel—Berth 300 feet long ; berth excavated to a depth of 23 feet.

Southern Oil Wharf.—Berth 500ft. long, excavated to a depth of 25ft. For the discharge of whale oil to the tanks of The Southern Oil Co. Ltd.

Mode Wheel Oil Wharves.—For the discharge and loading out of oil in bulk to and from the tanks of the Esso Petroleum Co. Ltd. Vessels can obtain supplies of fuel oil at this point.

Mode Wheel Locks, forming the entrance to the Manchester Docks– 600 feet by 65 feet and 350 feet by 45 feet ; width of Ship Canal below the locks 320 ft.

Manchester Dry Docks Company Ltd. Works, fitted with most modern equipment for ship repairing, comprising three graving docks—No. 1, 535 feet in length, 65 feet wide ; No. 2, 500 in length, 65 feet wide ; and No. 3, 450 feet in length, 65 feet wide.   No. 1 dock has 20 ft. 6 in. of water on blocks.   No. 2 dock has 18 feet of water on blocks.   No. 3 dock has 19 feet of water on blocks.   There is also a pontoon dry dock, 260 feet long, 45 feet wide, with a lifting capacity of 2,000 tons.

Salford Quay.   1,100 feet.

Docks 9, 8, 7, 6.—For ocean-going vessels.—See Manchester Docks section, this page.

British Oil and Cake Mills Ltd.—Works for the manufacture of cotton seed oil oil cake, feeding stuffs, etc., with wharf alongside.

Trafford Wharf.—1,653 feet.

Morrell Mills & Co. Ltd., Ship Repairers, Engineers, Boilermakers, Carpenters, Joiners, etc.

Co-operative Wholesale Society Ltd. Sun Mills.—Flour and Provender Mills with deepwater wharf alongside, 500 ft. long, and 170 ft. for small vessels.   Grain is discharged by the Society's elevators from vessel or barge alongside and conveyed by overhead conveyor direct into the mill.   The plant comprises three elevator legs, each of which is capable of lifting 125 tons per hour, and one elevator leg of 60 tons per hour capacity. An automatic weighing machine is provided at each leg.

Docks Railway Swing Bridge.—Carrying dock railways over the Ship Canal, also providing communication with Trafford Park.

Robertson Buckley & Co. Ltd.—Wharf 450 ft. long ; excavated to 15' 0" and warehouses.

Trafford Road Swing Bridge.—Span, 75 feet.   English & Scottish C.W.S.,

English & Scottish C.W.S.

R. & W. Paul Ltd.

Colgate Palmolive Ltd.

J. Jackson & Sons.

Trafford Mills Ltd.

Pomona Docks.—Nos 4, 3, 2, 1 for coastwise and near-Continental traffic.

Woden Street Footbridge.	**New Botany Shed.**
Hulme Locks Entrance to	**Marshall's Side Warehouse**
Bridgewater Canal.	(3 Storeys).
Regent Road Bridge.	**Victoria Warehouse** (5 Storeys).
Prince's Bridge.	**Albert Warehouse** (5 Storeys).
New Botany Warehouse (5 Storeys).	**Albert Shed.**

BRIDGES.

Provided the height of masts and/or funnels is not more than 71 ft. 6 ins from the water line vessels can pass under the fixed bridges on the Ship Canal under normal conditions.   As, however, the headway is necessarily less during periods of floods or high tides,-a vessel, in order to avoid detention, should reduce masts and funnels to 70 feet above the water–line.   Equipment is available at Eastham for removing and replacing the tops of masts and/or funnels.

DIMENSIONS OF LOCKS.	Rise Ft. In.	From Eastham Locks Miles
Queen Elizabeth II ....807 by 100 ft.	—	.. —
Eastham..............600 by 80 ft. and 350 by 50 ft. ..	—	.. —
Latchford ....600 by 65 ft. ,, 350 by 45 ft. ..	14 6	.. 21
Irlam ....600 by 65 ft. ,, 350 by 45 ft. ..	16 0	.. 25¾
Barton ....600 by 65 ft. ,, 350 by 45 ft. ..	15 0	.. 30¾
Mode Wheel ....600 by 65 ft. .. 350 by 45 ft. ..	13 0	.. 33¾

MANCHESTER DOCKS.

The Dock Estate covers an area of 700 acres, of which 179 acres is water space. Quays are 5¼ miles in length. The height of the quay wall is about 8 feet above ordinary water level.

The Dimensions of the Docks, etc., are :—

No. 1	..	780 by 120 feet.	No. 6	..	850 by 225 feet.
„ 2	..	600 by 150 „	„ 7	..	1,160 by 225 „
„ 3	..	600 by 150 „	„ 8	..	1,340 by 250 „
„ 4	..	560 by 150 „	„ 9	..	2,700 by 250 „

Trafford Wharf—Length, 1,653 feet.
Salford Quay—Length, 1,100 feet.

Queen Elizabeth II Dock, Eastham.—The dock covers an area of 19 acres in the form of a square and possesses four berths each capable of accommodating a super tanker.

Berth No. 1	...	800 feet	Berth No. 3	...	900 feet
Berth No. 2	...	725 „	Berth No. 4	...	730 „

Depth of water in dock ... ... 40 feet

EQUIPMENT.

The Dock equipment includes :—

CRANES—9 hydraulic, 48 steam, 191 electric luffing and jib cranes with radii of from 16 to 45 feet, capable of lifting from 1 to 7¼ tons to a height from rail level of from 13 to 70 feet; a floating, electric derricking crane with a lifting capacity of 120 tons to a height of 60 feet from water level with an out-reach of 30 feet (the crane can also be used for salvage duties up to a capacity of 250 tons and for the handling of lock gates) ; 57 electric hoists of various types ; a floating self-propelling derricking and revolving crane with a lifting capacity of 60 tons ; 30-ton steam crane.

Supplementary to the above are 32 mobile cranes ; 42 electric-battery trucks, 6 timber straddle carriers and other specialised mechanical equipment. A fleet of lighters and barges is also available.

RAILWAYS—75 locomotives and 2,900 railway wagons for the haulage of traffic over the Company's railways which exceed 200 track miles in extent serving the Canal system and completely intersecting the Dock Estate ; 11 hydraulic and 60 electric capstans on the quays and Dock Estate.

The dock system is connected to all main line railways, viz. :—

The London, Midland Region, and Eastern Region via Bridgewater Junction.

The London, Midland Region at Weaste Junction and New Barna Junction, Salford.

Traffic is conveyed in railway wagons between the various loading and discharging berths at the Docks and other places on the Ship Canal and over the above lines to every railway station in Great Britain.

Note.—All berths are rail connected.

QUAY SHEDS AND WAREHOUSES.

Quay sheds and warehouses have been provided as follows :—

Quay Sheds.		Warehouses.	
12 Single floor	Salford	13 Seven floor
1 Two „	Trafford Wharf	1 Single „
6 Three „	Irwell Park	4 Single „
5 Four „	Vere Street	3 Single „
16 Five „		

D

290

The schedule hereinbefore referred to:–

SCHEDULE OF SIGNALS 1990

I. SOUND SIGNALS

Number of Blasts	Meaning of Signal
1. **One Prolonged** .... (When inward bound)	To call attention generally, e.g. when i. Approaching another vessel; ii. Approaching or passing a lock; iii. Approaching a swing bridge which is required to be opened;
One Prolonged and one Short .... (When outward bound)	iv. Approaching a bend; or v. At intervals of not more than two minutes when navigating in or near an area of restricted visibility.
2. **One Prolonged and Two Short**	(To stern tug) – "Pull on port quarter"
3. **One Prolonged and Three Short** ..., ...	(To stern tug) – "Pull on starboard quarter'
4. **One Very Short ($\frac{1}{2}$ second duration)**	(To forward tug when getting under way) – "Ready, go ahead". (To stern tug) – "Cancel last signal".
5. **Three Short**	(To stern tug) – "Pull astern".
6. **Four Short**	(*a*) (To tugs) – "Hold ship in position". (*b*) "Am holding ship in position".
7. **One Prolonged, One Short and One Prolonged**	(To stern tug) – "Am about to pass another vessel".
8. **Four Short and One Prolonged**	"Vessel temporarily out of control".
9. **One Prolonged, Two Short and One Prolonged**	"About to swing".
10. **One Very Long of not less than 8 seconds duration**	"Have completed swing".
11. **Three Prolonged and Three Short**	"Attendance of boatman is required".

The following signals shall be given by means of MOUTH WHISTLE:–

Number of Blasts	Meaning of Signal
12. **One Prolonged and Two Short**	(To forward tug) – "Pull on port bow".
13. **One Prolonged and Three Short**	(To forward tug) – "Pull on starboard bow".
14. **One Short**	(To forward tug) – "Cancel last signal".

II. OTHER SIGNALS
(a) General

BY DAY (*i.e.* Between Sunrise and Sunset)	MEANING OF SIGNAL	BY NIGHT (*i.e.* Between Sunset and Sunrise)
15. Pennant half-mast	**Vessel moored in the canal** where traffic passes	(*a*) Two white lights on off side, one forward and one aft where best seen (*b*) On craft less than 50 metres long – one white light on off side where best seen
16.	**Tug engaged** in towing	As prescribed by rule 24 of the Collision Regulations except that no towing light need be shown above the stern light
17. Blue flashing light at Eastham crane berth	**Masting Crane** operations in progress (see bye-law 21)	Blue flashing light at Eastham crane berth
18. One white flashing light over one red flashing light at Ince	Outward bound vessels shall not proceed beyond Ince tying-up berth (see bye-law 24)	One white flashing light over one red flashing light at Ince

(b) Locks

BY DAY (*i.e.* Between Sunrise and Sunset)	MEANING OF SIGNAL	BY NIGHT (*i.e.* Between Sunset and Sunrise)
19. AT EASTHAM LOCKS **Vessels inward bound** (*a*) White light occulting every two seconds	**Lock available**	White light occulting every two seconds
(*b*) Red light occulting every two seconds	**Lock not available**	Red light occulting every two seconds
(*c*) Green light occulting every two seconds	**Lock gates open.** Water in the Mersey and the canal on the same level	Green light occulting every two seconds
(*d*) Two white circular shapes 1.2 metres in diameter spaced 2.4 metres apart in a horizontal place at a height of 15.7 metres above Mean High Water Springs	**Emergency signal** to inward bound vessels: large lock inoperative	One amber flashing light visible from seaward (two seconds flash, four seconds lapse) at a height of 17.5 metres above Mean High Water Springs and having a visibility of five miles
Vessels outward bound		
(*e*) White flashing light	**Lock available**	White flashing light
(*f*) Red flashing light	**Lock not available**	Red flashing light
(*g*) Green fixed light	**Lock gates open.** Water in the Mersey and the canal on the same level	Green fixed light

294

BY DAY (*i.e.* Between Sunrise and Sunset)	MEANING OF SIGNAL	BY NIGHT (*i.e.* Between Sunset and Sunrise)
20. AT QUEEN ELIZABETH II LOCK		
(*a*) Three fixed green lights in triangular form on outer bullnose	**Lock available**	Three fixed green lights in triangular form on outer bullnose
(*b*) Three fixed red lights in triangular form on outer bullnose	**Lock not available**	Three fixed red lights in triangular form on outer bullnose
(*c*) Three flashing red lights in triangular form on outer bullnose	**Lock not available** and lock sluicing in operation	Three flashing red lights in triangular form on outer bullnose
21. AT LOCKS OTHER THAN EASTHAM AND QUEEN ELIZABETH II LOCK		
(*a*) White flashing light	**Lock available**	White flashing light
(*b*) Red flashing light	**Lock not available**	Red flashing light

(c) Swingbridges
22. BRIDGE CLOSED

A red fixed light exhibited from the side structure of the bridge and positioned immediately over the centre of the fairway.

When the red fixed light is shown over the centre of the fairway no vessel shall approach except small craft able to pass safely under the bridge.

23. BRIDGE OPEN

In addition to the red fixed light (section 22) which will appear at the side of the fairway to which the bridge is swung an additional red fixed light showing in one direction and a green flashing light showing in the opposite direction.

This additional light is positioned at the top centre of the bridge structure at all swing bridges except Barton Road Swingbridge where it is displayed from a post at each extremity of the bridge island.

When two red fixed lights are shown at the side of the fairway the bridge is swung for another vessel proceeding in the opposite direction and the vessel signalled by two red fixed lights shall not attempt to pass the bridge but shall keep a reasonable distance away from it and make room for the safe passage of the vessel proceeding in the opposite direction.

When the red fixed light and the green flashing light are shown at the side of the fairway the bridge is open for the passage of the vessel signalled thereby and she may proceed.

No vessel shall proceed to pass a swingbridge until the bridge is seen to be completely swung open and the green flashing light is seen in addition to the red fixed light, whereupon she may proceed with caution.

24. EMERGENCY

A red flashing light in addition to or in place of signals 22 and 23 to indicate a bridge failure or other emergency.

The red flashing light indicates that the bridge cannot be fully opened due to mechanical fault or other cause and no vessel shall approach from either direction until the signal is cancelled whereupon a vessel may proceed with caution when signalled accordingly.

BRIDGE CLOSED (Do not approach)	BRIDGE OPEN (Do not approach)	BRIDGE OPEN (Proceed with caution)
RED FIXED LIGHT over centre of fairway	RED FIXED LIGHT and RED FIXED LIGHT at side of fairway	GREEN FLASHING LIGHT and RED FIXED LIGHT at side of fairway
EMERGENCY SIGNAL in any position – RED FLASHING LIGHT		

Note: Except in time of flood or high tide or with the permission of the harbour master no swingbridge will be swung for vessels which are fitted with appliances for lowering their masts and/or funnels to enable them to pass safely under the bridges.

[2 & 3 Geo. 5.] *Pilotage Act*, 1913. [Ch. **31.**]

CHAPTER 31.

An Act to consolidate and amend the Law relating to Pilotage. [7th March 1913.]

A.D. 1913.

BE it enacted by the King's most Excellent Majesty, by and with the advice and consent of the Lords Spiritual and Temporal, and Commons, in this present Parliament assembled, and by the authority of the same, as follows :

Part I.

Revision of Pilotage Organisation.

1. The Board of Trade shall take steps to obtain information with respect to pilotage organisation at the various ports in the United Kingdom, and, by the exercise of their powers under this Act to make Pilotage Orders, shall carry into effect any re-organisation or improvement of organisation which the Board may consider necessary or expedient at any port, and shall also at any port deal by Pilotage Order with any Act, order, charter, custom, byelaw, regulation, or provision in force at the port with a view to rendering the law relating to pilotage at the various ports in the United Kingdom accessible and, so far as possible, uniform.

Improvement of pilotage organisation.

2.—(1) The Board of Trade shall also take steps to obtain information with respect to the byelaws as to pilotage in force at the various ports in the United Kingdom, and, after consulting with the pilotage authority at the port and considering any byelaws proposed by that authority, shall, when necessary or expedient and with a view to securing, so far as practicable, uniformity of administration and to carrying out any changes consequent on the passing of this Act, make recommendations for the substitution of new byelaws for those in force at the port, or in case there are no such byelaws in force, for the making of such byelaws as may be required at the port.

Recommendations with respect to pilotage byelaws.

(2) If a pilotage authority fail to submit byelaws in accordance with the recommendations for confirmation by the Board of Trade under this Act, the Board may treat the byelaws

5

297

A.D. 1913. recommended by the Board as if they were byelaws submitted
— to them by the pilotage authority for confirmation, and those
byelaws, when confirmed by the Board of Trade in accordance
with this Act, shall have the same effect as if they had been so
submitted.

Commissioners for the purpose of Part I. **3.**—(1) The Board of Trade shall appoint such persons as
they think fit to act as Commissioners for the purposes of this
Act, but the appointment of any person appointed to be a
Commissioner under this section shall not have effect beyond
the first day of January nineteen hundred and seventeen, or such
date, not being more than five years later, as the Board of Trade,
with the approval of the Treasury, may determine.

(2) The Board of Trade may appoint and employ such
officers or other persons as they think fit to assist any persons
acting as Commissioners in the execution of their duties under
this Act.

(3) The salaries and remuneration of any persons acting as
Commissioners and of any persons so appointed or employed
shall be determined by the Board of Trade with the approval
of the Treasury, and any such salaries and remuneration, and
all expenses incurred by the Board of Trade in the execution of
this Act, shall be paid out of moneys provided by Parliament.

Schemes for reorganisation of pilotage at ports. **4.**—(1) With a view to the preparation of schemes for
the re-organisation or improvement of organisation of pilotage,
the Board of Trade shall cause local inquiries to be held by
any persons acting as Commissioners under this Act at the
various ports of the United Kingdom, except in cases where
the pilotage authority of the port has submitted, in accordance
with this Act, a scheme for the purpose to the Board of Trade,
and the Board of Trade are satisfied that the scheme so
submitted, with such modifications (if any) as may be made
by the Board, is adequate for the purpose, or the pilotage
authority have satisfied the Board of Trade that no scheme for
the re-organisation or improvement of organisation of pilotage
at the port is necessary or expedient. Any such local inquiry
may, if the Board think it necessary or desirable, include an
inquiry into the byelaws in force at the port where the inquiry
is held, and into the operation of those byelaws.

(2) Where any such inquiry is held at any port, the person
holding the inquiry shall make a report to the Board of Trade
recommending to the Board a scheme for the purpose of the
re-organisation or improvement of organisation of pilotage at
the port, or if a scheme has been submitted by the pilotage
authority, recommending any amendments which it appears
expedient to make in the scheme so submitted.

(3) The Board of Trade may, in any case they think fit,
group ports for the purpose of any such local inquiry, and in
that case the ports so grouped shall be dealt with at the same
inquiry.

6

[2 & 3 Geo. 5.]   *Pilotage Act*, 1913.   [Ch. **31.**]

(4) Any pilotage authority may, within three months after the passing of this Act, give notice to the Board of Trade of their intention to submit a scheme to the Board for the purpose of the re-organisation or improvement of organisation of pilotage at their port, and shall in such a case also give such public notice of their intention as the Board may require, and if such a scheme is so submitted to the Board within nine months after the passing of this Act, the scheme shall be treated as a scheme submitted to the Board in accordance with this Act.

A.D. 1913.
—

5.—(1) Notice of any local inquiry to be held under this Part of this Act shall be given and published in such manner as the Board of Trade think best fitted for giving information of the time and place of the inquiry to those concerned, and all persons interested shall be permitted to attend and make representations.

Provision as to local inquiries.

(2) Any person holding a local inquiry shall have power, by summons signed by him, to require the attendance of all such persons as he thinks fit to call and examine for the purpose of the inquiry, and shall have power to require the production of all books, papers, and documents which he considers important for that purpose.

(3) Any persons attending as witnesses at any such local inquiry shall be allowed such expenses as would be allowed to witnesses attending before a court of record, or in Scotland before the court of session, and in case of dispute as to the amount to be allowed, the dispute shall be referred by any person holding the local inquiry to a master or district registrar of the supreme court, or in Scotland to the auditor of accounts in the court of session, who on request signed by him shall ascertain and certify the proper amount of the expenses.

(4) If any person without reasonable excuse, the proof whereof shall lie on him, fails to comply with any summons or requisition of a person holding a local inquiry under this section, or impedes a person holding a local inquiry in the execution of his duty, he shall be liable on summary conviction in respect of each offence to a fine not exceeding five pounds, and, in addition, to a fine not exceeding one pound for every day during which the offence continues.

6. The Board of Trade, before making recommendations to a pilotage authority under this Act for the substitution of new byelaws for those in force in any port, and a pilotage authority, before submitting any scheme to the Board for the re-organisation or improvement of organisation of pilotage at their port shall, unless pilots are directly represented on the authority or on a pilotage committee of the authority, take steps to ascertain the opinion of the pilots at the port with respect to the matter in question.

Consultation with pilots as to byelaws and schemes.

7

A.D. 1913.

Part II.

General Pilotage Law.

Pilotage Orders.

Power of Board
of Trade
to make Pilot-
age Orders.

7.—(1) The Board of Trade may, by Order made under this Act (in this Act referred to as a Pilotage Order)—

(*a*) make such rearrangement of pilotage districts and pilotage authorities as the Board think necessary or expedient ; and

(*b*) establish new pilotage districts and new pilotage authorities and abolish existing pilotage districts and existing pilotage authorities in cases where it appears to the Board necessary or expedient ; and

(*c*) define the limits of pilotage districts, distinguishing as respects any pilotage district in part of which pilotage is compulsory and in part of which pilotage is not compulsory, the part of the district in which pilotage is compulsory ; and

(*d*) provide for the incorporation of any pilotage authority, and make such alteration in the constitution of any pilotage authority with reference to their powers and duties as pilotage authority, and such provisions as to the appointment of committees (including, if it is thought fit, persons not members of the authority), and as to the relations between the authority and the committee, as the Board think necessary or expedient ; and

(*e*) empower a pilotage authority to delegate to a committee thereof any of its powers and duties, and provide, if it seems necessary or desirable, that the decisions of the committee on questions so delegated shall not require confirmation by the pilotage authority ; and

(*f*) make such provision for the direct representation of pilots and shipowners on any pilotage authority or committee of a pilotage authority as the Board think necessary or expedient ; and

(*g*) in cases where a pilotage authority have powers and duties as to other matters as well as pilotage, provide for their accounts as pilotage authority being kept separate from their accounts in relation to other matters ; and

(*h*) provide that pilotage shall be compulsory in any area where it has previously not been compulsory, or provide, in connection with any rearrangement of a pilotage district, that pilotage shall be non-compulsory in any area where it has been compulsory, subject to provision being also made for the payment of compensation to the pilots concerned for any loss or damage which may be incurred by them in consequence of such rearrangement ; and

8

(*i*) authorise, where it appears expedient, any pilotage authority to make byelaws providing for the grant of certificates (in this Act referred to as deep sea certificates) certifying that persons are qualified to act as pilots of ships for any part of the sea or channels outside the district of any pilotage authority, so, however, that a pilot holding such a certificate shall not be entitled to supersede any other person as pilot of a ship ; and

(*j*) provide that any Act (other than this Act), order, charter, custom, byelaw, regulation, or provision shall, so far as it relates to pilotage, cease to have effect within any pilotage district or as respects any pilotage authority, but may re-enact the whole or any part thereof so far as is not inconsistent with the provisions of this Act ; and

(*k*) provide for compensation being paid to any pilots for any loss or damage which may be incurred by them in consequence of any Order abolishing or rearranging any pilotage districts ; and

(*l*) make any provisions which appear necessary or expedient for the purpose of giving full effect to the Order.

(2) Provision shall be made by Pilotage Order for the direct representation of pilots either on the pilotage authority or on the committee of the pilotage authority of any district where there are not less than six licensed pilots if a majority of the pilots licensed for the district signify in writing to the Board of Trade that they desire such representation, and, where such provision is made, provision shall also be made for the representation of shipowners on the authority or committee, as the case may be.

(3) A Pilotage Order establishing a pilotage authority for any pilotage district shall provide for the representation on the pilotage authority of any dock or harbour authority having jurisdiction within the district which was represented on the pilotage authority for the district at the time of the passing of this Act, and which desires to be so represented.

(4) A Pilotage Order shall not be made by the Board of Trade except—

(*a*) for any of the purposes of Part I. of this Act ; or

(*b*) on the application in writing of any person interested in the pilotage of any pilotage district or in the operation of the laws relating to pilotage in that district or the administration of those laws.

(5) A Pilotage Order shall require confirmation by Parliament—

(*a*) if it is an Order made for any of the purposes of Part I. of this Act ; and

(*b*) if, whatever the purpose for which it is made, a petition is presented to the Board of Trade against the Order

A.D. 1913.
——

9

[Cʜ. **31**.]   *Pilotage Act,* 1913.   [2 & 3 Gᴇᴏ. 5.]

A.D. 1913.   by any person appearing to the Board of Trade to be interested in the administration of pilotage in the district within six weeks after the Order is published and the petition is not withdrawn.

(6) A Pilotage Order which does not require confirmation by Parliament shall have effect as if enacted in this Act.

(7) The provisions contained in the First Schedule to this Act shall have effect with respect to Pilotage Orders.

Pilotage Districts and Authorities.

Pilotage districts and pilotage authorities.   **8.**—(1) For the purposes of this Act the districts established as pilotage districts under Pilotage Orders made under this Act shall be pilotage districts, and the pilotage authorities shall be the pilotage authorities as constituted by Pilotage Orders made under this Act.

(2) Until otherwise provided by Pilotage Order made under this Act, every pilotage district which is, at the time of the passing of this Act, a pilotage district shall continue to be a pilotage district, and every pilotage authority which is a pilotage authority at the time of the passing of this Act shall continue to be a pilotage authority.

Advisory Committee.

Power to appoint advisory committee.   **9.**—(1) The Board of Trade may appoint an advisory committee for the purpose of advising them with reference to the exercise of their powers or the performance of their duties under this Act, consisting of such persons as they may appoint, being pilots, shipowners, representatives of pilotage authorities, representatives of dock and harbour authorities,or other persons representing the interests principally affected, or having special knowledge of the subject-matter.

(2) There shall be paid to the members of any such committee out of moneys provided by Parliament such allowances and expenses as the Board of Trade may fix with the consent of the Treasury.

Compulsory Pilotage.

Continuation of existing compulsory districts and abolition of existing exemptions.   **10.**—(1) Subject to the provisions of any Pilotage Order, pilotage shall continue to be compulsory in every pilotage district in which it was compulsory at the time of the passing of this Act, and shall continue not to be compulsory in every pilotage district in which it was not compulsory at the time of the passing of this Act, and subject to the provisions of this Act all exemptions from compulsory pilotage in force at the date of the passing of this Act shall cease to have effect.

(2) Any reference in this Act to a pilotage district in which pilotage is compulsory shall, in the case of a district in which pilotage is compulsory only in part of the district, be construed, if the context so requires, as a reference to that part of the district only.

10

11.—(1) Every ship (other than an excepted ship) while navigating in a pilotage district in which pilotage is compulsory for the purpose of entering, leaving, or making use of any port in the district, and every ship carrying passengers (other than an excepted ship), while navigating for any such purpose as aforesaid in any pilotage district (whether pilotage is compulsory or not compulsory in that district) shall be either—

A.D. 1913.

Obligations where pilotage is compulsory.

> (a) under the pilotage of a licensed pilot of the district; or
> (b) under the pilotage of a master or mate possessing a pilotage certificate for the district who is bonâ fide acting as master or mate of the ship.

(2) If any ship (other than an excepted ship) in circumstances in which pilotage is compulsory under this section, is not under pilotage as required by this section, after a licensed pilot of the district has offered to take charge of the ship, the master of that ship shall be liable in respect of each offence to a fine not exceeding double the amount of the pilotage dues that could be demanded for the conduct of the ship.

(3) For the purposes of this Act the following ships are excepted ships :—

> (a) Ships belonging to His Majesty ;
> (b) Pleasure yachts ;
> (c) Fishing vessels ;
> (d) Ferry boats plying as such exclusively within the limits of a harbour authority ;
> (e) Ships of less than fifty tons gross tonnage ;
> (f) Ships exempted from compulsory pilotage by byelaw as hereinafter provided in this section.

(4) A pilotage authority may by byelaw made under this Act exempt from compulsory pilotage in their district any of the following classes of ships, if not carrying passengers, up to such limit of gross tonnage in each case as may be fixed by the byelaw, that is to say :—

> (i) Ships trading coastwise ;
> (ii) Home trade ships trading otherwise than coastwise ;
> (iii) Ships whose ordinary course of navigation does not extend beyond the seaward limits of a harbour authority, whilst navigating within those limits or within such parts thereof as may be specified in the byelaw :

Provided that, if any such byelaw appears to the Board of Trade to exempt from compulsory pilotage ships of any class or description which were not at the date of the passing of this Act in practice exempted in the district to which the byelaw relates, the Board shall not confirm the byelaw, but may, if they think fit, submit to Parliament a Bill confirming the byelaw with or without modifications. and such Bill shall be treated as if it were a Bill confirming a Pilotage Order, and the provisions of this Act with respect to such Bills shall apply accordingly.

11

[Ch. **31**.]   *Pilotage Act*, 1913.   [2 & 3 Geo. 5.]

A.D. 1913.
———

(5) For the purposes of this section, a ship which habitually trades to or from any port or ports outside the British Islands shall not be deemed to be trading coastwise, and a ship which habitually trades to or from any port outside the home trade limits shall not be deemed to be a home trade ship, by reason only that she is for the time being engaged on a voyage between ports in the British Islands, or within the home trade limits, as the case may be.

Exemption from compulsory pilotage of ships belonging to certain public authorities.

12. The provisions of this Act with respect to compulsory pilotage shall not apply to tugs, dredgers, sludge-vessels, barges, and other similar craft—

(*a*) belonging to or hired by a dock, harbour or river authority whilst employed in the exercise of the statutory powers or duties of the authority and navigating within any pilotage district which includes within its limits the whole or any part of the area of the authority ; or

(*b*) belonging to a local authority whilst employed in the exercise of the statutory powers or duties of the authority and navigating within the pilotage district within which the port to which they belong is situate :

Provided that, where in any pilotage district any of the classes of vessels aforesaid were at the time of the passing of this Act in practice subject to compulsory pilotage, the pilotage authority may by byelaw provide that any of such classes of vessels shall continue to be so subject.

Provision with respect to ships calling at a port for the purpose only of taking pilot.

13. A ship calling at a port in a pilotage district for the purpose only of taking on board or landing a pilot belonging to some other pilotage district shall not, for the purpose of the provisions of this Act relating to compulsory pilotage, be deemed to be navigating in the first-mentioned district for the purpose of entering, leaving, or making use of that port.

Provision against extension of defence of compulsory pilotage.

14. Notwithstanding anything in any Pilotage Order made under this Act, any area in which pilotage was not compulsory at the date of the passing of this Act shall be deemed to be an area in which pilotage is not compulsory for the purpose of determining the liability of the owner or master of a ship being navigated in the area for any loss or damage occasioned by or arising out of the navigation of such ship.

Liability of owner or master in the case of a vessel under pilotage.

15.—(1) Notwithstanding anything in any public or local Act, the owner or master of a vessel navigating under circumstances in which pilotage is compulsory shall be answerable for any loss or damage caused by the vessel or by any fault of the navigation of the vessel in the same manner as he would if pilotage were not compulsory.

(2) This section shall not take effect until the first day of January, nineteen hundred and eighteen, or such earlier date as His Majesty may fix by Order in Council, certifying that it

12

2 & 3 GEO. 5.]　　　*Pilotage Act, 1913.*　　　[CH. **31.**]

is necessary to bring the section into operation in order to enable　A.D. 1913.
His Majesty to comply with an international convention.

(3) As from the date of the coming into operation of this
section, section six hundred and thirty-three of the Merchant　57 & 58 Vict.
Shipping Act, 1894, shall cease to have effect.　　　c. 60.

Power of Pilotage Authorities to license Pilots and make Byelaws.

16. Subject to the provisions of this Act, a pilotage authority　Powers of
may license pilots for their district, and do all such things as　pilotage autho-
may be necessary or expedient for carrying into effect their　pilots for their
powers and duties.　　district.

17.—(1) A pilotage authority may by byelaws made under　Power of pilot-
this Act—　　age authorities
to make bye-

　(a) determine the qualification in respect of age, physical　laws.
　　　fitness, time of service, local knowledge, skill, character,
　　　and otherwise to be required from persons applying
　　　to be licensed by them as pilots; provide for the
　　　examination of such persons, and fix the term for
　　　which a licence is to be in force, and the conditions
　　　under which a licence may be renewed ; and

　(b) fix the limit (if any) on the number of pilots to be
　　　licensed, and provide for the method in which and
　　　the conditions under which the list of pilots is to be
　　　filled up ; and

　(c) provide generally for the good government of pilots
　　　licensed by the authority, and of apprentices, and in
　　　particular for ensuring their good conduct and con-
　　　stant attendance to and effectual performance of their
　　　duties, whether at sea or on shore ; and

　(d) determine the system to be adopted with respect to the
　　　supply and employment of pilots, and provide, so far
　　　as necessary, for the approval, licensing, and working
　　　of pilot boats in the district, and for the establish-
　　　ment and regulation of pilot boat companies ; and

　(e) provide for the punishment of any breach of any byelaws
　　　made by them for the good government of pilots or
　　　apprentices by the infliction of fines not exceeding
　　　twenty pounds (to be recoverable as fines are re-
　　　coverable under the Merchant Shipping Acts, 1894
　　　to 1907), without prejudice to their powers under
　　　this Act to revoke or suspend the licence in the case
　　　of any such breach of byelaw ; and

　(f) fix for the district the rates of payments to be made
　　　in respect of the services of a licensed pilot (in this
　　　Act referred to as pilotage dues), and define the
　　　circumstances and conditions under which pilotage
　　　dues may be payable on different scales and provide
　　　for the collection and distribution of pilotage dues ;
　　　and

13

No tides to Stem

A.D. 1913.

(g) if and so far as it appears to the authority to be generally desired by the pilots concerned, provide for the pooling of pilotage dues earned by the licensed pilots or by any class of pilots in the district ; and

(h) provide for a deduction being made from any sums received by pilots of any sums required for meeting the administrative expenses of the authority, or any contributions required for any fund established for the payment of pensions or other benefits to pilots, their widows or children (in this Act referred to as a pilots' benefit fund) ; and

(i) provide, if and so far as it appears to the authority to be generally desired by the pilots, for bonds (the penalty of which shall not in any case exceed one hundred pounds) being given by pilots for the purpose of the provisions of this Act limiting pilots' liability ; and

(j) establish, either alone or in conjunction with any other pilotage authority, pilots' benefit funds, and provide for the direct payment to any such fund of any contributions by pilots towards the fund, or of any part of the ordinary receipts of the pilotage authority, and also for the administration of any such fund and for the conditions of participation in any such fund ; and

(k) provide for the method of conducting the examination of masters and mates applying for pilotage certificates so as to maintain a proper standard of efficiency ; and

(l) prohibit the grant of pilotage certificates to masters or mates who do not hold at least a mate's certificate of competency recognised under Part II. of the Merchant Shipping Act, 1894 ; and

(m) provide that a pilotage certificate shall not be renewed without re-examination unless the master or mate has made not less than a specified number of visits to the port as master or mate of any ship in respect of which the certificate is granted ; and

(n) if the pilotage authority are an authority authorised to grant deep sea certificates by virtue of a Pilotage Order made with reference to that authority, provide for the grant of deep sea certificates ; and

(o) apply any byelaws made under this section for the good government of pilots and the punishment of any breach of any such byelaw, with any necessary modifications, to masters and mates holding pilotage certificates ; and

(p) require the owners of ships, whose masters or mates hold pilotage certificates, to contribute towards the pilot fund or account of the pilotage district, and require the holders of such certificates to make a periodical return to them of the pilotage services rendered by

14

them; provided that the contribution so required A.D. 1913. from an owner shall not exceed such proportion of the pilotage dues which would have been payable in respect of the ship if the master or mate had not held a pilotage certificate, as may be fixed by the Board of Trade ; and

(*q*) provide for any matter for which provision is to be made or may be made under this Act by byelaw.

(2) A byelaw shall not take effect unless it has been submitted to the Board of Trade and confirmed by them with or without modifications.

(3) Notice of any byelaw proposed to be submitted for confirmation under this section shall, before it is so submitted be published in such manner as the Board of Trade direct.

18.—(1) If at any port either—

(*a*) a majority of the licensed pilots belonging to the port; or

(*b*) any number of persons, not less than six, being masters, owners, or insurers of vessels using the port ; or

(*c*) a dock or harbour authority not being the pilotage authority ;

Power of Board of Trade on representation to revoke or vary byelaws or require pilotage authority to make byelaws.

object to any byelaw in force at the port, or desire that any byelaw should be in force at the port which is not in force therein, they may make a representation to the Board of Trade to that effect, and the Board of Trade if the representation appears to them reasonable after giving the pilotage authority, and, if they think fit, any other persons, an opportunity of making representations on the subject, may, by order, revoke, vary, or add to any byelaw to which objection is made, or require the pilotage authority to submit to them for confirmation a byelaw for the purpose of giving effect to the representation.

(2) Any byelaw revoked by any such order shall cease to have effect, and any byelaw to which additions are made or which is varied or added to, shall have effect with the variations or additions made by the order.

(3) If a pilotage authority fail to submit to the Board of Trade for confirmation a byelaw in accordance with an order made under this section, the Board of Trade may treat the byelaw which they have required the pilotage authority to submit to them as a byelaw submitted to them by the authority, and confirm it accordingly, and the byelaw so confirmed shall have effect as if it had been made and confirmed in accordance with this Act.

. **19.** The grant or renewal of a licence to a pilot by a pilotage authority under the powers given to them by this Act does not impose any liability on the authority for any loss occasioned by any act or default of the pilot.

Licensing of pilots by pilotage authority not to involve any liability.

15

[CH. **31**.]   *Pilotage Act, 1913.*   [2 & 3 GEO. 5.]

A.D. 1913.

Form of pilot's licence, and production and return of pilot's licence to pilotage authority.

20.—(1) A pilot's licence shall be in a form approved for the time being by the Board of Trade.

(2) A licensed pilot shall, when required by the pilotage authority by whom the licence has been granted, produce his licence to the authority, and, in case his licence is revoked or suspended, shall deliver up his licence to the authority.

(3) On the death of a licensed pilot, the person into whose hands his licence comes shall without delay transmit it to the pilotage authority by whom it was granted.

(4) If any licensed pilot or other person fails to comply with the requirements of this section, he shall be liable in respect of each offence to a fine not exceeding ten pounds.

Receipts and expenses of pilotage authority.

21.—(1) All receipts of a pilotage authority in their capacity as such (other than any money received by them on behalf of and paid over to any pilot, or if the authority administer a pilots' benefit fund, any sums received by them as direct payments for that fund), shall be paid into a separate fund or account, to be called the pilot fund or account of the pilotage district.

(2) All expenses incurred by a pilotage authority in the exercise of their powers or performance of their duties as such authority shall be paid out of their pilot fund or account, and, except so far as may be provided to the contrary by byelaw, subject to the payment of those expenses, the balance shall in each year be applied for the purposes of any pilots' benefit fund established in the district, and so far as not required for that purpose shall be applied for the benefit of pilots in such manner as may be determined by the pilotage authority with the approval of the Board of Trade.

(3) A separate account shall be kept by any pilotage authority who administer a pilots' benefit fund of all moneys received by them as payments to that fund, or for the benefit of that fund, and money standing to the credit of that account shall not be applicable to any purpose other than the purposes of the fund.

(4) Nothing in this section shall prevent a pilotage authority which owns or hires the pilot boats for the district from keeping a separate account in respect of such boats.

Returns to be furnished and statements of accounts to be sent to Board of Trade by pilotage authorities.

22.—(1) Every pilotage authority shall deliver triennially, or, if the Board of Trade so direct, at shorter intervals, to the Board, in the form and at the time required by the Board, returns giving such particulars as the Board may by order prescribe with respect to pilotage in their district, and any returns so delivered shall, as soon as may be, be laid before both Houses of Parliament.

(2) Every pilotage authority shall in addition furnish annually to the Board of Trade, at such time as the Board direct, a statement of their accounts in the form prescribed by the Board, duly audited, including a statement of the average gross and net earnings of pilots during the past year, and, where the authority administer a pilots' benefit fund, the separate accounts of that fund, including particulars of the investments if any.

16

(3) Every pilotage authority shall allow the Board of Trade, A.D. 1913. or any person appointed by the Board for the purpose, to inspect any books or documents in the possession of that authority relating to any matter in respect of which a return is required to be delivered or a statement is required to be furnished under this section.

(4) If a pilotage authority refuse or fail without reasonable cause to deliver any return or furnish any statement to the Board of Trade in accordance with this section, His Majesty may by Order in Council suspend the pilotage authority for such time as His Majesty may direct, and thereupon the Board of Trade shall by order direct that, in the meantime, the powers of the authority shall be exercised, and the duties of the authority shall be performed, by such person as they may appoint for the purpose, and any such order shall take effect as if it were enacted in this Act.

Masters' and Mates' Certificates.

23.—(1) A pilotage authority may grant a certificate (in this Grant of Act referred to as a pilotage certificate) to any person who is masters' and bonâ fide the master or mate of any ship if that person applies ficates by pilot-for such a certificate, and if, after examination, they are satisfied age authorities. that, having regard to his skill, experience, and local knowledge, he is capable of piloting the ship of which he is master or mate within their district :

Provided that—

(a) A pilotage certificate shall not be granted to the master or mate of a ship unless he is a British subject, except in the cases for which special provision is made by this Act ; and

(b) In any district where a byelaw is in force prohibiting the grant of pilotage certificates to masters or mates who do not hold at least a mate's certificate of competency recognised under Part II. of the Merchant Shipping Act, 1894, the pilotage authority shall not grant a certificate except to a master or mate holding such a certificate of competency.

(2) A pilotage certificate shall be in a form approved for the time being by the Board of Trade, and shall contain (in addition to any other particulars which may be prescribed) the name of the person to whom the certificate is granted, the name and draught of water of the ship or ships in respect of which it is granted, the limits of the district in respect of which the certificate is granted, and the date on which it was granted.

(3) A pilotage certificate shall not be in force for more than a year from the date on which it is granted, but may be renewed annually by the pilotage authority, subject to the provisions of any byelaw made by that authority as to re-examination.

(4) A pilotage certificate may be granted so as to extend to more than one ship belonging to the same owner, while the

B   17

[Ch. **31**.]   *Pilotage Act,* 1913.   [2 & 3 Geo. 5.]

A.D. 1913. master or mate is bonâ fide acting as master or mate of any
such ship, provided that they are ships of substantially the same
class.

(5) A pilotage authority may, on the application of the
master or mate of a ship, alter his pilotage certificate so as to
relate to any other ship or ships of a not substantially greater
draught of water or tonnage than that to which the certificate
formerly related, to which the master or mate may be transferred,
or so as to cover any ships of substantially the same class and
belonging to the same owner as the ships to which the certificate
already relates.

(6) A pilotage authority may, for the purposes of this section,
treat ships which are shown to their satisfaction to be bonâ fide
under the management of the same person as manager, managing
owner, demisee, or time charterer, as being ships owned by that
person.

Power to grant
certificate to
a master or
mate, not being
a British sub-
ject, under
special circum-
stances.

24.—(1) Notwithstanding anything in this Act, the provisions of this Act as to the renewal of a pilotage certificate shall
apply, with respect to the renewal of a pilotage certificate
granted before the first day of June nineteen hundred and six,
to a master or mate who is not a British subject in the same
manner as they apply to a pilotage certificate granted to a
master or mate who is a British subject.

(2) If any master or mate who is not a British subject shows
to the satisfaction of the Board of Trade that he is the master or
mate of a ship which is of substantially the same class, and is
trading regularly between the same ports as a foreign ship
which, on the first day of June nineteen hundred and six, was
exempt from the obligation to carry a licensed pilot, or had
habitually been piloted by a master or mate of the ship who
held a pilotage certificate, the Board of Trade may authorise the
master or mate to apply to the pilotage authority for a pilotage
certificate under this Act, and the provisions of this Act as to
the granting of a pilotage certificate shall, notwithstanding
anything in this Act, extend to a master or mate so applying for
a certificate, although he is not a British subject, as they extend
to a master or mate who is a British subject :

Provided that if the Admiralty at any time consider that, on
the grounds of public safety, the provisions of this subsection
should not be applicable with respect to any pilotage district or
part of a pilotage district, they may make an order excluding
that district or part of a district from the operation of those
provisions ; and while any such order is in force with respect to
any such district or part of a district, a certificate granted under
those provisions shall not be of any effect within that district or
part of a district.

Provision with
respect to
foreign certifi-
cates of com-
petency.

25. For the purposes of this Act, references to certificates
of competency recognised under Part II. of the Merchant
Shipping Act, 1894, shall be deemed to include references to

18

any certificate of competency granted by the government of a foreign country, being a certificate of a class approved by the Board of Trade for the purpose.

A.D. 1913.
—

Supplementary Provisions as to Licences and Certificates.

26. A pilotage authority may suspend or revoke any pilot's licence or any pilotage certificate granted by them if it appears to them, after giving the holder thereof an opportunity of being heard, that he has been guilty of any offence under this Act or of any breach of any byelaw made by the authority, or of any other misconduct affecting his capability as a pilot, or that he has failed in or neglected his duty as a pilot, or that he has become incompetent to act as pilot; and a licence or certificate, if so revoked, shall cease to have effect, and, if so suspended, shall cease to have effect for the period for which it is suspended :

Suspension or revocation of a pilot's licence or a pilotage certificate.

Provided that in any case where pilots are directly represented on a committee of a pilotage authority, that committee may, until a Pilotage Order is made regulating the relations between the authority and the committee, exercise the powers conferred on a pilotage authority by this section with respect to pilots' licences as though they were the pilotage authority.

27.—(1) If a complaint is made to the Board of Trade that a pilotage authority have—

Appeal by pilot, master, or mate, against action of pilotage authority with respect to pilot's licence or pilotage certificate.

(a) without reasonable cause refused or failed to examine any candidate for a pilot's licence, or a master or mate for a pilotage certificate, or to grant such a licence or certificate after examination ; or

(b) conducted any examination for a pilot's licence or a pilotage certificate improperly or unfairly ; or

(c) imposed conditions on the granting of a pilot's licence or a pilotage certificate which they have no power to impose or which are unreasonable ; or

(d) without reasonable cause refused or failed to renew a pilotage certificate, or, having obtained possession of any such certificate, refused or failed to return it; or

(e) without reasonable cause suspended or revoked a pilotage certificate ; or

(f) in any other manner failed properly to perform their duties under this Act with respect to the matters above-mentioned in this section, or improperly exercised any of their powers under this Act with respect to those matters ;

the Board of Trade shall consider the complaint, and, if they are of opinion that the complaint is in any respect well founded, shall make such order as they think fit for the purpose of redressing the matter complained of, and the pilotage authority shall give effect to any order so made by the Board of Trade.

(2) If a pilotage authority refuse or fail to give effect to any such order of the Board of Trade, the Board of Trade may, for the purpose of giving effect to the order, exercise any powers of

B 2   19.

[CH. **31.**]   *Pilotage Act*, 1913.   [2 & 3 GEO. 5.]

A.D. 1913.
___

Appeal by pilot against action of pilotage authority in suspending, &c. pilot's licence.

the pilotage authority, and anything done by the Board of Trade in the exercise of those powers shall have the same effect as if it had been done by the pilotage authority.

28.—(1) If a pilot is aggrieved by the suspension or revocation by the pilotage authority of his licence, or by the refusal or failure of the pilotage authority to renew his licence, or by the refusal or failure of the pilotage authority who have obtained possession of his licence to return it to him, or by the imposition upon him by the pilotage authority of a fine exceeding two pounds, he may either appeal to a judge of county courts having jurisdiction within the port for which the pilot is licensed, or to a metropolitan police magistrate or stipendiary magistrate having jurisdiction within that port.

(2) For the purpose of hearing the appeal, the judge or magistrate shall sit with an assessor of nautical and pilotage experience selected and summoned by the judge or magistrate.

(3) Objection may be taken to any person proposed to be summoned as an assessor, either personally or in respect of his qualification, and by either party to the appeal.

(4) The judge or magistrate may confirm or reverse the suspension or revocation of the licence, or make such order in the case as may seem just, and his decision shall be final, unless special leave to appeal from the same to the High Court on a question of law or a question of mixed law and fact is given by the judge or magistrate, or by the High Court, and in such case the decision of the High Court shall be final.

(5) The costs incurred by a pilotage authority under this section shall be payable out of any fund applicable to the general expenses of the pilotage authority.

(6) Rules with respect to the procedure under this section (including costs and the remuneration of assessors) may be made, as respects county court judges, by the authority having power to make rules of practice under the County Courts Act, 1888, and as respects metropolitan police and stipendiary magistrates by a Secretary of State, but in either case with the concurrence of the Treasury as to fees.

51 & 52 Vict. c. 43.

(7) In Scotland the appeal under this section shall be to the sheriff having jurisdiction at the port where the decision is given, and may be heard by the sheriff sitting with an assessor as provided in this section, and rules may be made by the Court of Session by Acts of sederunt with respect to the procedure in case of those appeals in Scotland (including costs and the remuneration of assessors), subject to the concurrence of the Treasury as to fees. In the application of this section to Scotland, references to the Court of Session shall be substituted for references to the High Court.

(8) In the application of this section to Ireland—

    (a) The expression " judge of county courts " and " judge " shall respectively mean a county court judge and chairman of quarter sessions, and include recorder ;

2υ

312

[2 & 3 GEO. 5.]   *Pilotage Act*, 1913.   [CH. **31.**]

(b) The expressions "stipendiary magistrate" and "ma- A.D. 1913.
gistrate" shall respectively mean a magistrate ———
appointed under the Constabulary (Ireland) Act, 6 & 7 Will. 4.
1836 ;   c. 13.

(c) Rules with respect to the procedure in case of appeals
under this section (including costs and the remuneration of assessors) may from time to time be
made, as respects county court judges and chair-
men of quarter sessions, by the authority having
power to make rules and orders for regulating the
practice under the County Officers and Courts 40 & 41 Vict.
(Ireland) Act, 1877, and as respects stipendiary c. 56.
magistrates, by the Lord Lieutenant of Ireland in
Council, but in either case with the concurrence of
the Treasury as to fees.

29. Such fees shall be payable on the examination for a Fees in respect
pilot's licence, or for a pilotage certificate, and on the grant, of pilots'
renewal, or alteration of any such licence or certificate, as may pilotage cer-
be fixed by byelaw made under this Act. tificates. .

Rights and Obligations of Licensed Pilots.

30.—(1) A pilot licensed for a district may supersede any Right of
pilot not so licensed who is employed to pilot a ship in the licensed pilot
district. to supersede
                                                                                        unlicensed
(2) Where a licensed pilot supersedes an unlicensed pilot persons.
the master of the ship shall pay to the latter a proportionate
sum for his services, and shall be entitled to deduct the sum
so paid from the sum payable in respect of the services of the
licensed pilot.

Any question as to the proportion payable to the licensed
pilot and to the person whom the licensed pilot has superseded
shall be referred to the pilotage authority by whom the licensed
pilot has been licensed, and their decision on the question shall
be final.

(3) If in any pilotage district a pilot not licensed for the
district pilots or attempts to pilot a ship after a pilot licensed
for that district has offered to pilot the ship, he shall be liable in
respect of each offence to a fine not exceeding fifty pounds.

(4) If the master of a ship knowingly employs or continues
to employ a pilot not licensed for the district to pilot the ship
within any pilotage district after a pilot licensed for that district
has offered to pilot the ship, or, in the case of an outward bound
ship, without having taken reasonable steps (proof whereof
shall lie on the master) to obtain a licensed pilot, he shall be
liable in respect of each offence to a fine not exceeding fifty
pounds.

(5) If any person other than the master or a seaman being
bonâ fide one of the crew of the ship is on the bridge of a ship,
or in any other position (whether on board the ship or else-
where) from which the ship is navigated, that person shall, for

21

A.D. 1913.   the purposes of this section, be deemed to be piloting the ship
———   unless the contrary is proved.

Declaration as
to draught of
ship.

    31.—(1) A licensed pilot may require the master of any
ship which he is piloting to declare her draught of water,
length and beam, and the master shall comply with any such
request.

    (2) If the master of a ship refuses to comply with any such
request of a pilot, or makes or is privy to any other person
making any false statement to the pilot in answer to the request,
he shall be liable in respect of each offence to a fine not
exceeding fifty pounds.

Provision as
to ships within
a harbour,
dock, &c.

    32.—(1) A ship while being moved within a harbour which
forms part of a pilotage district shall be deemed to be a ship
navigating in a pilotage district, except so far as may be
provided by byelaw in the case of ships being so moved for the
purpose of changing from one mooring to another mooring or of
being taken into or out of any dock :

    Provided that a byelaw shall in every case be made for the
purpose aforesaid in any pilotage district where any class of
persons other than licensed pilots were in practice employed at
the date of the passing of this Act for the purpose of changing
the moorings of ships or of taking ships into or out of dock.

    (2) A ship whilst being navigated within any closed dock,
lock, or other closed work in a pilotage district shall notwithstanding anything in this Act be deemed to be navigating in a
district in which pilotage is not compulsory.

Copies of pilotage provisions
to be furnished
to pilots.

    33.—(1) The pilotage authority shall cause every pilot
licensed by them to be furnished with a copy of this Act as
amended for the time being, and with a copy of any Pilotage
Order for the time being in force in the district, and of any
byelaws so in force.

    (2) A licensed pilot shall produce any copy so furnished to
him to the master of any ship or other person employing him
when required to do so, and if he fails without reasonable cause
to do so, he shall be liable in respect of each offence to a fine
not exceeding five pounds.

Allowance to
licensed pilot
taken out of
his district.

    34.—(1) A master of a ship shall not, except under circumstances of unavoidable necessity, take a licensed pilot without
his consent beyond the district for which he is licensed, or
beyond the point up to which he has been engaged to pilot the
ship, and if a master of a ship acts in contravention of this
section, he shall be liable in respect of each offence to a fine not
exceeding twenty pounds.

    (2) Where a pilot is taken beyond the district for which he
is licensed, or beyond the point up to which he has been engaged
to pilot the ship, either without his consent or under circumstances of unavoidable necessity, he shall be entitled, over and
above his pilotage dues, to maintenance and to the sum of ten

    22

shillings and sixpence a day, recoverable in the same manner as A.D. 1913.
pilotage dues.

(3) The sum so to be paid shall be computed from and inclusive of the day on which the ship passes beyond the district for which the pilot is licensed, or the point up to which the pilot was engaged to pilot her, and up to and inclusive of either the day of his being returned in the said ship to the place where he was taken on board, or, if he is discharged from the ship at a distance from that place, such day as will allow him sufficient time to return thereto; and in the last-mentioned case he shall be entitled to his reasonable travelling expenses.

35.—(1) A licensed pilot, who has given a bond in conformity with byelaws made for the purpose under this Act, shall not be liable for neglect or want of skill beyond the penalty of the bond and the amount payable to him on account of pilotage in respect of the voyage in which he was engaged when he became so liable. Limitation of pilots' liability where bond is given.

(2) Any bond given by a pilot in conformity with byelaws made for the purpose under this Act shall not be liable to stamp duty, and a pilot shall not be called upon to pay any expense in relation to the bond other than the actual expense of preparing the same.

(3) Where any proceedings are taken against a pilot for any neglect or want of skill in respect of which his liability is limited as provided by this section, and other claims are made or apprehended in respect of the same neglect or want of skill, the court in which the proceedings are taken may determine the amount of the pilot's liability, and, upon payment by the pilot of that amount into court, may distribute that amount rateably among the several claimants, and may stay any proceedings pending in any other court in relation to the same matter, and may proceed in such manner and subject to such regulations as to making persons interested parties to the proceedings, and as to the exclusion of any claimants who do not come in within a certain time, and as to requiring security from the pilot, and as to payment of any costs as the court thinks just.

36.—(1) Every licensed pilot when acting as such shall be provided with his licence, and shall, if requested, produce it to any person by whom he is employed, or to whom he offers his services as pilot. Obligation on licensed pilot to produce his licence to employer.

(2) If a licensed pilot refuses to produce his licence in accordance with this section, he shall be liable, in respect of each offence, to a fine not exceeding ten pounds.

37. If any person not being a licensed pilot for a district falsely represents himself to be a licensed pilot for that district, either by means of using a licence which he is not entitled to use or by any other means, he shall be liable in respect of each offence to a fine not exceeding twenty pounds. Penalty on fraudulent use of licence.

23

No tides to Stem

Pilot Boats and Pilot Signals.

Approval of
pilot boats.
    38. All vessels regularly employed in the pilotage service of any pilotage district (in this Act referred to as " pilot boats.") shall be approved and licensed by the pilotage authority of the district, and that authority may, at their discretion, appoint and remove the masters of those pilot boats.

Characteristics
of pilot boats.
    39.—(1) Every pilot boat shall be distinguished by the following characteristics, namely :—

    (*a*) On her stern the name of her owner and the port to which she belongs, painted in white letters at least one inch broad and three inches long, and on each bow the number of her licence :

    (*b*) In all other parts a black colour, painted or tarred outside, or such other colour or colours as the pilotage authority of the district, with the consent of the Board of Trade, direct :

    (*c*) When afloat a flag (in this Act called a pilot flag) of large dimensions compared with the size of the pilot boat, and of two colours, the upper horizontal half white, and the lower horizontal half red, to be placed at the mast head, or on a sprit or staff, or in some equally conspicuous situation.

    (2) It shall be the duty of the master of the pilot boat to see that the pilot boat possesses all the above characteristics, and that the pilot flag is kept clean and distinct, so as to be easily discerned at a reasonable distance ; and also that the names and numbers aforesaid are not at any time concealed ; and if a master fails, without reasonable cause, to comply with the requirements of this section, he shall be liable in respect of each offence to a fine not exceeding twenty pounds.

Pilotage order
not to diminish
powers of
pilotage autho-
rities as to pilot
boats.
    40. A Pilotage Order in dealing with any Act, order, charter, custom, byelaw, regulation, or provision shall not provide for abolishing or diminishing any power of a pilotage authority to acquire, own, hire, build, renew, maintain, or work pilot boats.

Display of
pilot flag when
pilot is on
board ship.
    41.—(1) When a ship is navigating in a pilotage district, and has on board a pilot licensed for that district, or a master or mate holding a pilotage certificate for that district, the master of the ship shall cause a pilot flag to be exhibited ; and if he fails, without reasonable cause, to do so, he shall be liable in respect of each offence to a fine not exceeding fifty pounds.

Penalty on
ordinary boat
displaying
pilot flag.
    42. A pilot flag, or a flag so nearly resembling a pilot flag as to be likely to deceive, shall not be displayed on any ship or boat not having a licensed pilot or a master or mate holding a pilotage certificate on board, and, if any such flag is displayed on any such ship or boat, the master of that vessel shall, unless

24

in the case of· the display of a flag likely to deceive he proves A.D. 1913 that he had no intention to deceive, be liable for each offence to a fine not exceeding fifty pounds.

43.—(1) The master of a ship (other than an excepted ship) shall when navigating in circumstances in which pilotage is compulsory under this Act, display a pilot signal, and keep the signal displayed until a licensed pilot comes on board.

Obligation to display signal for pilot in certain circumstances.

(2) The master of a ship, whether navigating in circumstances in which pilotage is compulsory or not, which is being piloted in a pilotage district by a pilot not licensed for the district, shall display a pilot signal and keep the signal displayed until a licensed pilot comes on board.

(3) If the master of any ship fails to comply with this section, he shall be liable in respect of each offence to a fine not exceeding twenty pounds.

44.—(1) The master of a ship (other than an excepted ship) which, in circumstances in which pilotage is compulsory under this Act, is not under pilotage as required in these circumstances, shall, if a licensed pilot of the district makes a signal for the purpose of offering his services as pilot, by any practical means consistent with the safety of his ship, facilitate the pilot getting on board the ship, and shall give the charge of piloting the ship to that pilot, or, if there are two or more licensed pilots offering at the same time, to such one of them as may, according to any byelaws for the time being in force in the district, be entitled or required to take charge of the ship.

Facilities to be given for pilot getting on board ship.

(2) Where the master of a ship, whether in circumstances in which pilotage is compulsory or not, accepts the services of a licensed pilot, he shall, by any practical means consistent with the safety of his ship, facilitate the pilot getting on board the ship.

(3) If the master of any ship fails to comply with the provisions of this section, he shall be liable in respect of each offence to a fine not exceeding double the amount of pilotage dues that could be demanded for the conduct of the ship.

45.—(1) His Majesty may by Order in Council make rules as to the signals to be used or displayed where the services of a pilot are required on any· vessel, and those signals are in this Act referred to as pilot signals.

Signals to be displayed by ships requiring a pilot.

(2) If a vessel requires the services of a pilot, the master of that vessel shall use or display the pilot signals.

(3) If a master of a vessel uses or displays, or causes or permits any person under his authority to use or display, any of the pilot signals for any other purpose than that of summoning a pilot, or uses or causes or permits any person under his authority to use any other signal for a pilot, he shall be liable in respect of each offence to a fine not exceeding twenty pounds.

25

No tides to Stem

[Cʜ. **31**.]   *Pilotage Act*, 1913.   [2 & 3 Gᴇᴏ. 5.]

A.D. 1913.

Offences by Pilots.

Penalty on
pilot endan-
gering ship,
life, or limb.

46. If any pilot, when piloting a ship, by wilful breach of
duty or by neglect of duty, or by reason of drunkenness—

> (a) does any act tending to the immediate loss, destruction,
> or serious damage of the ship, or tending immediately
> to endanger the life or limb of any person on board
> the ship ; or
>
> (b) refuses or omits to do any lawful act proper and requisite
> to be done by him for preserving the ship from loss,
> destruction, or serious damage, or for preserving any
> person belonging to or on board the ship from danger
> to life or limb ;

that pilot shall in respect of each offence be guilty of a mis-
demeanour.

Penalty on
person obtain
ing charge of a
ship by mis-
representation.

47. If any person, by wilful misrepresentation of circumstances upon which the safety of a ship may depend, obtains, or
endeavours to obtain, the charge of that ship, that person and
every person procuring, abetting, or conniving at the commission
of the offence shall, in addition to any liability for damages, be
liable in respect of each offence to a fine not exceeding one
hundred pounds.

Offences by
pilots.

48.—(1) If a licensed pilot, either within or without the
district for which he is licensed,—

> (a) himself keeps, or is interested in keeping by any agent,
> servant, or other person, any premises licensed for the
> sale of intoxicating liquors, or sells or is interested in
> selling any intoxicating liquors, tobacco, or tea ;
>
> (b) is in any way directly or indirectly concerned in any
> corrupt practices relating to ships, their tackle,
> furniture, cargoes, crews, or passengers, or to persons
> in distress at sea or by shipwreck, or to their moneys,
> goods, or chattels ;
>
> (c) lends his licence ;
>
> (d) acts as pilot whilst suspended ;
>
> (e) acts as pilot when in a state of intoxication ;
>
> (f) employs, or causes to be employed, on board any ship
> which he is piloting any boat, anchor, cable, or other
> store, matter, or thing beyond what is necessary for
> the service of that ship, with intent to enhance the
> expenses of pilotage for his own gain or for the
> gain of any other person ;
>
> (g) refuses or wilfully delays, when not prevented by illness
> or other reasonable cause, to pilot any ship within
> the district for which he is licensed, upon the signal
> for a pilot being made by that ship, or upon being
> required to do so by the master, owner, agent, or
> consignee thereof, or by any officer of the pilotage
> authority by whom the pilot is licensed, or by any
> chief officer of Customs and Excise ;

26

(h) unnecessarily cuts or slips, or causes to be cut or slipped, A.D. 1913.
    any cable belonging to any ship ;

(i) refuses, otherwise than on reasonable ground of danger
    to the ship, when requested by the master, to conduct
    the ship which he is piloting into any port or
    place within the district for which he is licensed ; or

(k) quits the ship, which he is piloting, before the service
    for which he was engaged has been performed and
    without the consent of the master of the ship ;

that pilot shall, in addition to any liability for damages, be
liable in respect of each offence to a fine not exceeding one
hundred pounds.

(2) If any person procures, aids, abets, or connives at the
commission of any offence under this section, he shall, in
addition to any liability for damages, be liable to a fine not
exceeding one hundred pounds.

(3) The provisions of the law relating to Customs with
respect to the recovery of penalties under that law, and the
application of such penalties, shall apply in the case of any
prosecution by any officer of Customs and Excise for the recovery
of a fine in respect of any offence against this section.

Recovery, &c. of Pilotage Dues.

49.—(1) The following persons shall be liable to pay Recovery of
pilotage dues for any ship for which the services of a licensed pilotage dues.
pilot are obtained, namely :—

(a) the owner or master ;

(b) as to pilotage inwards, such consignees or agents as have
    paid or made themselves liable to pay any other
    charge on account of the ship in the port of her
    arrival or discharge ;

(c) as to pilotage outwards, such consignees or agents as
    have paid or made themselves liable to pay any other
    charge on account of the ship in the port of her
    departure ;

and those dues may be recovered in the same manner as fines
of like amount under the Merchant Shipping Act, 1894, but
that recovery shall not take place until a previous demand has
been made in writing.

(2) Any consignee or agent (not being the owner or master
of the ship) who is hereby made liable for the payment of
pilotage dues in respect of any ship may, out of any moneys
received by him on account of that ship or belonging to the
owner thereof, retain the amount of all dues paid by him,
together with any reasonable expenses he may have incurred
by reason of the payment of the dues or his liability to pay
the dues.

50. A licensed pilot shall not demand or receive, and a Receiving or
master shall not offer or pay to any licensed pilot, dues in offering im-
respect of pilotage services at any other rates, whether greater proper rates
of pilotage.

27

A.D. 1913.
—

or less, than the rates which may be demanded by law, and, if a pilot or master acts in contravention of this enactment, he shall be liable in respect of each offence to a fine not exceeding ten pounds.

Pilotage rate
for leading
ships.

51. If any boat or ship, having on board a licensed pilot, leads any ship which has not a licensed pilot on board when the last-mentioned ship cannot, from particular circumstances, be boarded, the pilot so leading the last-mentioned ship shall be entitled to the full pilotage rate for the distance run as if he had actually been on board and had charge of that ship.

Special Provisions as to the Trinity House.

Trinity House
outport dis-
tricts.

52.—(1) For the purposes of this Act, any district which at the time of the passing of this Act is under the authority of sub-commissioners appointed by the Trinity House and any pilotage district which may be declared after the passing of this Act to be a Trinity House outport district, shall be deemed to be a Trinity House outport district.

(2) The powers and duties of the Trinity House under this Act as the pilotage authority of an outport district shall be exercised and performed through a committee appointed for the district in such manner and subject to such conditions as may be determined by a Pilotage Order, under the name of Sub-Commissioners or such other name as may be fixed by the Order, and any such Order may be made so as to apply to all or any one or more of the outport districts.

Trinity House
Pilot Fund.

53. Nothing in this Act shall oblige the Trinity House to maintain separate pilot funds for each of the pilotage districts of which they are the authority, and, if they maintain a single pilot fund for all those districts, the provisions of this Act as to pilot funds shall apply as if all the districts of which they are the pilotage authority were a single pilotage district.

Power of
Trinity House
to make pro-
visions as to
exempt pilots.

54. Notwithstanding anything in this Act, the Trinity House may permit any person who, at the date of the passing of this Act, was licensed to pilot an exempted vessel in the Thames or Medway, to continue to pilot any vessel in those rivers belonging to a class which, at the date of the passing of this Act, were exempted vessels, and were, in the opinion of the Trinity House, in practice piloted by such persons, and any such person while so acting shall be deemed, for the purposes of this Act, to be a licensed pilot.

Collection of
pilotage dues
in Port of
London by
officers of
Customs and
Excise.

55.—(1) The following pilotage dues in respect of foreign ships, not being excepted ships, trading to and from the port of London, namely :—

  (*a*) as to ships inwards, the full amount of pilotage dues for the distance piloted ; and
  (*b*) as to ships outwards, the full amount of dues for the distance required by law ;

28

shall be paid to the chief officer of Customs and Excise in the A.D. 1913.
port of London by the master, or by any consignees or agents of
the ship who have paid, or made themselves liable to pay, any
other charge for the ship in the port of London.

(2) The chief officer of Customs and Excise, on receiving any
pilotage dues in respect of foreign ships, shall give to the person
paying the dues a receipt in writing for the dues, and in the
port of London the ship may be detained until the receipt is
produced to the proper officer of Customs and Excise of the
port.

(3) The chief officer of Customs and Excise shall pay over
to the Trinity House the pilotage dues received by him under
this section, and the Trinity House shall apply the dues so
received—

(a) in paying to any licensed pilot who produces to them
sufficient proof of his having piloted the ship such
dues as would have been payable to him for pilotage
services if the ship had been a British ship, after
making any deductions which they are authorised to
make by byelaw under this Act; and

(b) in paying to any person not being a licensed pilot who
produces to them sufficient proof of his having, in
the absence of a licensed pilot, piloted the ship, such
amount as the Trinity House think proper, not
exceeding the amount which would, under similar
circumstances, have been payable to a licensed pilot
after making the said deductions; and

(c) in paying over to the Trinity House pilot fund the
residue, together with the amount of any deductions
made as aforesaid.

(4) Nothing in this section shall affect the application of the
provisions of this Act as to the recovery of pilotage dues.

Miscellaneous and General Provisions.

56. The expenditure under this Act out of money provided Limit on ex-
by Parliament shall not exceed six thousand pounds in any one penditure.
year.

57. The Board of Trade Arbitrations, &c. Act, 1874, shall Application of
apply as if this Act were a special Act within the meaning of 37 & 38 Vict.
the first-mentioned Act. c. 40.

58. Notwithstanding anything in this Act, where a pilotage Saving for
authority is entitled by statute at the time of the passing of pilotage autho-
this Act to receive moneys in the name of pilotage and to power to apply
apply part of such moneys to purposes other than those autho- money received
rised under this Act, a Pilotage Order made under Part I. of in name of
this Act in respect of that authority may provide for the other pur-
apportionment of the moneys so received as between the pilot poses.
fund or account and such other purposes.

29

A.D. 1913.
—
Commence-
ment of Act.

59. This Act shall (except as expressly provided) come into operation on the first day of April nineteen hundred and thirteen : Provided that any enactment, order, charter, custom, byelaw, regulation, or provision with reference to pilotage affecting any pilotage district in particular, and in force at the time of the passing of this Act, including any exemptions from compulsory pilotage taking effect thereunder, shall remain in force notwithstanding anything in this Act or any repeal effected by this Act, until provision is made by Pilotage Order, or in the case of a byelaw by byelaw, made under this Act superseding any such enactment, order, charter, custom, byelaw, regulation, or provision. '

Repeal.

60.—(1) The enactments mentioned in the Second Schedule to this Act are hereby repealed to the extent specified in the third column of that schedule.

Provided that—

> (*a*) Any order in council, licence, certificate, byelaw, rule, or regulation made or granted under any enactment hereby repealed or in pursuance of any power which ceases in consequence of this Act, shall, subject to the provisions of this Act, continue in force as if it had been made or granted under this Act ; and

> (*b*) Any officer appointed, any body elected or constituted, and any office established under any enactment hereby repealed shall continue and be deemed to have been appointed, elected, constituted, or established, as the case may be, under this Act ;

> (*c*) Any document referring to any Act or enactment hereby repealed shall be construed to refer to this Act or to the corresponding enactment of this Act.

52 & 53 Vict.
c. 63.

(2) The mention of particular matters in this section shall not be held to prejudice or affect the general application of section thirty-eight of the Interpretation Act, 1889, as regards the effect of repeals.

Extent of Act.

61. This Act extends to the United Kingdom and the Isle of Man, and applies to all ships, British and foreign.

Short title.

62. This Act may be cited as the Pilotage Act, 1913, and shall be construed as one with the Merchant Shipping Act, 1894, and the Acts amending the same ; and the Merchant Shipping Acts, 1894 to 1907, and this Act may be cited together as the Merchant Shipping Acts, 1894 to 1913.

30

SCHEDULES.   A.D. 1913.

FIRST SCHEDULE.   Section 7

PROVISIONS AS TO PILOTAGE ORDERS.

1. Subject to the provisions of this schedule, the Board of Trade may make rules in relation to applications for Pilotage Orders, and to the payments to be made in respect thereof, and to the publication of notices and advertisements, and the manner in which and the time within which representations or objections with reference to any application are to be made, and as to the publication of Pilotage Orders.

2. Notice of an application for an Order shall be published once at least in each of two successive weeks in the month immediately succeeding the date of the application in such manner as may be prescribed by the rules made by the Board of Trade.

3. The notice shall state the object which it is proposed to effect by the Order.

4. The Board of Trade on receiving any application for an Order shall refer the application to the pilotage authority of the district, if the authority are not themselves the applicants, and shall consider any objections which may be made to the proposed Order whether by the pilotage authority or by other persons appearing to the Board of Trade to be interested, and for that purpose shall allow at least six weeks to elapse between the date on which the application is referred to the authority and that on which the Order is made.

5. The Board of Trade may submit to Parliament for confirmation any Order which requires confirmation by Parliament.

6. If and when a Bill confirming any such Order is pending in either House of Parliament, a petition is presented against any Order comprised therein, the Bill, so far as it relates to that Order, may be referred to a Select Committee, or, if the two Houses of Parliament think fit so to order, to a Joint Committee of those Houses, and the petitioner shall be allowed to appear and oppose as in the case of private Bills.

7. Any Act confirming an Order under this Act may be repealed, altered, or amended by any subsequent Order made under this Act.

8. The Board of Trade may revoke, either wholly or partially, any Order made by them before the Order is confirmed by Parliament, but such revocation shall not be made whilst the Bill confirming the Order is pending in either House of Parliament.

9. The making of an Order shall be primâ facie evidence that all the requirements of this Act in respect of proceedings required to be taken previously to the making of the Order have been complied with.

31

MANCHESTER SHIP CANAL.

REGULATIONS

AND

BYE-LAWS.

Revised to date,

November 1st, 1903.

1

Canal Superintendents :

From Eastham Locks (including approach channel) to Point Turnbridge Ferry,

Captain HEASLEY,

No Man's Land, Runcorn.

From Point Turnbridge Ferry to Rixton Junction,

Captain WARING,

Latchford Locks, Latchford.

From Rixton Junction to Coastwise Cattle Wharf,

Captain DUDLEY,

Irlam Locks, Irlam.

DOCK MASTER:

From Coastwise Cattle Wharf (below Mode Wheel) to Woden Street Bridge (including the Docks),

Captain WILLIAMS.

DOCK OFFICE:

Trafford Road, Old Trafford, Manchester.

325

Manchester Ship Canal.

NAVIGATION AND DOCK REGULATIONS.

Upon receiving a copy of these Regulations the Captains and Owners of all vessels Navigating the Canal must abide by and conform to them in all respects, and also satisfy all requirements of the Company's officers made in conformity therewith. Captains and Owners will be held responsible for all consequences that may ensue from any failure on their part to comply with these Regulations.

The expression " Canal " in these Regulations shall be held to include the Ship Canal, Approach Channels, Locks, and Docks.

The expression "navigating the Canal" shall be held to include entering, leaving, and mooring in, the Ship Canal, Approach Channels, Locks, and Docks.

1. The Manchester Ship Canal Company do not take any charge of or assume any responsibility whatever in respect of any vessel, boat, barge, lighter, or other craft navigating the Canal, all craft under such circumstances being at the sole risk of the owners, who alone are responsible for the safety and security of their vessels and moorings, *Vessels in Canal at owner's risk*

326

3

and also for any damage done by their vessels or servants to the premises or property of the Company, or to vessels or goods in or upon any part of the Company's premises.

Anchors to be stowed, sails furled, &c., whilst in Canal

2. All vessels navigating the Canal must have their anchors properly stowed and a strong kedge aft ready for use in case of emergency, their sails furled, all boats swung inboard, flying jib-boom and jib-boom rigged in, all out-riggers unshipped, and yards braced fore and aft or cockbilled, so that nothing projects over the ship's side, except fenders.

Declaration of cargo, &c.

3. The Captain or other person in charge of every vessel must, on entering the Canal, declare the particulars of the vessel and cargo, draft of water, and any other information required by the Company's officers.

Speed

4. The maximum speed in the Canal must not exceed 6 miles an hour, unless a special permit has been obtained from the Company's General Superintendent.

Sails not to be used

5. Sails must not under any circumstances be used in the Canal without the permission of the Dockmaster or Canal Superintendent.

Vessels to be navigated with care

6. Vessels must at all times be navigated with care and caution, and in such manner as will not involve risk of collision, or endanger the safety of other vessels or their moorings, or cause damage thereto, or to the banks of the Canal, or to any other part of the Company's property. Special care and caution must be used when approaching the locks, where the banks of the Canal are under or waiting repair, when passing vessels moored or employed in dredging or other work, small craft, or workmen engaged in repairs or otherwise, under which circumstances vessels must reduce their speed to dead slow, or if necessary stop altogether.

4

7. If the safety of any vessels or their moorings is endangered, or if damage is caused thereto or to the banks of the Canal by a passing vessel, the onus shall lie upon the master of such vessel to show that she was navigated with care and caution, and at such a speed and in such manner as directed by these regulations.

8. All vessels navigating the Canal must provide and use good and sufficient ropes or warps of their own, which must be kept ready to send ashore when required. When ropes are sent on board by the Company's officers they are only intended to be used in aid of the ship's own ropes, and the Company do not hold themselves liable for any damage in the event of ropes breaking. Such fenders as may be necessary must be provided by the ship, and must be of such material as will not sink if lost overboard.

9. All vessels navigating the Canal must carry and use proper signals in accordance with the schedule attached hereto.

10. The signals at the swing-bridges consist of a black ball hoisted on a mast near the centre of the bridges by day, and at night a red light is shown from the bridges midway across the Canal when closed, and a green light at the side when open. If, when approaching any swing-bridge, the ball signal is seen to be hoisted, that will signify that the bridge is being got ready to be swung, but unless the bridge is completely open, or by night a green light is shown, no vessel must attempt to pass through. All vessels must approach the swing-bridges at moderate speed in case any accident should occur to the machinery whilst swinging. If the ball is not hoisted, or having been hoisted is lowered, or a red light is shown, any vessel approaching such bridge must immediately stop. If the ball should be lowered,

or a red light be shown, while two vessels are approaching a swing-bridge from the same direction, at the same time, the bridge being open, that will indicate that the bridge is being closed against the second vessel, which must stop until the ball is again hoisted, or a green light shown.

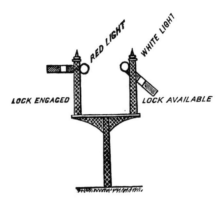

Signals at Locks   11. Whenever a signal is against a vessel approaching any lock she must signal in accordance with the schedule attached hereto, and no vessel must make for any lock by day unless signalled to do so by the lowering of the semaphore, or by night by the changing of the red light to white, and then only for the lock for which she has been signalled.

Vessels not to impede entrances to locks   12. No vessel must approach so near to any lock as to impede the entrance to or departure from such lock of any other vessel when the semaphore is raised or a red light is shown.

Lock-masters' instructions absolute   13. The Lock-master or other Officer in charge shall fix the order and position in which vessels may enter or leave any lock, and his instructions shall be absolute.

Vessels in locks   14. When the stern ropes of a vessel entering a lock are ashore, the engines must <u>not</u> be moved ahead until she is ready to leave the lock.

15. When vessels proceeding in opposite directions Vessels meeting
are approaching one another, each vessel must be steered
as closely as possible with safety to her own starboard
side of the Canal, so that they may pass on the port side
of each other; each vessel must reduce her speed to dead
slow, or, if necessary, stop the engine while passing
each other, so as to ensure their passing in safety.
When vessels meet in the tidal portion of the Canal
when the tide is running in or out, the vessel proceeding
against the tide must give way, or tie up if necessary,
until the vessel coming with the tide or stream has
passed, and when vessels meet in the non-tidal portion
of the Canal, or in the tidal portion during slack water,
the vessel bound up the Canal must give way, or tie up
if necessary, until the vessel coming down has passed.

16. When one vessel is following another without Vessels following
the intention of passing, she must not approach
nearer to the leading vessel than one furlong or
eighth of a mile.

17. No vessel must overtake another within half a Vessels over-taking
mile of any lock or swing-bridge. Every vessel when
being overtaken must keep as far as possible to
starboard of mid-channel; and if after sunset, a white
light must be shown over the stern. The vessel
overtaking must pass on the port side of the vessel
overtaken.

18. Wherever the slopes of the Canal will permit, Small craft
small craft must be kept entirely out of the track
of sea-going vessels.

19. Whenever vessels under way require to depart Vessels crossing
from the course laid down for them in these regulations, for the purpose, for instance, of proceeding to or
from any quay, wharf, works, or lock, or for any other
reason, the responsibility of doing so in safety, having
regard to passing traffic and to works in operation,
or otherwise, will rest upon the person in charge
and the owners of such vessel.

dge gauges 20. Special care must be taken when vessels are approaching the bridge gauges over the Canal to see that there is a clear headway, and when passing down the Canal no spars must be hoisted until the bridge gauge at Runcorn has been passed.

Dredgers 21. When dredgers are working in the Canal in daylight a ball will be hoisted on the side of the dredger which is clear for vessels to pass, and this will be replaced by a white light when working at night. A red light will be shown on the side of the dredger where there is no clear passage. When moored, dredgers will exhibit the ordinary lights by night.

Hopper doors 22. Except by special permission in writing from the Company's Engineer, hopper doors must not be opened in the Canal.

Obstructions or damage to be reported 23. An efficient lookout must be kept on board all vessels navigating the Canal, and any obstruction or danger—particularly timber or other articles observed in the Canal, or damaged buoys or perches—must be reported at the first lock or swing-bridge.

Rubbish 24. Ballast, cinders, or rubbish of any kind whatever must not be deposited in the Canal, or upon any portion of the Company's property, except by consent of the Company in writing. Rubbish, ashes, &c., must not be allowed to remain on the deck or gangway of vessels in the Canal.

Material discharged by accident to be reported 25. When by accident or otherwise any material of any kind whatever falls overboard or is discharged in the Canal, the circumstances, quantity, nature of the material, and position, must be immediately reported to the Dock Master, Canal Superintendent, or at the first lock or swing-bridge.

Sunken vessels 26. Immediate notice of the sinking of any vessel must be given to the Dock Master or Canal Superintendent, and signals must be displayed as provided for in the schedule attached hereto.

8

27. Every vessel must be kept at all times so Vessels to be properly ballasted loaded or ballasted as to be safely navigated or moored in the Canal.

28. Vessels must be moored only at such quays Mooring and lights and other places as are provided for that purpose by the Company, and, except in cases of emergency, or unless specially ordered to do so by the Company's Officers, no vessel must be brought up or stopped or remain moored or anchored in the fairway of the Canal. When a vessel is moored in places where traffic is passing, a pennant must be hoisted at half mast by day, and at night two white lights must be exhibited where they can be best seen, one forward and one aft, on the side of the vessel which is open to the Canal. No master or other person having or taking upon himself the command or management of any vessel in the Canal, nor any other person employed in or about any such vessel, shall make fast, or cause, permit, or suffer, any rope, chain, or tackle of any description to be made fast from such vessel to the pillars or any other part of any shed, or to the rails, railway wagons, or to any other property of the Company, excepting the bollards, mooring posts, or rings specially provided for the purpose. When a vessel is moored the engines must not be set in motion without the express permission of the Dock Master or Canal Superintendent, nor until a suitable look-out has been first placed fore and aft.

29. A competent watchman must be in charge Competent watchman to be on board both day and night on board every vessel in the Canal, except small boats, and the latter must be moored clear of the traffic.

30. Vessels must be removed on the first intimation Vessels to be moved under orders of Company's officers from the Dock Master or Canal Superintendent; and Masters or other persons in charge and owners of vessels must obey the directions of, and must not offer any obstruction to, such Officers as to the mooring, unmooring, or moving of any vessel, or in

9

regulating the position for loading and discharging of any vessel, and the quay space to be occupied by them, and no vessel must be removed from one berth to another without the express permission of the Dock Master. All vessels must be moved by the persons in charge and their crews, under the direction of the Dock Master, his assistants, or deputies.

Towing   31. No vessel may tow any other vessel unless licensed or authorised by the Company to do so; tow lines must not exceed 50ft. within the Canal, and the stern of the hindmost vessel towed must not be distant more than 500ft. from the bow of the vessel **towing** when between Eastham and Mode Wheel Locks, and not more than 400ft. when above Mode Wheel Locks. Two trains of vessels towed must not exceed 40ft. in width, and must be properly secured by breast ropes. When the vessels are towed in single line, the tow rope must be made fast on the port bow of the vessels towed, and no vessel, barge, or craft of any description must be moved in the fairway of the Canal without the assistance of a tug or her own propelling power without the special permission of the Dock Master or Canal Superintendent.

Fires and lights   32. No person shall have or keep any fire, lighted candle, or lamp, in any portion of the Docks or in any vessel in the Canal, unless such candle or lamp be at all times enclosed in a lantern, or unless such fire consume only coal or coke, and be safely secured. When a fire is observed to have broken out on board any vessel, an alarm should be raised by ringing a bell on board such vessel, and at the same time an alarm given through one of the Gamewell Fire Alarms, which are fixed up in various places about the Docks. Every vessel must have on board hose pipe of sufficient length and section, in good working order, and capable of being immediately attached to the force pump, for the purpose of extinguishing fire. When a fire is observed to have broken out in any warehouse, shed, or

10

elsewhere on the Company's property, the nearest Gamewell Fire Alarm should be immediately made use of. Signalling a fire through a Gamewell Fire Alarm notifies the position of the fire simultaneously to both the Company's Dock Fire Office and also the Fire Office of the Manchester Corporation in the City.

33. No ship or boat laden wholly or in part with any explosive substance will be allowed to enter the Canal without the special permission of the Company in writing. *Explosives not to be carried without permission*

34. No timber or other Merchandise must be discharged into the Canal without the consent of the Dock Master or Canal Superintendent. *Timber not to be floated without consent*

35. No Master or other person in charge of any vessel lying in the Canal shall permit such vessel to be discharged or loaded, or shall permit such vessel or her masts, spars, or tackle to be repaired, in such manner as to allow any substance to fall into the Canal, or without providing a canvas or other protection, if necessary, so secured from the side of such vessel during the whole of the time occupied by such discharge, loading, or repairs, as effectually to prevent any substance from falling into the Canal. *Vessels not to be discharged, loaded, or repaired without steps being taken to prevent material from falling into the dock*

36. It is the duty of the owner of every vessel to provide ladders or stages, and of the officer in charge of the vessel to see that the same are securely placed and duly protected so as to form a safe gangway on board or over such vessel, and that they are properly replaced whenever it is necessary to shift the same, or alter the moorings; and the Company are not responsible for the sufficiency or security of any ladder or stages which may be lent to vessels for such purpose. *Gangways*

37. Cargo must not be deposited near the edge of the quays, and no obstacle of any kind must be allowed to interfere with the free and safe use of the quays, mooring posts, bollards, hydrants, or hydraulic connections. *Quays to be kept clear of cargo,&c*

11

Nuisances not to be committed

38. Privies and urinals are provided for the convenience of persons using the Docks. All closets on board any vessel or craft must be kept closed during the whole time such vessel or craft is in the Canal.

Dogs, and dangerous animals and reptiles

39. Dogs must be properly secured by the person in charge of them, or otherwise responsible for their control. Ferocious animals, or birds, or dangerous reptiles will not be permitted on board any vessel, barge, lighter, or other craft, or upon any of the Company's premises, unless properly secured.

Smoking

40. Smoking is strictly prohibited upon any part of the docks, wharves, or premises of the Company, except at places specially provided. Smoking upon any vessel, barge, lighter, or other craft is also prohibited in respect of any vessel loading or discharging cargo damageable by fire.

Defacing dock premises

41. All persons are prohibited from writing upon, soiling, defacing, marking, or injuring any of the sheds, barricades, railings, fences, posts, or any other part of the premises of the Company in any way whatever.

Horses and vehicles

42. No vehicle of any description, and no horse or beast of burden, will be allowed to remain unattended upon any of the Company's roads or quays, or for a longer time than is necessary for the loading or unloading of goods, or for taking up or setting down passengers.

Interference with cranes, &c.

43. No person other than an authorised Officer of the Company shall make use of any crane, jigger, hydraulic lead, hydraulic lift, hydraulic levers at the docks or locks, or any other machinery or working appliances of the Company, and any other person interfering or tampering with any such machinery or working appliances will be liable to prosecution.

12

44. No person will be allowed to load or discharge, or to assist in loading or discharging, vessels in the docks, or to handle traffic upon the quays or in the sheds, unless authorised to do so, or employed by the Dock Traffic Superintendent of the Company.

Labour not to be employed without permission

45. No goods will be allowed to be removed from the premises of the Company until an authorised pass has been delivered in respect of them.

Passes to be delivered before goods leave the Company's premises

46. The Master or other person in charge must give reasonable notice to the Dock Master or Canal Superintendent of the time when his vessel is intended to leave her berth.

Vessels leaving berth

47. Any person who assaults, resists, obstructs, or impedes any Officer of the Company in the execution of his duty, or disobeys his lawful orders, or uses abusive or offensive language, or aids or incites others to do so, will be liable to prosecution.

Obstructing Officers

The Officers of the Company are hereby instructed to report every offence against any of the foregoing Regulations.

SCHEDULE OF SIGNALS.
1903

During the Day, between Sunrise and Sunset	Reason for Signal	During the Night, between Sunset and Sunrise
		{ *Lights in accordance with the provisions for avoiding collisions at sea.*
Whistle... ... ... {	When approaching other vessels, boats, or rafts...	} *Whistle.*
Whistle ... ... {	When overtaking another vessel with intention to pass ...	} *Whistle.*
Three blasts of Whistle— one short, one long, and one short blast ... ... }	If obliged to stop when another vessel is following	{ *Three blasts of whistle— one short, one long, and one short blast.*
Whistle. Approaching from Manchester, one long and one short blast of whistle; from Eastham, one long blast of whistle; but whistle not to be sounded if semaphore lowered at lock or ball hoisted at swing-bridge	When approaching a lock or swing-bridge and requiring to pass through ...	{ *Whistle. Approaching from Manchester, one long and one short blast of whistle; from Eastham, one long blast of whistle.*
Comply with the rule of the road ... ... }	During fog, mist, or falling snow	{ *Comply with the rule of the road.*
Three black balls or shapes in a vertical line one over the other, not less than three feet apart, to be placed on the mast where they can be seen by those navigating the Canal both ways. Bell to be rung on the approach of any other vessel	Vessels aground or disabled	{ *Three red lights in globular lanterns in a vertical line one over the other, not less than three feet apart, to be placed on the mast where they can be best seen by those navigating the Canal both ways. One bright circular light aft. Bell to be rung on the approach of any other vessel*

Table of Distances.

[illegible]	Side of Canal.	Canal Sectional No.	Distance from Eastham L'cks Miles	Distance from Manchester. Miles	Canal Superintendent.
***Eastham Locks** 6 miles from Prince's Landing Stage, Liverpool; 19 miles from Bar Lightship	—	1	—	36	Capt. Heasley
Bankfield Wharf	S	3—4	0⅝	35⅜	"
Hooton Wharf	S	6	1¼	34¾	"
Mount Manisty	N	8—9	1⅞	34⅛	"
Pool Hall Wharf	S	11	2⅝	33⅜	"
Ellesmere-Port	S	16—17	3¼	32¾	"
Stuart Wharf	S	18	3½	32½	"
Pontoon and Ship Repairing Yard	S	19	3¾	32¼	"
Stanlow Wharf	S	21	4	32	"
Coal Tip...	S	22	4	32	"
Ince Rock Cutting—Lay-Bye for large vessels	S	31	6	30	"
Ince Ferry	S	31—32	6⅛	29⅞	"
Ince Wharf	S	34	6⅝	29⅜	"
Weaver Sluices	N	43—44	10	26	"
Weston Point	S	48—49	10¾	25¼	"
Weston Mersey Lock	N	48	10¾	25¼	"
Delamere Dock	S	49—50	11	25	"
Bridgewater Jetties and Coal Tip ...	S	51	11¼	24¾	"
Runcorn Lay-Bye	S	52	11½	24½	"
Bridgewater Lock...	N	53—54	11¾	24¼	"
Runcorn Docks	S	54—55	12	24	"
Runcorn Railway Bridge (fixed) ...	—	59	12½	23½	"
Runcorn (Old Quay) Lock...	N	61	13	23	"
Old Quay Lock Wall Lay-Bye	N	62	13⅛	22⅞	"
Runcorn (Old Quay) Swing Bridge...	—	65—66	13¼	22¾	"
United Alkali Co., Wigg's Works ...	N	67—68	13¾	22¼	"
Turnbridge Ferry...	—	69—70	14	22	"
Stone Delph Lay-Bye...	S	74—75	15	21	Capt. Waring
Old Randles Sluices	N	76	15¼	20¾	"
Pumping Station	N	77—78	16⅛	19⅞	"
Moss Lane Wharves	N	77—78	16½	19½	"
Moore Lane Swing Bridge...	—	80—81	17	19	"
Haydock Coal Wharf and Lay-Bye	N	80—81	17½	18½	"
L. & N. W. and G. W. Railway Viaduct (fixed)	—	81	17¾	18¼	"
Walton Lock Cutting (Lay-Bye for large vessels)...	S	81—82	18½	17½	"
Walton Wharf	S	81—82	18⅝	17⅜	"
Stag Inn Swing Bridge	—	81—82	18¾	17¼	"
Warrington Dock Entrance and Walton Lock	N	82	18⅞	17⅛	"
Northwich Road (Wilderspool) Swing Bridge	—	84	19⅜	16⅝	"
20-Steps Lock (Junction with Runcorn and Latchford Canal) ...	N	84	19⅜	16⅝	"
Latchford High Level Bridge—Chester Road—(fixed)...	—	89	20	16	"
Knutsford Road Swing Bridge	—	89—90	20⅜	15⅝	"
Lay-Bye for large vessels	N	90	20½	15½	"
L. & N. W. Railway Viaduct (fixed)	—	90	20⅝	15⅜	"
***Latchford Locks** (rise 16ft. 6in.)	—	90—91	20⅞	15⅛	"
Thelwall Ferry	—	93	21¾	14¼	"
Statham Wharf	S	96—97	22⅞	13⅛	"
Statham Brick Yard	N	96 *	23	13	"
Rixton Junction (Junction with Mersey and Irwell Navigation)	N	99	23⅞	12⅛	"

* Fresh water may be obtained at these places.

TABLE OF DISTANCES.—*Continued.*

	Side of Canal.	Canal Sectional No.	Distance from Eastham L'cks	Distance from Manchester.	Canal Superintendent.
			Miles	Miles	
Warburton Wharf	S	102	24⅞	11⅛	Capt. Dudley
Warburton High Level Bridge (fixed)	—	102—103	25⅛	10⅞	,,
Warburton Wharf	S	102—103	25¼	10¾	,,
Hollins Ferry	—	102—103	25½	10½	,,
Millbank Wharf	S	104	26	10	,,
Cadishead Wharf...	N	108	26⅝	9⅜	,,
Cheshire Lines Viaduct (fixed) ...	—	109—110	26⅞	9⅛	,,
Partington Coal Basin and Lay-Bye	N & S	111-112	27⅛	8⅞	,,
Peaksnook Wharf	S	112	27¼	8¾	,,
Carrington Wharf (M'chest'r C'rpor'n	S	113	27¾	8¼	,,
Manchester and Salford Corporation Wharves	N	114			
Mersey Weir...	S	115	28	8	,,
Cheshire Lines Viaduct—Liverpool & Manchester (fixed)	—	115—116	28	8	,,
Co-operative W'sale Society's Wharf	N	116	28	8	,,
Irlam Locks (rise 16 feet)	—	117—118	28¼	7¾	,,
Irlam Ferry	—	119	28½	7½	,,
Flixton Wharf	S	119			
BoysnopeWharf (M'chester C'rporat'n	N	122	29⅝	6⅜	,,
Hulme's Bridge Ferry...	—	122			
Barton Locks (rise 15 feet)... ...	—	125—126	30⅜	5⅝	,,
Stickens Wharf, Davyhulme (Manchester Corporation)	S	127	30⅝	5⅜	,,
Bromyhurst Wharf	S	127—128	31	5	,,
Eccles Wharf	N	129	31½	4½	,,
Barton Road Swing Bridge	—	129—130	31¾	4¼	,,
Barton Swing Aqueduct	—	130	31¾	4¼	,,
Barton Wharf, South...	S	131	32	4	,,
***Irwell Park Wharf and Lay-Bye**	N	133	32⅛	3⅞	,,
Eccles Oil Wharf...	N	134	32½	3½	,,
Eccles Landing Stage	N .	135	32⅝	3⅜	,,
Trafford Park, private wharves ...	S	136—137	33	3	,,
Jetty	N	136—137	33⅜	2⅝	,,
Coastwise Cattle Wharf	N	137	33½	2½	Capt. Williams
Weaste Wharf	N	137—138	33½	2½	,,
Wharf (Frozen Meat)...	N	137—138	33½	2½	,,
Oil Wharves	S	138	33⅞	2⅛	,,
Foreign Animals Wharf (M/c. Corp.)	S	138	33⅞	2⅛	,,
Mode Wheel Locks (rise 13ft.)	—	138—139	34	2	,,
Pontoon and Dry Dock ...	S	138—139	34	2	,,
***Grain Elevator**	S	139	34¼	1¾	,,
Salford Quay...	N	139	34—34½	2—1½	,,
Coaling Crane (25 tons)	N	139	34¼	1¾	,,
Trafford Wharf	S	139—140	34¼—34⅞	1¾—1⅛	,,
30-ton Crane...	N	139—140	34⅜	1⅝	,,
***Docks**, Nos. 8, 7, 6...	N	139—140	34½—34⅞	1½—1⅛	,,
Dock Railway & Swing Bridge... ...	—	139—140	34⅞	1⅛	,,
Manchester & Liverpool Transport Co.'s Wharf	S	140	35	1	,,
Ferry Landing Stage	S	140	35	1	,,
Trafford Road Swing Bridge	—	140			
Dock Office (temporary)	S	140			
Throstle Nest Wharf	S	140			
***Docks**, Nos. 4, 3, 2, 1	S	142	35½—35¾	0⅝—0¼	,,
Cornbrook Wharf...	S	142	35¾	0¼	,,
Woden Street Foot Bridge (fixed) ...	—	—	36	—	,,

* Fresh water may be obtained at these places.